Teacher Education at Hispanic-Serving Institutions

Documenting the collaborative work of staff at the University of Texas Rio Grande Valley over the course of several years, this text explores the many ways in which teachers and faculty must engage with the institutional designation of Hispanic-Serving Institution (HSI). In doing so, the volume illustrates how colleges of education might provide Latinx students with the education, support, and environment they require to thrive.

As the number of HSIs continues to grow, this text provides much needed insight into how colleges and universities can better enact their HSI status. Chapters document the practices and experiences of faculty as they look to increase family engagement, utilize social and cultural values to inform instruction, and acknowledge historically institutionalized legacies of oppression and marginalization. By highlighting the successes and challenges associated with serving Latinx students, the text draws out the ways in which teacher education and development might be structured at an HSI, in order that the institutional identity is reflected in curricula, pedagogy, scholarship, and community engagement. The text also explains important distinctions between HSIs and other minority-serving institutions and illustrates the importance of HSIs to Latinx students.

This text will be of great interest to graduate and postgraduate students, researchers, academics, libraries, professionals, and policy makers in the field of higher education, multicultural education, educational leadership, teacher education, and Race & Ethnicity Studies.

Janine M. Schall is Associate Professor and Chair in the Department of Bilingual and Literacy Studies at the College of Education and P-16 Integration at the University of Texas Rio Grande Valley, USA.

Patricia Alvarez McHatton is Executive Vice President for Academic Affairs, Student Success, and P-16 Integration at the University of Texas Rio Grande Valley, USA.

Eugenio Longoria Sáenz is Deputy Director at Educate Texas for RGV FOCUS and a Lecturer in the College of Education at the University of Texas Rio Grande Valley, USA.

Routledge Research in Higher Education

For more information about this series, please visit: www.routledge.com/
Routledge-Research-in-Higher-Education/book-series/RRHE

Teacher Education at Hispanic-Serving Institutions

Exploring Identity, Practice, and Culture

Edited by
Janine M. Schall,
Patricia Alvarez McHatton,
Eugenio Longoria Sáenz

Routledge
Taylor & Francis Group

NEW YORK AND LONDON

First published 2020
by Routledge
52 Vanderbilt Avenue, New York, NY 10017

and by Routledge
2 Park Square, Milton Park, Abingdon, Oxon, OX14 4RN

Routledge is an imprint of the Taylor & Francis Group, an informa business

Library of Congress Cataloging-in-Publication Data
A catalog record for this title has been requested

ISBN: 978-0-367-18828-3 (hbk)
ISBN: 978-0-429-19856-4 (ebk)

Typeset in Sabon
by codeMantra

We dedicate this book to our students, their families, and their communities and to the rich linguistic and cultural heritage of the Rio Grande Valley that guides our work.

Contents

Contributors

Jair J. Aguilar holds a Ph.D. in STEM education with a concentration in Mathematics from the University of Texas, Austin. Before studying his doctorate, he earned a B.S. in Information System Engineering with a concentration in Mathematics and Computer Science from the Monterrey Tech., a Master of Education from the Monterrey University, and an MBA from the Regiomontana University. Dr. Aguilar has over 20 years of teaching experience ranging from middle school to higher education. His research has been focused on the development of mathematical skills in preservice elementary teachers when they solve open-ended problems and non-routine tasks.

Isela Almaguer is a Professor and Endowed Chair in Education at the University of Texas Rio Grande Valley in the Department of Bilingual and Literacy Studies. She earned an Ed.D. from the University of Houston in Curriculum and Instruction with an emphasis in Literacy Studies. Her research interests center on literacy and biliteracy development of English Language Learners, dual language education, and language issues impacting Latino students and communities. Dr. Almaguer's research has been published in a variety of national and international scholarly journals and books.

Gerardo Aponte-Safe is an Assistant Professor of Global Education at the University of Wisconsin-La Crosse, teaching courses in global and multicultural education. Dr. Aponte-Safe's research integrates teacher education and social studies education, considering how teachers navigate conflicting cultural lenses in curriculum and pedagogy for teaching diverse learners. Recent work has focused on how teacher educators approach culturally sustaining pedagogy for future Latinx and LGBTQ+ teachers. Originally from Puerto Rico, he grew up traveling throughout Latin America, living for six years in Belize and Perú. He has worked as a social studies teacher in Florida and a teacher educator in Michigan, Texas, and the Dominican Republic.

Alyssa G. Cavazos is an Associate Professor of Rhetoric, Composition, and Literacy Studies in the Department of Writing and Language

Studies at the University of Texas Rio Grande Valley. She teaches undergraduate and graduate coursework in writing studies. Her pedagogical and scholarly interests include language difference in the teaching of writing, translingual writing, multilingualism across communities, border rhetoric, and Latinas/os in higher education. As reflected by her 2017 Regents' Outstanding Teaching Award, she is committed to designing linguistically inclusive pedagogies, which can lead to students' academic success across academic disciplines in higher education.

Angela Chapman has a Ph.D. in Curriculum and Instruction with an emphasis in Science Education. Her area of expertise is diversity, equity, and inclusion in STEM, including underrepresented populations. One aspect of her research seeks to better understand the intersection of science teacher identity and agency of STEM teachers for culturally and linguistically diverse populations. In addition, she examines practices and factors that improve K-12 student engagement and success in STEM.

Leticia De Leon holds an Ed.D. in Curriculum and Instruction from the University of Houston and is a Professor in the Department of Teaching and Learning at the University of Texas Rio Grande Valley. Her research interests include digital literacies and how to integrate technology in teacher preparation.

Miryam Espinosa-Dulanto is a faculty member in the Department of Teaching and Learning at the University of Texas Rio Grande Valley. She holds a Ph.D. in Curriculum Theory and Educational Policies for Linguistic Minorities from the University of Wisconsin-Madison. Dr. Espinosa-Dulanto's writing, as well as her academic research, emerges from her identity as a woman of color, a Borderlands Mestiza, and a non-mainstream person in the U.S. From that perspective, she explores the construction and transmission of knowledge. She is an avid ethnographer who uses narrative inquiry, photography, and poetry as tools to learn and communicate.

J. Joy Esquierdo is a Professor in the Department of Bilingual and Literacy Studies at the University of Texas Rio Grande Valley. She is also the Director for the Center for Bilingual Studies as part of the B3 Institute. Dr. Esquierdo's academic interests center on bilingual/dual language education, gifted and talented education and the cognitive development of bilingual children. Additionally, her research agenda includes topics that focus on the academic performance of bilingual-dual language students in various areas such as content biliteracy development (English and Spanish), and overall best teaching practices for bilingual-dual language learners that focus on academic rigor.

Veronica L. Estrada is a Professor at the University of Texas Rio Grande Valley in the Department of Teaching and Learning. She earned her Ph.D. at The Ohio State University in Education Studies with an emphasis in English Education and Language, Literacy, and Culture. Her research interests include teacher development and preparation, literacy and identity, and teaching with mixed-reality virtual teaching environments. She is an active member of several professional education boards and has served her department as Interim Department Chair and Program Coordinator of the Secondary/All Level program.

Ariana Garza Garcia has an M.Ed. in Curriculum and Instruction with an emphasis in Science Education. She has been a chemistry high school teacher of diverse populations for four years. Her research interests involve the analysis of how race, language, and immigration status influence students' identity. She is also interested in self-reflection to better understand her own identity and agency as a Mexican American female teaching in STEM.

Kip Austin Hinton is an Associate Professor in the Department of Bilingual and Literacy Studies at the University of Texas Rio Grande Valley. His research interests include language ideology, critical race theory, immigrant students, and educational equity within bilingual education programs. He is a guitarist who plays traditional country music. He also plays bass in a feminist punk rock band.

Hitomi Kambara is an Assistant Professor of Literacy Education in the Department of Bilingual and Literacy Studies at the University of Texas Rio Grande Valley. She received her Ph.D. in Instructional Leadership and Academic Curriculum with Specialization in Language and Literacy Education at the University of Oklahoma. Her research focuses on literacy motivation, attitudes, habits, and practices across different racial and ethnic groups and also in international contexts by employing quantitative, qualitative, and mixed methods research.

Jacqueline B. Koonce is an Assistant Professor in the Department of Bilingual and Literacy Studies at the University of Texas Rio Grande Valley. She received her Ph.D. in Curriculum, Instruction, and Teacher Education with a specialization in Language and Literacy Education from Michigan State University. Dr. Koonce's current research focuses on early literacy development, the impact of caring on students, the experiences of women faculty of color at Hispanic-Serving Institutions (HSIs), and African American women's language and literacy practices.

María G. Leija is an Assistant Professor of Early Childhood Education in the Department of Interdisciplinary Learning and Teaching at The

University of Texas at San Antonio. She earned her Ph.D. from The University of Texas at Austin in Curriculum and Instruction with an emphasis in Bilingual/Bicultural Education. Her research focuses on ways bilingual teachers effectively leverage Latinx students' cultural and linguistic resources through their literacy practices to support their academic vocabulary development, acquisition of content knowledge, and the development of students' bilingual, biliterate, and bicultural identities.

Gilberto P. Lara earned his Ph.D. in Curriculum and Instruction with an emphasis in Bilingual and Bicultural Education from The University of Texas at Austin. He is an Assistant Professor in the Bicultural-Bilingual Studies Department at The University of Texas at San Antonio. His research considers the intersectionality of Latinos in the U.S. including language, immigration, ethnicity, culture, identity, phenotype, and sexuality. A particular interest of his is how people situate themselves as bilingual, bicultural, raced, and gendered beings through linguistic practices.

Karin Ann Lewis is an Associate Professor in the Department of Teaching and Learning at the University of Texas Rio Grande Valley. Dr. Lewis holds a Ph.D. in Educational and Counseling Psychology from the University of Kentucky. Her scholarly focus takes on complexities of identity and agency from a social justice perspective meant to open up transdisciplinary discourses by seeking ways to transcend the current educational paradigm through transformative, culturally responsive pedagogy. Her scholarship is grounded in qualitative, collaborative, collective ethnographic methodologies.

Alcione N. Ostorga is a Professor in the Department of Bilingual and Literacy Studies at the University of Texas Rio Grande Valley. She teaches undergraduate and graduate courses in the bilingual education program. Her scholarly work focuses on developing border pedagogies for addressing contextual mitigating factors in the identity development of Latinx teacher candidates such as specific pedagogies for the development of cultural and professional identities, teacher agency, and academic Spanish abilities.

Patricia Alvarez McHatton received her Ph.D. in Curriculum and Instruction with an emphasis in Special Education and Urban Education from the University of South Florida. She is the Executive Vice President for Academic Affairs, Student Success, and P-16 Integration for the University of Texas Rio Grande Valley. Her research focuses on teacher preparation, collaboration, and data-based decision-making. Currently, Dr. Alvarez McHatton, in collaboration with faculty from within and beyond the College of Education and P-16 Integration (CEP), is focused on exploring what it means to be a Hispanic-Serving

Institution and what we do as a Hispanic-Serving Institution to ensure the success of Hispanic learners.

Sandra I. Musanti is an Associate Professor in the Department of Bilingual and Literacy Studies at the University of Texas Rio Grande Valley. She received her Ph.D. in Educational Thought and Sociocultural Studies from the University of New Mexico. She was a postdoctoral fellow for the Center for the Mathematics Education of Latinos/as, a project funded by the NSF. Presently, her research interests focus on preservice and in-service bilingual teacher development across content areas, practice-based, and translanguaging approaches in bilingual teacher preparation, novice bilingual teachers' repertoire of practice development and identity construction, and translanguaging pedagogies in Hispanic-Serving Institutions.

Noushin Nouri received her Ph.D. in Curriculum and Instruction with an emphasis in Science Education from the University of Arkansas. She is an Assistant Professor in the College of Education and P-16 Integration for the University of Texas Rio Grande Valley. Her research focuses on nature and history of science and culturally relevant teacher preparation. Currently, Dr. Nouri tries to combine research in nature of science with components of Hispanic culture to ensure the success of Hispanic preservice teachers and their readiness to be a culturally responsible teacher.

Dagoberto E. Ramirez received his Ed.D. in Educational Leadership from the University of Texas-Pan American. He is a Learning Framework Lecturer and Academic Advisor in the University College at the University of Texas Rio Grande Valley. His current research primarily focuses on the first-year experience of first-generation Hispanic students at Hispanic-Serving Institutions. He also explores issues connected to bilingualism, leadership development of Mexican American superintendents in the Rio Grande Valley, and culture and literacies of recent immigrants from Mexico.

Patricia Ramirez-Biondolillo received her Master's degree in Curriculum and Instruction with an emphasis in Secondary Science from the University of Texas at Brownsville. Patricia is a Lecturer in the Department of Teaching and Learning at the University of Texas Rio Grande Valley (UTRGV). Patricia is currently a doctoral student at UTRGV in the Science Education Ed.D. program. Her research focuses on elementary science teacher preparation in a Hispanic-Serving Institution.

Alma D. Rodríguez received her Ed.D. in Curriculum and Instruction from the University of Houston. She is the Dean of the University of Texas Rio Grande Valley College of Education and P-16 Integration.

Her research has focused on bilingual and ESL teacher preparation from three interconnected dimensions: issues of language and how those impact teaching and learning; the use of culturally and linguistically relevant approaches to teacher preparation with the goal of impacting teacher candidates' practice; and the improvement of teacher preparation programs with an emphasis on meeting the needs of Latina/o emergent bilingual students, teachers, and communities.

Felicia Rodriguez has a B.S. in Chemistry with secondary certification and is a chemistry high school teacher in the Rio Grande Valley. Her research interests involve using counter-storytelling and autoethnography to develop teacher agency.

Cinthya M. Saavedra is an Associate Professor, Academic Program Director of Mexican American Studies, and Associate Dean of Interdisciplinary Programs and Community Engagement. Her research centers Chicana/Latina feminist epistemology in education research. In addition, Dr. Saavedra's scholarship addresses critical methodologies such as testimonios, pláticas, and critical reflexivity.

Eugenio Longoria Sáenz is the Deputy Director for the RGV FOCUS collective impact initiative of Communities Foundation of Texas's (CFT) Educate Texas in the Rio Grande Valley. Prior to joining CFT, Eugenio was the Executive Director of the Eastern North Philadelphia Youth Services Coalition. He was also awarded two international research training opportunities in Geneva, Switzerland, by the World Health Organization, and in Cape Town, South Africa, by the Human Sciences Research Council. Eugenio holds a Bachelor's of Business Administration in economics and international business from Baylor University and a Master's in education and human development from George Washington University.

Janine M. Schall is an Associate Professor and Chair of the Department of Bilingual and Literacy Studies at the University of Texas Rio Grande Valley. She received her Ph.D. in Language, Reading and Culture from the University of Arizona. Her research interests focus broadly on literacy education and teacher preparation with an emphasis on culture, identity, and language. She studies how marginalized populations are represented in children's literature and how children of all backgrounds can be connected with multicultural and global literature. She also studies language and literacy practices of Latinx students in higher education, particularly within a Hispanic-Serving Institution.

Elena M. Venegas earned a Ph.D. in Curriculum and Teaching from Baylor University. Presently, she is an Assistant Professor in the Department of Bilingual and Literacy Studies at the University of Texas

Rio Grande Valley. Dr. Venegas' research interests center on social issues within education, student-centered approaches to literacy instruction, social-emotional learning, and Latinx students.

Vejoya Viren is an Associate Professor of Early Childhood Studies in the Department of Human Development & School Services at the University of Texas Rio Grande Valley. Dr. Viren holds a Ph.D. in Human Development from the Virginia Polytechnic Institute and State University. Her research currently has a diverse focus ranging from infant toddler language environment, context-based play and learning, to identity and teaching. Vejoya also leads early childhood teacher workshops in Nepal and India.

Christian E. Zúñiga is an Assistant Professor in the Department of Bilingual and Literacy Studies at the University of Texas Rio Grande Valley. Her research has focused on teacher education and language policy, and how these influence bilingual/biliteracy development for minoritized communities, especially in borderland communities.

Acknowledgments

The editors would like to acknowledge RGV FOCUS for their support, collaboration, and belief in the work that we do as we strive to ensure the success of Latinx learners. We would also like to acknowledge the Hispanic Association of Colleges and Universities (HACU), particularly Alicia Diaz, for their tireless work on behalf of Hispanic-Serving Institutions and Latinx learners.

We must also acknowledge and thank the contributors of this volume and our colleagues across the country who served as peer reviewers throughout this process.

1 The Hispanic-Serving Designation and Educator Preparation

Patricia Alvarez McHatton, Janine M. Schall and Eugenio Longoria Sáenz

What I also like is that UTRGV resembles the heart of a Hispanic- they are strong, willing, determined, and most importantly fearless in every situation.

Leonardo Daniel Carmona, UTRGV student

Hispanic-Serving Institutions (HSIs) are defined by the U.S. Department of Education (n.d.) as an institution of higher education that is an eligible institution and has an enrollment of full-time equivalent students that is comprised of at least 25% Hispanic[1] students. The way HSIs came into being is an important distinction compared to other minority-serving institutions, most of which were specifically created to serve a particular population. For example, the mission of Historically Black Colleges and Universities (HBCUs) was and is the education of black Americans (The Higher Education Act of 1965). Similarly, tribal colleges and universities are controlled and operated by American Indian tribes and serve that population.

The creation of the HSI designation resulted from decades of advocacy efforts to ensure access to resources and recognition as institutions that served many Latinx students (Valdez, 2015). Texas was at the forefront of efforts to create the HSI designation (De La Trinidad, Guajardo, Kranz, & Guajardo, 2017) due to long-term lack of access to quality education, deficit views, and negative stereotypes about the Latinx population, and an expectation for individuals from culturally and linguistically diverse backgrounds to assimilate into the dominant culture. During the 1980s leaders were cognizant of the challenges Latinx students faced in completing their degree and the limited financial support provided to institutions that served predominately Latinx populations. The desire to improve educational outcomes for Latinx students led to the inception of the Hispanic Association of Colleges and Universities (HACU), which was formed in 1986 with the express mission "to engage in activities that heightened the awareness among corporations, foundations, governmental agencies and individuals of the role that member colleges and universities play in educating the nation's Hispanic youth" (HACU, 2011). The formal recognition of and targeted federal appropriations for HSIs in 1992 was made possible through the efforts of HACU and its members. HACU continues to play an integral role in ensuring positive outcomes for Latinx learners through its advocacy efforts.

Considering the shifting demographics of our nation, it is not surprising that the number of HSIs has grown significantly since 1986. HSIs comprise over 15% of non-profit colleges and universities. The majority are in urban areas, and 83% of all HSIs are located in California, Texas, Florida, New York, Illinois, New Mexico, and Puerto Rico. Since 1994, the number of HSIs has grown from 189 to 523, with an average increase of 30 institutions per year since 2009. An additional 328 are classified as emerging HSIs; these are institutions with 15–24.9% Latinx undergraduate full-time equivalent enrollment (Excelencia in Education, n.d.). Sixty-six percent of undergraduate Latinx students (Excelencia in Education, 2018; HACU, 2019) or nearly 1.97 million Hispanic students attend HSIs (Pennamon, 2018). Thus, HSIs serve a critical role in the education of Latinx students. The main reasons cited by Latinx students for attending HSIs are access, location, cost, and representation, or the opportunity to attend an institution at which they feel a sense of belonging.

Given that institutions of higher education achieve the HSI designation based on meeting a predetermined threshold, HSIs are highly diverse and serve a variety of missions (Núñez, Crisp & Elizondo, 2016). Research suggests that obtaining the designation does not necessarily result in institutions building identity to align with their HSI status (Contreras, Malcom, & Bensimon, 2008; Garcia & Dwyer, 2018; Santiago, 2012). Garcia (2017) proposes the need for institutions to examine who they are as a Latinx-serving organization. She identifies the ideal Latinx-serving identity as one with "high productivity (in regard to legitimized outcomes) [e.g., graduation rates, graduate school enrollment, and employment] and provides a culture that enhances the experience of Latinx students" (p. 122S). This means the ideal HSI examines its historical legacy regarding the education of Latinx students, implements culturally responsive and sustaining practices which recognize and value the cultural and linguistic capital the students possess, and has faculty and staff that connect with students on various levels.

In addition to recognition as institutions that serve the majority of Latinx students, the HSI designation provided increased funding and services to assist these institutions in their efforts to offer a high-quality education to Latinx students. Such support is important but insufficient to the success of Latinx students. We believe an HSI designation demands attention to the whole student from an ecological perspective that examines and attends to the student within his or her immediate environment, recognizes family as a partner in the education of the child, utilizes social and cultural values and diverse ways of knowing to inform instruction, and acknowledges and attends to historically institutionalized legacies of oppression, disenfranchisement, and marginalization. It is this belief that led us to explore what it means to be a Hispanic-Serving College of Education (HSCOE) and how we can make this designation meaningful.

What Led Us to This Work?

Patty

We emigrated to the U.S. shortly after Castro took over Cuba. My ethnic identity blurred due to assimilation demands that permeated my environment. I found myself struggling with the need to retain my cultural heritage while wanting to belong in my new environment. It was during my doctoral studies that I became cognizant of my desire to reconnect fully with my identification as a Latina.

Early in my career in higher education, I had the honor of teaching and ultimately serving as chair of John's[2] dissertation committee. I remember being in awe of John's strong sense of self as a Black male, and deep understanding of his cultural roots. As we got to know each other throughout his doctoral journey, he shared his educational experiences at an HBCU. He credited the institution with providing a supportive environment that fostered a sense of community, valued his cultural heritage, and engendered his racial development.

I joined the University of Texas Rio Grande Valley (UTRGV) in its inaugural year as the Founding Dean of the College of Education and P-16 Integration (CEP). As a Latina, serving at an HSI allowed me an opportunity to reflect on my own educational experiences and strengthen my connection to my own cultural and ethnic heritage. John often came to mind as I explored the extent to which we actually "served" our students. Would they describe their experiences with us in the same manner that John did his experiences at his HBCU?

Janine

When I graduated college there were almost no teaching jobs in the Midwest, so I expanded my job search to places across the U.S. where I thought my knowledge of Spanish would be a competitive advantage. I ended up getting hired to teach fifth grade in a rural school district in the South Texas borderlands. It was a community that was predominately Latinx, Spanish-speaking, and low income, but I was sure that my excellent teacher certification program had prepared me for my first year of teaching and that my year abroad in Spain had prepared me for any cultural or linguistic differences I might find. This was, of course, deeply naïve.

I returned to South Texas after earning my doctorate, working predominately with Latinx preservice teachers at The University of Texas (UT)-Pan American. I tried to make my classroom culturally affirming and sustaining, using culturally relevant materials whenever I could and encouraging bilingual students to be comfortable using Spanish as well as English in our classroom.

When UTRGV was created, the idea of us becoming a premiere bilingual, bicultural, and biliterate HSI was built into our foundation, but there wasn't yet much discussion of what that meant. At the same time, I was named Chair in a new department that housed courses about multicultural and bilingual education. As chair, I wanted to help the faculty in my department build research capacity. I also felt it was vital for the success of our students to engage in critical conversations about how to support Latinx preservice teachers.

Eugenio

As a kid from the Rio Grande Valley (RGV), I am not supposed to be an author of this book, or everything else that was a pre-cursor to becoming an author of this book. These were not possibilities I was socialized to believe could be a part of my lived experiences. Nonetheless, I am here. I am here despite the many deficits we have normalized about Latinx and other minoritized students and their academic and professional achievements. I am here because there is a young boy that still resides in me. This young boy is the "I" that still sees himself in every student in the RGV, and, in doing so, knows that every student in the Valley can see themselves in him too. I am linked to this region in this way forever – we are past, current, and future state reflections of each other. Speaking at a conference not too long ago, I remember saying, "They are not the Us in this room anymore; They are a new We." This was in reference to the current academic achievements of the newest generation of learners growing up in the RGV today. "They are perhaps the greatest generation of learners from the Rio Grande Valley to ever enter the higher education pipeline," I continued. They are what brought me to this work. This work is in service to them, and that young boy part of me that I still see in them.

The three of us came together and engaged in substantive discussion on what it meant to be an HSI in general and specifically what it meant to be a HSCOE. More precisely, what did it mean to prepare predominately Latinx teachers who will be teaching in Hispanic-Serving School Districts (HSSDs) in which most students also are Latinx? These conversations led us to the development of a research initiative focused on exploring the question: What does it mean to be a HSCOE and how do we make this designation meaningful?

The Context in Which We Do Our Work

The Region

The RGV is in Deep South Texas. It spans a four-county area along the northern bank of the Rio Grande, which separates the U.S. from Mexico. Much of the population in the RGV is of Mexican heritage, comprised of recent immigrants and long-established local families who settled in this region when it was still a territory of Spain. It is a vibrant, predominately bilingual community that values family and a strong work ethic and is fiercely proud of its cultural and linguistic heritage. Concurrently, it is also one of the poorest regions in the nation, and has been underserved and often overlooked, undervalued, or misunderstood by those outside of the RGV.

According to the U.S. Census Bureau (2019), the population of the RGV in 2018 was 1,375,887, 91.75% of whom are Hispanic. Per the *State of Texas Children 2017* (Tingle, Haynes, & Li, 2017), Cameron and Hidalgo, two of the four counties comprising the RGV, account for 94% of children living in the RGV. Ninety-five percent of those children are Hispanic and are U.S. citizens, with approximately 75% of them having at least one parent who is a U.S. citizen by birth. It is estimated that by 2050 more than 600,000 children will live in this two-county area.

The population in the Valley has lower high school graduation rates, lower college attendance rates, and higher rates of living in poverty compared to the state at large (Tingle et al., 2017). The percent of children living in high-poverty neighborhoods in the RGV is 68% compared to 18% in the state of Texas. A number of these children live in *colonias*. Barton, Perimeter, Blum, and Marquez (2015) define *colonia* as an unincorporated settlement of land along the Texas-Mexico border that may lack some of the most basic living necessities, such as access to drinking water and sewer systems, electricity, paved roads, and safe and sanitary housing. Some of the nation's poorest counties exist along the Texas border as the per-capita median income average is approximately half of the overall Texas state median income rates, and the percentage of individuals living below poverty level is almost double that of the state average (Ura, 2016).

While socioeconomic status is a strong predictor of academic success, students in the RGV are performing at impressive academic levels. Academic success occurs when we work as a collective body to ensure all students, and the systems that serve them, are provided the resources necessary to achieve equitable life outcomes. Figure 1.1 demonstrates 12 Cradle-To-Career educational pathway indicators that have been tracked for the past seven years as part of a larger collective impact initiative called RGV FOCUS. As of 2018, the RGV met or exceeded the state performance in 9 of those 12 indicators (RGV FOCUS, 2019b).

Additionally, RGV school districts outperform the statewide average by 22% in the number of students who attends an "A" or "B" school based on the Texas Education Agency (TEA) Accountability Rating System (2019). Figure 1.2 compares the RGV districts' accountability performance to other major districts or regions in the state.

Finally, in the U.S., the RGV also has the highest concentration of teachers with similar ethnic and lived experiences as their students (RGV

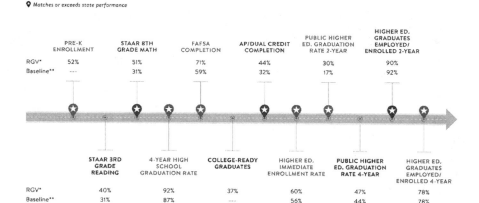

MAKING A DIFFERENCE ALONG THE CRADLE-TO-CAREER
EDUCATIONAL PATHWAY

Figure 1.1 Academic performance comparison: RGV and Texas.

87% of Rio Grande Valley Students Attend "A" or "B" Schools vs. 65% Statewide, 61% in Dallas County, and 52% in Bexar County

Percent of Students Attending Campuses by TEA Accountability Rating, by State and for Major Counties/ Regions, 2018-19 School Year

Figure 1.2 TEA accountability rating comparison.

FOCUS, 2019a). Ninety percent of teachers in the RGV identify as Latinx compared to 27% for the state and 9% for the U.S. Comparatively, 97% of students in the RGV identify as Latinx compared to 52% for the state and 26% for the U.S.

The University

The UTRGV is a distributed campus that primarily serves the RGV community. It was established in 2015 through legislative action, becoming the first major public university of the 21st century in Texas. This allowed UTRGV the opportunity to expand educational opportunities and established a new School of Medicine. The university assumed the assets and liabilities of The UT-Pan American, located in Edinburg, Texas, and The University of Texas Brownsville-Texas Southmost College, located in Brownsville, Texas, which are considered our legacy institutions. Figure 1.3 shows how the work of the university revolves around five core priorities and four additional areas of focus (UTRGV, 2017).

Central to our work is the need to serve our regional population; improve educational outcomes for Latinx students across the region, state, and country; and serve as a national model for the success of Latinx students. Furthermore, we were committed to building upon strong cultural and linguistic assets by becoming a bicultural, bilingual, and biliterate institution.

In fall 2018, UTRGV enrolled 28,644 students (UTRGV, 2019). Eighty-eight percent self-identified as Latinx, making it one of the highest Hispanic-enrolling institutions in the nation. Of those, 92.6% came from the four-county area that makes up the RGV and an additional 2% are Mexican Nationals, students who are born in Mexico and may continue to live there, crossing into the U.S. to attend classes. Most of our students receive some form of financial aid; for example, 60.3% are Pell grant eligible. We consistently rank as one of the most affordable institutions of higher education in the nation and in the performance of first-generation students and Pell recipients (Kelchen, 2018). What is more important to know but is often less documented is that

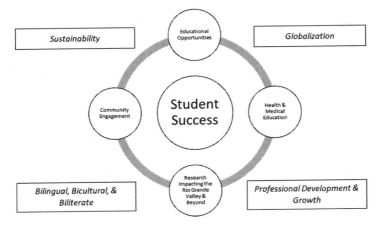

Figure 1.3 UTRGV core priorities and other focus areas.

our students are committed to family, believe in giving back to community, understand and are willing to assume responsibility, and persevere in their endeavors. Further, their families understand the value of an education, support their child's pursuit of an education, and want to be included their child's progress in higher education.

The College

The fall 2018 enrollment in the UTRGV CEP was 2,868, 94.6% of whom are native to the RGV and 89% of whom identify as Latinx (UTRGV Strategic Analysis and Institutional Reporting). Most of our graduates return to their communities to begin their teaching career and are retained in the profession at higher rates than the state overall. Similarly, 96.9% of PK-12 students in the RGV identify as Latinx (RGV FOCUS, 2019b). Thus, graduates from our HSCOE enter districts that are also designated as Hispanic-Serving based on their demographics.

Based on the demographics of our region, our districts, and our institution, our teacher preparation programs should exemplify an educational experience with culturally responsive pedagogy that entails asset-based approaches, culturally mediated instruction, and curricula that allow students an opportunity to learn about the contributions of their ancestors as well as about topics and issues relevant to their background and culture. Furthermore, the linguistic diversity in our region also demands we employ culturally sustaining pedagogy which withstands "...the cultural and linguistic competence of [students'] communities while simultaneously offering access to dominant cultural competence" (Paris, 2012, p. 95). While some of our faculty may have taken the cultural and linguistic knowledge of our students into account in their teaching, overall our curriculum, programs, and policies have not. This is not unusual for HSIs, where often the college experience is traditional and tailored to fit white, middle-class university students (Garcia & Dwyer, 2018; Ledesma & Burciaga, 2015). Our discussions on what it means to be an HSI take on a new urgency because of our responsibility preparing teachers, many of whom will teach in an HSSD and will affect PK-12 children for decades to come.

The Structure of This Book

This book is the outcome of several years of collaborative engagement with a committed group of faculty devoted to serving Latinx students and ensuring their success. Chapter 2 details the process we engaged in as we implemented Special Interest Research Groups (SIRGs) charged with responding to our guiding question: *What does it mean to be a Hispanic-Serving College of Education and how do we make this designation meaningful?* Chapters 3 through 10 describe the work of eight of our

SIRGs. In Chapter 3, Leija, Lara, Aponte-Safe, and Kambara describe how they participated in a collaborative self-study as first-year assistant professors at an HSI in which they critically examined their pedagogical practices. In Chapter 4, Lewis, Espinosa-Dulanto, Koonce, and Viren illustrate their journey as transplants to the RGV and UTRGV through individual and collective narratives. In Chapter 5, Saavedra, Esquierdo, Ramirez, and Almaguer put forth recommendations about decolonializing community-based research. In Chapter 6, Musanti, Cavazos, and Rodríguez examine how their students explored their perceptions of language difference and negotiated their understanding of bilingualism and the use of translanguaging in the classroom. In Chapter 7, Venegas, Estrada, Schall, and De Leon investigate the language and literacy practices of bilingual education preservice teachers. In Chapter 8, Garcia, Rodriguez, and Chapman highlight Garcia and Rodriguez' lived experiences as they worked to develop a sense of self and teacher agency as Latina women in STEM education. In Chapter 9, Nouri, Aguilar, and Ramirez-Biondolillo engage Latinx preservice teachers in exploring the nature of science through autobiographies revealing the importance of culturally responsive and sustaining approaches to teaching science. In Chapter 10, Ostorga, Zúñiga, and Hinton describe their process as they worked to develop a border pedagogy for Latinx teacher development. Finally, in Chapter 11, we explore the questions that serve as the impetus for this work and discuss the cross-cutting themes that emerged from each of the studies. We share lessons learned to date and detail next steps for our continued development as an HSI and an HSCOE. We end by reinforcing the importance of this work and a call to action by other HSIs and HSCOEs.

Notes

1 Because the term 'Hispanic' has been commonly used by the U.S. government, we include it when it is part of a federal designation or when it is used in an original source. However, we prefer the term Latinx, which we feel better recognizes the heterogeneity of the U.S. population with Latin American ancestry or origin.
2 Pseudonym.

References

Barton, J., Perlmeter, E., Blum, E., & Marquez, R. (2015). *Las Colonias in the 21st century – Progress along the Texas-Mexico border*. Dallas, TX: Community Development Department and Public Affairs Department.
Contreras, F. E., Malcom, L. E., & Bensimon, E. M. (2008). Hispanic serving institutions: Closeted identity and the production of equitable outcomes for Latino/a students. In M. Gasman, B. Baez, & C. S. Turner (Eds.), *Understanding minority-serving institutions* (pp. 71–90). Albany, NY: SUNY Press.

De La Trinidad, M., Guajardo, F., Kranz, P. L., & Guajardo, M. (2017). The University of Texas Rio Grande Valley: Reframing HSIs through a multi-sited ethnography. *Association of Mexican American Educations (AMAE) Journal, 11*(3), 50–83.

Excelencia in Education. (2018). Hispanic-serving institutions (HSIs): 2017–2018. Washington, DC: *Excelencia in Education.*

Excelencia in Education. (n.d.). Hispanic-serving institutions (HSIs). https://www.edexcelencia.org/research/hispanic-serving-institutions-hsis).

Garcia, G. A. (2017). Defined by outcomes or culture? Constructing an organization identify for Hispanic-serving institutions. *American Educational Research Journal, 54*(1S), 111S–134S.

Garcia, G. A., & Dwyer, B. (2018). Exploring college students' identification with an organizational identity for serving Latinx students at a Hispanic serving institution (HSI) and an emerging HSI. *American Journal of Education, 24,* 191–215.

Higher Education Act of 1965. [P.L. 89-329; Approved November 8, 1965]. https://legcounsel.house.gov/Comps/Higher%20Education%20Act%20Of%201965.pdf

Kelchen, R. (2018). America's best bank for the buck colleges 2018. *Washington Monthly,* p. 42–110.

Núñez, A. M., Crisp, G., & Elizondo, D. (2016). Mapping Hispanic serving institutions: A typology of institutional diversity. *The Journal of Higher Education, 87*(1), 55–83.

Paris, D. (2012). Culturally sustaining pedagogy: A needed change in stance, terminology, and practice. *Educational Researcher, 41*(3), 93–97. doi:10.3102/0013189X12441244

Pennamon, T. (2018, June 5). HSI increases reflect growing student enrollment, matriculation. *Diverse Issues in Higher Education.* Retrieved from https://diverseeducation.com/article/117645/

RGV FOCUS. (2019a). *A celebration of collective impact in the Rio Grande Valley: A report on educational initiatives in South Texas.* Retrieved from https://issuu.com/educatetexas0/docs/edtx-cigatesreport-r10-singlepages

RGV FOCUS. (2019b). *Contigo: 2018 annual report.* Retrieved from https://www.edtx.org/getattachment/c50e678a-8c3a-4f93-b329-248e24e9f368/RGV-Focus-2019-AR-Contigo

Santiago, D. A. (2012). Public policy and the Hispanic serving institutions: From invention to accountability. *Journal of Latinos and Education, 11,* 163–167.

Texas Education Agency. (2019). 2019 Accountability rating system. Retrieved from https://tea.texas.gov/Student_Testing_and_Accountability/Accountability/State_Accountability/Performance_Reporting/2019_Accountability_Rating_System

The Hispanic Association of Colleges and Universities. (2011). 1986–2011: 25 years of championing Hispanic higher education – A historical review and a glimpse into the future. Retrieved from https://www.hacu.net/images/hacu/about/HACU_History_1986-2011F.pdf

The Hispanic Associate of Colleges and Universities. (2019). 2019 fact sheet: Hispanic higher education and HSIs. Retrieved from https://www.hacu.net/hacu/HSI_Fact_Sheet.asp

Tingle, K., Haynes, M., & Li, D. (2017). State of Texas children 2017. Retrieved from https://forabettertexas.org/images/2017_SOTC_RioGrande.pdf

Ura, A. (2016). Latest census data shows poverty rate highest at border, lowest in suburbs. *The Texas Tribune*. Retrieved July 9, 2019, from https://www.texastribune.org/2016/01/19/poverty-prevalent-on-texas-border-low-in-suburbs/

U.S. Census Bureau. (2019). Quick facts. Retrieved from https://www.census.gov/quickfacts/fact/table/willacycountytexas,starrcountytexas,cameroncountytexas,hidalgocountytexas,US/PST045218

U.S. Department of Education. (n.d.). White House Initiative for Educational Excellence for Hispanics. Retrieved from https://sites.ed.gov/hispanic-initiative/hispanic-serving-institutions-hsis/

UTRGV. (2017). Transforming your world strategic plan. Retrieved from https://www.utrgv.edu/strategic-plan/_files/documents/pdf/16094_aa_strategic_plan_full_document_proof_4.pdf

UTRGV. (2019). *Fast Facts 2018*. Retrieved from https://www.utrgv.edu/sair/fact-book/2018_fast-facts.pdf

Valdez, P. (2015). An overview of Hispanic serving institutions' legislation: Legislation policy formation between 1979 and 1992. In J. P. Mendez, F. Bonner, J. Mendez-Negrete & R. Palmer (Eds.), *Hispanic serving institutions in American higher education: Their origin, and present and future challenges* (pp. 5–29). Sterling, VA: Stylus.

2 The Hispanic-Serving College of Education Special Interest Research Group Initiative

Building a Community around a Question

Janine M. Schall, Patricia Alvarez McHatton and Eugenio Longoria Sáenz

What does it mean to be a Hispanic-Serving College of Education (HSCOE) and how do we make that term meaningful in ways that will further student success? While some of the faculty at our HSCOE were designing classes, developing curriculum, and teaching in ways that built upon students' cultural and linguistic assets, as a college we lacked a coherent identity related to our status as an HSCOE. Although we enrolled and graduated large numbers of Latinx students, we believed that we could improve their higher education experience through *serving* them by designing curriculum, programs, and policies that were culturally and linguistically affirming and sustaining (Paris & Alim, 2017) and by consciously and deliberately attending to the needs of our Latinx students, faculty, and staff.

We established the Hispanic-Serving Institution Special Interest Research Group (HSI SIRG) initiative as one way to become consciously skilled at addressing the question of what it means to be an HSCOE. By *consciously skilled* we mean that rather than continuing to have random, uncoordinated bursts of individual effort, we hoped to work together as a college to develop a strategic set of tools, concepts, and methods through a deliberate, critical, and reflective process that would allow us to consider our overarching question and related questions both now and through recursive future initiatives.

As we planned for the first year of the initiative, we developed a structure that would facilitate faculty explorations around the question of what it means to be an HSCOE and to enable us to meet multiple goals. The original call for proposals described the initiative as follows:

> Using the overarching question *what does it mean to be an HSCOE and how do we make this term meaningful for postsecondary education* as a guide, research teams should develop a focus for in-depth exploration. For example, one SIRG may focus on leadership preparation within an HSI while another SIRG examines the needs of transnational

preservice teachers. Although each SIRG will have a different focus, we expect all SIRGs to struggle with broad questions such as the following:

- How do we support the identity that is being an HSI for University of Texas Rio Grande Valley (UTRGV)?
- How is an HSI different from other institutions?
- How is a College of Education at an HSI different from other Colleges of Education?
- How do we effectively address the unique student population at an HSI?
- How does an HSI designation affect recruitment, college readiness, and the teacher pipeline?
- What are initiatives within an HSI that can inform our work with educator preparation?

While the broad, overarching goal was to explore what it means to be an HSCOE in order to improve student experience and success, we also hoped to accomplish a number of other things through the initiative. We believed that this initiative would help us build community among faculty through coming together to explore a focused topic. Even though this initiative was limited to the College of Education and P-16 Integration (CEP), with 5 different departments and over 90 faculty members, participants did not necessarily know each other. In addition, our university had recently integrated faculty from two different campuses, which had different campus cultures. We also wanted to help develop faculty in terms of their knowledge of Latinx students and culturally sustaining and affirming pedagogy (Paris & Alim, 2017). We intended to build research capacity and plant the seeds for future grant writing and larger research projects. Finally, we wanted to position UTRGV as a leader in Latinx student education.

We decided to structure the initiative around three central events: a beginning of the year retreat, a mid-project pulse check, and an end of the year exhibition and celebration. We also made strategic decisions about SIRG membership and in what ways participation would be encouraged or required. Finally, we decided each SIRG cycle would last one academic year, which would provide adequate time for small projects and could serve as pilots for larger studies or grant proposals.

Work with a Collective Impact Organization as a Thought Partner

For this initiative, the CEP partnered with RGV FOCUS, a collective impact collaborative with Educate Texas—the statewide educational initiative of Communities Foundation of Texas. RGV FOCUS provided some financial support for this initiative, but more importantly became a thought partner in this work. Collective impact is a structured form of collaboration, supported by various backbone organizations, and built around a common agenda, among a committed group of important actors from different sectors, working to create lasting solutions for critical social issues. The common agenda for RGV FOCUS is for all RGV learners to achieve a degree or credential that leads to a meaningful career. In order to realize this vision, RGV FOCUS joined UTRGV as a thought partner, with Eugenio serving as our most regular contact with the organization.

SIRG Participants

In order to encourage collaboration but to keep the size of the groups manageable, we required all SIRGs to consist of three to five members, who could be drawn from multiple disciplines or a single discipline. The lead needed to be from the College of Education, and the expectation was that the majority of group members would be from the CEP. However, SIRGs could include faculty from other colleges as well as students at either the undergraduate or graduate level. Participants could only participate in one SIRG at a time.

Proposal and Review Process

Because one of our goals was to develop research capacity in our college, we patterned the application process after a competitive grant's request for proposals (RFPs) (see Appendix 1 for the full RFP). We developed a call that described the initiative; laid out the requirements for participation, including mandatory attendance at all SIRG events, and the proposal format; and asked for proposals for a year-long research project around the overarching question. We also developed an evaluation rubric (see Appendix 2) that was distributed to faculty. We scheduled an informational meeting several weeks before proposals were due where we addressed questions and emphasized that the requirements listed in the call were mandatory and we expected strict adherence.

Once proposals were submitted, they were peer reviewed and we awarded proposals that demonstrated substantial potential to be strong research projects. While there was some discussion at the beginning of this initiative about whether or not we should commit to projects that were weak but could potentially be developed if we had the funding, we decided that we would enforce a high standard for awarded proposals even if that meant we accepted less than our capacity. Every submitted proposal—awarded or not—received substantial feedback as to its strengths and areas of improvement. The review process happened quickly so that we could get the projects started as close the beginning of the semester as possible.

Commitment and Accountability

College faculty are busy and pulled in many directions, and we knew that it would be easy for SIRG research to lose out while other priorities demanded attention. As facilitators, we needed to build in accountability measures to support SIRG participants following through on their commitment to this work. Each SIRG pledged to participate in all the initiative activities and to produce a tangible deliverable—a manuscript, grant submission, etc.—by the end of the cycle. In our second year of the SIRG initiative we added an end-of-year report so we could more easily keep track of the outcomes from the SIRG.

While accountability measures such as end-of-year reports were particularly important for the HSI SIRG facilitators, for the participants what mattered most was the way they provided accountability to each other within and across the different SIRGs. We knew that accountability had to be structured in ways that was supportive of the work, not punitive. As facilitators we deliberately included community-building experiences and times for participants to share their work with others. Participants knew that they would report on their work at each of the three main SIRG events. This, in itself, provided a powerful accountability measure; no one wanted to be in a position to share that no progress had occurred between SIRG events. Facilitators also kept in touch with SIRG members informally, and members of various SIRGs interacted in multiple ways throughout the year; it was common to have a quick, informal 'how's it going' conversation when SIRG members connected at college meetings or in the hallway.

Support and Critique

While a fundamental component of the SIRG initiative was the need for accountability, the opportunity to provide various kinds of support was equally, if not more, important. Financial support was offered through the funding each SIRG received. While minimal, the Dean's Office provided $1,250 for each awarded SIRG which could be spent on any SIRG-related activities; SIRGs spent their funds on anything from transcription services, to travel, to purchasing books and other supplies. Our decisions about the amount of funding were based on the limitations of the college budget; we wanted the amount to be small since this is intended to be seed money, but large enough that it would be purposeful.

More significant support occurred through the engagements at each of the required events and the development of a research community. Because the climate was supportive, not competitive, SIRG members were honest about their successes and their challenges; participants provided each other encouragement and suggested potential solutions to challenges. Many times an issue one group was struggling with was something another SIRG had successfully navigated already.

SIRG Events

We established three mandatory events; these included a kick-off retreat, a mid-project pulse check, and the final exhibition and celebration where each group presented its research.

Kick-off retreat. SIRGs participated in a two-day retreat intended to build community, engage in feedback allowing SIRGs to refine research questions and methodology, and finalize project timelines and outcomes. During this retreat, SIRG members moved between individual group and collective group work and served as critical friends to each other. A critical friend is a "trusted person who asks provocative questions, provides data to be examined through another lens, and offers critique of a person's work as a friend" (Costa & Kallick, 1993, p. 49).

A major goal of the kick-off retreat was to begin building community and establishing a common understanding of the overarching question guiding the initiative. To this end, we began with setting ground rules and establishing expectations for the day, then participated in a journey lines engagement to help us get to know each other. In the journey lines engagement, each person used chart paper to sketch out their journeys to this project; what in their personal or professional life led them to this work in the context of an HSCOE? Each person then shared with the larger group. Most people chose to share personal information about their background, sharing about families, immigration stories, transformative moments, and more. This was a powerful way for SIRG members to begin building relationships as a group; we saw commonalities across experiences that connected us and differences that explained our unique perspectives. Because we were sharing what brought us to this work, the journey line engagement helped SIRG members see each other as fellow humans, foster a sense of openness and receptivity, and also built a foundation for our continued discussion about why this work matters.

Throughout the rest of the retreat, we moved from a whole group macro discussion to meso, then micro discussions within each SIRG to refine their project. The macro discussion was based on the broad, overarching question *what does it mean to be an HSCOE and how do we make this term meaningful* and the sub-questions listed in the original RFP. This provided us, as facilitators, an opportunity to learn how the participants were thinking about the question and their initial understandings. It also allowed the group to begin building common understandings of the question and the language we would use throughout the initiative.

In the meso discussions, we asked each group to consider how their project contributed to the exploration of the overarching question, using the following guide:

- How does our project contribute to the question: What does it mean to be a HSCOE and how do we make this term meaningful for post-secondary education?

- How does our project contribute to understandings in the field about Latinx post-secondary education and learning?
- What does our project tell us about the CEP student population?
- How does our project inform the identity that is being an HSI at UTRGV?
- How does our project contribute to knowledge about student success, recruitment, college readiness, and the teacher pipeline?
- How does our project inform CEP programs and initiatives?

SIRGs met in their individual groups to discuss the question. During this process, the SIRGs began narrowing their projects to clearly align with the overarching question. Significant elements of their project were then captured on chart paper, which was posted on the wall so we could engage in a feedback carousel (Table 2.1).

Feedback was structured through the use of a quadrant, which was posted next to each project outline (see Figure 2.1). SIRGs then rotated throughout the room, reading about each project and posting feedback in the appropriate quadrant. This experience not only provided each SIRG with significant critical feedback about their project, but also helped SIRGs understand the type of feedback that we expected from the SIRG members as they served as critical friends. Once the SIRGs had rotated through all projects, we debriefed as a whole group.

Table 2.1 Meso discussion project outline

Research project's significant elements
Research question
Research methods
Literature/theory
Outcomes/goals
Relevance to HSI
Budget allocation

Clarifying Questions	Probing Questions
Recommendations	Resources

Figure 2.1 Feedback carousel quadrant.

At this point, SIRGs had received three rounds of significant feedback: from the proposal reviewers, the macro discussions, and the meso discussion and feedback carousel. On the second day of the retreat, we concluded with micro discussions, with each SIRG expected to focus on refining and strengthening their projects based on the feedback received the previous day. Focus questions for this discussion included:

- How did we refine our project based on the discussions we had yesterday?
- What revisions did we make in our project question and description?
- How did we strengthen our connection with the overarching HSI SIRG questions?
- How did we refine our research design?
- What do we still need to know as we begin our projects?
- What is the most productive use of our financial award?
- What are realistic project goals, outcomes, and products?

Many SIRGs significantly revised their projects during this process. One common issue was overambitious research plans, with SIRGs proposing projects that would realistically take several years to complete. Other SIRGs realized that their proposed projects only shallowly addressed the focus of the SIRG initiative and more tightly aligned their project with the HSI SIRG overarching question. In other cases, SIRGs reworded questions or revisited research protocols to avoid deficit perspectives. This was, perhaps, the most important shift we began to see; although SIRG members were participating in this initiative because they valued their students and wanted to improve their education, it was clear that some had conscious or unconscious deficit views of their students and the RGV community. It was essential for us as facilitators and as SIRG participants to tease out and push back against these ways of thinking whenever we came across them; deficit views of Latinx students and communities are so deeply engrained into U.S. educational institutions that confronting and deconstructing deficit views happened regularly throughout each cycle. This process not only helped us—facilitators and SIRG members—become consciously aware of our unconscious biases, it also forefronted the need for asset pedagogies within our SIRG projects and within an HSCOE identity.

During the micro discussions, SIRGs also completed a project template, which laid out their plan for completing the work over the year. This work was completed using the Pomodoro method, with repeated times of focused work, interspersed with quick reporting out and break time. We wrapped up the kick-off retreat with a debriefing session, and established expectations for the SIRGs in the next months before our mid-point pulse check.

Pulse check. Midway through each cycle, SIRGs met at a local restaurant to provide an update on their projects and again obtain feedback from their colleagues. SIRG participants reported on their accomplishments to date and shared resources, suggested professional readings, and helped each other troubleshoot issues in data collection. In each cycle, the discussions at the pulse check were animated and energetic, as participants pushed each other to consider new ideas, find connections between projects, and contribute to shaping emerging ideas about our HSCOE identity. It was during the pulse check in the initial cycles that we began to identify common threads—an ethic of care, community, agency, and inquiry—among the projects that we believe began to shed light on what it means to be an HSCOE.

Final exhibition. At the end of the year, SIRGs presented their work at the final exhibition, which took place off campus. Faculty from throughout the institution were invited to attend. Similar to the pulse check this event provided an opportunity for SIRGs to share their research with a larger audience. SIRGs also explicitly addressed how their research was beginning to inform the question of what it means to be an HSCOE. In a reflective discussion at the conclusion of the first cycle's final exhibition, participants noted concrete ways the HSI SIRG initiative supported their research, such as the ways that the SIRG structure helped them stay on task and fostered a sense of accountability. Members also shared the power of the collective and how they appreciated the framework for collective inquiry, the growing research community, and the ways that the initiative fostered critical self-reflection. Participants left the final exhibition with new questions to explore a renewed sense of themselves as researchers, and a deepened commitment to the education of Latinx students and to their own role as faculty in an HSCOE.

HSI SIRG Initiative Growth and Evolution

At the time of this writing, the HSI SIRG initiative is entering its fourth cycle. While the basic structure has remained the same, in each cycle we have refined our own work as facilitators and the SIRG engagements, based on the feedback from SIRG participants and the needs of each cycle's participants.

While SIRG participants all committed to and valued this work, it is easy for research work to be put aside in the face of more immediate demands of teaching and service. As facilitators, we structured the initiative to enforce participation and accountability standards so that the work of each SIRG continued to move forward. In the second year of the initiative, we added an end-of-year report to help us track project outcomes.

We found that in some cycles the participants were willing and able to serve as critical friends right away, and in other cycles they needed support in this area. As facilitators, we sometimes needed to do a lot of this work in the initial stages as a way to model what we expected, then were able to step back as SIRG members moved into more active roles as critical friends.

We also found that despite the overarching question explicitly addressing HSIs, a number of SIRGs needed support in strongly aligning their research to the HSCOE experience. Some SIRGs developed projects that used Latinx participants and/or that took place at UTRGV, but that did not explicitly address the HSI experience. In our second year, we revised the RFP to emphasize this point and also provided explicit opportunities in each SIRG event for groups to discuss this issue.

After our second cycle, we became dissatisfied that so many projects were gathering information, but not moving forward to action. We believed that it was necessary but not sufficient to learn more about our students, faculty, and context; transformation required action built upon what these projects learned. In each cycle, we became more explicit about asking 'so what' and 'what does this mean for our college,' and pushing SIRG members to think about how their research should inform our actions as a college.

By the end of our third cycle, a significant number of CEP faculty members had participated in at least one SIRG. Over the initial 3 cycles, we funded 13 unique projects, with 4 projects renewed at least once (see Appendix 3). We saw that this question of serving Latinx students and of transforming our college through culturally sustaining and affirming practices was becoming a central conversation in our college. We also saw an increased sense of community and increased research capacity. However, we realized that our students belong not just to our college, but to our university, and that this initiative needed to expand to include faculty across the university. Because of this, for our fourth cycle we partnered with the Division of Academic Affairs and solicited proposals from across the university. In addition, we revised the RFP to emphasize action; our new overarching question is *what do we do as a HSI and as a faculty in an HSI to ensure the success of our student population?*

After three cycles of the HSI SIRG initiative, we realize that there is no one answer to our original question of what it means to be an HSCOE. However, the process of exploring that question has helped us get closer to being *consciously skilled*; the structure of the initiative supports the deliberate, critical, and reflective exploration of our overarching question. The ethics of care, community, agency, and inquiry that have emerged from our work are an initial framework that demands further investigation and development; we look forward to future cycles of the HSI SIRG initiative.

References

Costa, A., & Kallick, B. (1993). Through the lens of a critical friend. *Educational Leadership, 51*(2), 49–51.

Paris, D., & Alim, H. S. (2017). *Culturally sustaining pedagogies: Teaching and learning for justice in a changing world.* New York, NY: Teachers College Press.

3 Reflections on Teacher Education Practices of First-Year Tenure-Track Professors at an HSI

*María G. Leija, Gilberto P. Lara,
Gerardo Aponte-Safe and Hitomi Kambara*

Research on Hispanic-Serving Institutions (HSIs) has often focused on student outcomes on the basis of graduation rates (Bensimon, Hao, & Bustillos, 2006; Garcia, 2013) or enrollment rates (Malcom, 2010; Santiago, 2012). In answering the call for HSIs to examine the ways in which they serve their Latinx students (Flores & Park, 2013; Garcia, 2017), this chapter draws on data from a self-study of us, as teacher educators, at an HSI—specifically a Hispanic-Serving College of Education (HSCOE), reflecting on our learning and practice of Culturally Sustaining Pedagogy or CSP (Paris & Alim, 2017). This one-year self-study as first-year tenure-track faculty members included a weekly book study where we examined our pedagogical practices through a CSP lens, with the following research questions: What does it mean to be a professor at an HSI?; how am I inclusive of my students' knowledge, experiences, language(s), and culture(s)?; and what activities do I engage in as I work toward becoming a professor that encourages the sustainment of my students' culture(s) and language(s)? The book study created a space for each of us to support one another in critically reflecting about our role as teacher educators by engaging in weekly dialogues facilitated by discussions about a professional book on CSP. We must always keep in mind that Latinx students are a heterogeneous group with a variety of ethnicities, races, social classes, and nationalities (Oboler, 1995). For this reason, it is critical for HSI faculty to examine how their pedagogical practices support the academic success of the diverse student population they serve without essentializing a one-size-fits-all approach toward all Latinx populations.

Review of the Literature

As the enrollment of Latinx students continues to increase at HSIs and additional universities are designated as HSIs, it is vital to examine the role of faculty in the academic and personal success of Latinx students; 66% of all Latinx undergraduate students are served at HSIs (Excelencia in Education, 2019). Latinx students are least likely to obtain their bachelor's degree when compared to other racial and ethnic groups (Astin & Oseguera, 2003). Although colleges and universities offer federally funded and campus-wide programs to support Latinx students' adjustment and retention in higher education (Reyes, 2007; Seidman, 2005), historically, Latinx college students have encountered obstacles such as lack of financial resources (Núñez & Bowers, 2011) and college navigational capital (Espinoza & Espinoza, 2012), which they must overcome.

In regard to HSIs, scholars have found instrumental non-academic measures leading to student success as important. These include connections with faculty and sharing a common language (Sebanc, Hernandez, & Alvarado, 2009) and a sense of belonging to campus (Arbelo-Marrero & Milacci, 2016; Maestas, Vaquera, & Zehr, 2007). Other social aspects of successful HSIs include characteristics such as promoting a positive racial and ethnic identity (Garcia, Patrón, Ramirez, & Hudson, 2016), availability of Chicana/o Studies courses (Muñoz, Jaime, McGrill, & Molina, 2012), and culturally relevant pedagogy (Garcia & Okhidoi, 2015; Núñez, Ramalho, & Cuero, 2010). Garcia (2017) noted that the HSI organizational identity has been constructed/studied through legitimized norms that value measures such as graduation rates. She argues for obtaining the perspectives of students, administrators, tenure-track professors, and staff in order to understand institutional and cultural perspectives. Echoing this, other scholars note the importance of faculty in providing culturally relevant curriculum and pedagogy at HSIs (Garcia & Okhidoi, 2015). Nuñez, Ramalho, and Cuero (2010) touted the importance of introspection as they examined the pedagogical practices of three diverse female faculty at an HSI, in terms of personal experiences, bilingualism, and female role models for their Latinx students. Given the dearth of literature in the scope of faculty looking at their pedagogy and practices, this study aims to fill that gap.

Theoretical Framework

The theoretical framework of Latino Critical Race Theory (LatCrit) (Solorzano & Bernal, 2001) and CSP (Paris & Alim, 2017) informs the study. LatCrit shifts the focus away from a Black/White binary (Perea, 1997) to include the history of struggles against segregation and for equality, identity, and the role that racism has played specifically in Latinxs' lived experiences (Perea, 1997; Valdes, Culp, & Harris, 2002). LatCrit extends Critical Race Theory (Valdes, 1996) to address issues of subordination based on immigration status, language, ethnicity, culture, phenotype, identity, and sexuality (Solorzano & Bernal, 2001). LatCrit's focus is to provide a platform to hear the experiences, voices, and concerns of marginalized Latinxs. CSP, the complementary theory, challenges educators to act beyond acknowledging the diversity of their students and inclusion of their diverse backgrounds. Sustaining makes for an intentional, sometimes subversive, attempt to create spaces where power relations are uncovered when discussing the experiences and the inclusion of marginalized learners. In conclusion, CSP seeks to foster teachers who are responsive and seek to sustain cultural pluralism, linguistic repertoires, and literacies of their students as a way to address systemic racism (Paris & Alim, 2017).

Methodological Considerations

Through a qualitative research study (Merriam & Tisdell, 2016), we employed a self-study approach (Zeichner & Noffke, 2001) that served to reflect on our pedagogical practices as we documented our weekly book study meetings and discussions of the book *Culturally Sustaining Pedagogies: Teaching and Learning for Justice in a Changing World* (Paris & Alim, 2017). Data sources consisted of weekly chapter reflections and discussions, transcribed audio recording of book study meetings, and course syllabi. Through analysis of the interview transcripts and artifacts collection, we generated initial codes, patterns, and emerging themes through a constant comparative method (Glaser & Strauss, 1967).

We began the study as four first-year tenure-track assistant professors hired in the College of Education and P-16 Integration during the 2017–2018 year. María's multiple positionalities include first-generation college graduate, bilingual (Spanish and English), bicultural, and biliterate Chicana.[1] She immigrated to the U.S. as a child and was raised in the Pacific Northwest. Gilberto self-identifies as Chicano. His parents are Mexican immigrants. As a transnational child, he grew up in both México and the Pacific Northwest U.S. He is bilingual, bicultural, and biliterate. Gerardo is originally from Puerto Rico, and spent his teenage years in Belize and Peru, where he developed a multilingual and multicultural identity. He arrived in the U.S. for higher education. Hitomi is a first-generation immigrant and bilingual in Japanese and English. She was raised in Japan and immigrated to Oklahoma at the age of 18 to pursue college degrees. María and Hitomi are faculty in the Literacy program, Gilberto is in the Bilingual Education program, and Gerardo teaches in the Secondary Education program.

The University of Texas Rio Grande Valley (UTRGV), a four-year HSI, had an undergraduate full-time equivalent enrollment of 17,336 undergraduate Hispanic students during the 2018–2019 academic year (UTRGV, 2019a). UTRGV, the institution with the highest Latinx undergraduate student enrollment in the state of Texas, is located in deep South Texas. It is situated along the U.S.-México border, an area referred to as the Rio Grande Valley (RGV) or the Valley. As noted previously, each of us grew up outside of the Valley. Consequently, all four of us had unique etic perspectives. For the most part, we had all been schooled in U.S. university contexts in primarily white privileged spaces or Pre-dominantly White Institutions (PWIs). During the fall 2017 semester, we learned about the Special Interest Research Groups (SIRGs) focused on HSIs (Chapter 2 in this volume) and worked collaboratively to submit a proposal that met our collective research interests.

Critical Reflection

As part of our discussions of the guiding Paris and Alim text (2017), we examined ways that our course policies, our instructional materials and resources, and our interactions with students were connected to the culture of the students. A key component of these discussions was critical reflection. Critical reflection involved taking a good, often hard, look at our teaching practices as well as the rationales behind such practices. Moreover, we sought to uncover how our academic and professional formation, our family upbringing, and our cultural mindsets—our socialization—shaped how we understood the students we taught as well as the goals we set for their learning (Harro, 2013). Given that a basic principle in our conversations was to recognize the way that defining the students' cultures involved power hierarchies (a principle in line with CSP), our critical reflection served as a key space to wrestle with the tensions of navigating the dynamics of such hierarchies.

We engaged in deep introspection of a variety of experiences throughout our research time. For example, one particular conversation that took place early in the project related to attendance and timeliness procedures for students in our classes. We wrestled with the policy practices we brought from our previous PWIs, such as "Students should notify the instructor prior to being absent and follow up with the instructor to make up classwork." This policy was justified as an important part of developing preservice teachers' "professional dispositions," comparing it to developing responsibility for communicating with school administrators and making substitute teacher plans. One of the authors indicated that in spite of his course policy, there were still some occasional absences; students may have missed class or were unable to meet with the instructor citing significant outside obligations such as family and multiple jobs. At the heart of this problem of practice—setting classroom policies that foster professional dispositions while being attentive to student circumstances—the author who brought this situation to the book study group intended to guard against having deficit mindsets of the students in the class, while also taking into consideration student circumstances without lowering standards and expectations.

This issue was brought to the group to unpack how the policy and its rationales revealed assumptions about students, including assumptions about students in the PWIs such as "come from wealth," "don't have to work," and "Mom and dad pay for all their tuition," as well as assumptions about students at the HSI like "different SES" and "family comes first." Identifying such assumptions helped us to push back on definitions of "professionalism" and how those definitions are imposed on students, labeling them unprofessional or uncaring, in relation to generating classroom policies and procedures. As we uncovered our assumptions, we acknowledged how our position as faculty members enforcing such policies was tied to problematic readings of the students, sometimes overtly simplifying or essentializing our students and their cultures.

Yosso (2005) highlights how familial capital means recognizing kinship ties that are important in maintaining a "healthy connection to the Latino community" (p. 79). This wider network of support provides and models lessons in caring, coping, providing *consejos, respeto, y educación* (Elenes, Gonzalez, Bernal, & Villenas, 2001). In this new context, the participants of this study were forced to consider the importance of family in the success of students. Fránquiz, Salazar, & DeNicolo (2011) ask that teachers and teacher educators deconstruct "majoritarian tales" or racist norms that cloud how educators "view themselves, schooling, families, and students" (p. 282). Viewing the student no-shows from a white middle-class point of view that values individualism would undoubtedly bring up deficit notions of Latinxs. Valencia (2002) expands on this "myth that Mexican Americans do not value education," and how it "stems from the general model of deficit thinking, and from the specific variant of familial deficits" (p. 83). Valencia goes on to add how deficit arguments assume that Latinxs "fail in school because they and their families have internal defects, or deficits, that thwart the learning process" (p. 83). Considering that many first-generation students are still developing the navigational capital (Yosso, 2005) necessary for academic institutions, it is useful to look beyond a white deficit lens and inquire whether students must also give back or take care of the wider community that is pooling its resources together to help them be successful in college.

Throughout the research meetings, we returned to this tension – how the practices we implemented at PWIs applied in our HSI, how we fostered a teaching practice that lifted up our students and did not penalize them for their circumstances and instead avoided reinforcing deficit mindsets. Our process of collective critical reflection guided by the CSP mentor text followed what Toshalis (2015) called *critical friends' groups*, an "intentional and sustained gathering of colleagues who meet regularly to analyze issues of context and practice in a focused, collaborative, and reflective setting" (p. 36). This critical reflection and engagement required mutual respect, honoring the vulnerability of opening up about our practice, our assumptions, and our biases. As we engaged in the tenets of CSP and reflected on our practice, we created a space where we could be vulnerable with each other so we could uncover our lenses, sometimes problematic, through which we read our students.

De-centering Whiteness and Recognizing White Gaze

In the process of recognizing the lenses that shaped our notions about teacher education through critical reflection, we first reflected on the ways in which we all formed our narratives, and named the narratives we espoused in terms of what it meant to be a teacher educator of Latinx students at an HSI. We reflected on our own biases and how beliefs or prejudices may have kept us from acknowledging the counter-narratives. Seeing our largely Latinx population from a PWI lens would undoubtedly position them as deviant. Yet the act of moving to "the Valley" presented some opportunities for us to begin recognizing the vestiges of having lived in white spaces. Hitomi shared, "Working with Latino students, now I'm trying to understand their cultures, but I'm having culture shock." This sense of dissonance was also echoed by Gilberto, "At first I had to do a double take because all the students on the website and flyers were Latinos, in the labs, cheerleading, sports- everywhere!" This was something that Gilberto had not seen since living a few years in México as a child. In the authors' new normal, Latinxs were not a minority, but rather a critical mass in the borderlands region.

As previously mentioned, Hitomi was raised in Japan which is a relatively homogeneous country with less diversity. In the process of learning about CSP, she reflected on her experiences and acknowledged what she called "her unconsciousness." First, she mentioned that in Japan there was a lot of discrimination toward foreigners and Korean-Japanese people. This painful process of introspection toward how she had viewed foreigners allowed her to recognize her socialization as normal in the process of othering. She confirmed that she was just as accepting of her societal upbringing and never questioned the problematic aspects. Upon coming to the U.S., she became a minority and a foreigner herself, the tables turned, and she experienced marginalization (Jang, 2017; Lee, 2002; Stanley, 2006). Her own marginalization awakened her to the dynamics by which others were placed on the periphery. She described the process as follows:

> In Oklahoma, I didn't interact with a lot of Hispanics. The only time I saw them was in Asian supermarkets, and they were cutting meat... So, my perception was so different back then. I was hired here, and when I got here, my perception changed. I'm more passionate about Latino students now.

As Hitomi expressed her unconscious beliefs, she understood how her ontological shift had been precipitated by being positioned as an outsider. In Oklahoma, she would always be a forever foreigner (Tuan, 1998). However, Hitomi recognized her privilege in that space, being "privileged enough to have the means to study abroad." In the largely white area where she lived, there were congruent immigrant narratives that she had heard at home in Japan but this time for Latinxs as immigrants, complete with the trope of unskilled laborers. In her new institution and surroundings where the Latinx population numbered close to 100%, it meant having to reevaluate the meta-narratives of Latinx as immigrants that she had come to believe up until that point.

Disrupting the Narratives We Carry and Challenging Dominant Ideologies

The "overwhelming presence of whiteness" in teacher education programs leads to the silencing of people of color (Sleeter, 2001, p. 101). Whiteness permeates teacher education, in terms of "principles, morals, values, and history of white culture" (Urrieta, 2005, p. 173). Urrieta purposefully uses the term "whitestream" to de-center whiteness as dominant, and to illustrate the propensity for folks of color to "play the game" as a way to exist within dominant institutions but does not rule out individual's agency in acts of transformational resistance (Solorzano & Bernal, 2001). All four of the participants in this study at one point or another learned to walk a fine line between "selling out" and "playing along" to thrive in academic institutions (Urrieta, 2005). Returning to Sleeter's silencing effect (2001) of whiteness, the propensity for any languages other than English to also be included in teacher education proved to be problematic in an institution that sets out to be the first bilingual university of its kind. These tensions are illustrated by Gerardo's comment below as the CSP group set out to tackle the complexity of Spanish use in their classrooms.

> I'm going like, "I need to stop them from speaking Spanish." And I'm like, "I can't stop them from speaking Spanish, this is exactly why…this is exactly why I came to this institution in the first place." And then, I'm like, "But there are students who can't understand this, or might not…or even if they can speak Spanish, they can't understand everything that is being said." You know, all this stuff and this moderator role that you (as instructor) play, as the authority in the classroom. That's one thing that I think about a lot in terms of, how can the choices I make about how I structure the class, about how I modulate their behaviors, reflect culturally sustaining pedagogies?

While Gerardo's particular course is not designated as a course taught in Spanish, the majority of his students for that particular class were bilingual education majors who are accustomed to having to speak in Spanish in their courses to build their academic Spanish and Spanish fluency. This hegemony of English (Shannon, 1995) as the official language of academia permeates so deeply that it forces us to take stock of what it means in a bilingual university with a Latinx majority.

Similarly, an exchange took place as the group discussed a section in Bucholtz, Casillas, and Lee's chapter, *Language and Culture as Sustenance*, in Paris & Alim's text (2017). In that chapter, a student is deliberate with her use of Spanish during a family night where students presented their linguistic autobiography projects which showcased their translanguaging, writing, and speaking using both Spanish and English to accurately communicate their identities.

GERARDO: Language has power... So we need to empower people by allowing them to speak their language. The problem is, that doing that, is a power move as well. Then you're othering whoever doesn't speak Spanish. Which in our context, is a big deal, because Spanish has power here.

MARÍA: But what's wrong with that? I think that's what they (the authors) would argue. What's wrong with putting English monolinguals in that situation? Well, that is the purpose, troubling English and the dominance that it has. When people are put in that position, then it's the same as people who can't understand English. I think it was beautiful, and I think that her doing this, it's not just about her language, it's about her identity. She's saying, "I'm bilingual, and this is how I can identify myself, as being a bilingual person; being able to translanguage." That was really neat! Then the other girl, she had a conversation about language and power, and identity and then the fact that she's able to take that and criticize the system, and say, "Wait a minute, this is a celebration about my accomplishments, about my family support along the way. For them [her family] to not be able to understand what I'm saying, at this significant event, is wrong."

Gerardo saw the use of the heritage language in the speech as a power move, flipping the table of language power dynamics by giving the young ladies in the chapter a forum to showcase their identity. María's take on whether some folks are othered or excluded versus de-centering the whiteness of accommodating to the monolingual English crowd offers insight on the mestiza consciousness (Anzaldúa, 1987; Bernal, 2001) that enables Latinx students to recognize how white supremacy places an emphasis on assimilating and adopting the values of the mainstream. Mestiza consciousness means engaging in a balancing act of juggling cultures and languages, all the while an inward gaze of what it means to be Latinx from the white point of view (Anzaldúa, 1987). As a self-identified Chicana, María recognized that language is one of the forms of racial and intersectional subordination (Solorzano & Bernal, 2001) including gender. The young ladies in the chapter being discussed speak from the standpoint of being female and Latina, empowering them to use their full linguistic repertoires engaging in transformational resistance and challenging dominant ideologies (Solorzano & Bernal, 2001). We recognized these challenges to the centrality of whiteness, which were also indicative of the process through which we wrestled through the complexity of disrupting the master narratives and de-centering whiteness in our own practices.

Centering Students' Cultural and Language Assets

As outsiders to the culture of the region we all came in with varied histories and experiential knowledge. Within our group of four, we had various cultural backgrounds that allowed us to appreciate the beauty and complexity of the borderland experience beyond what our students often positioned as mundane and ordinary. As former graduates of PWIs all four of us had originally inhabited white-centric spaces where our own cultures had rarely been validated. What was validated was a Eurocentric and Western way of conducting research. Now, in a university touted as the first university to embark on efforts to integrate bilingualism, biculturalism, and biliteracy, it was important for us to take stock of the various cultures our students brought with them into the university setting. We sought to reflect on how we could place at the center of our pedagogy and our courses the students' cultural and linguistic assets. Below María illustrates how the marriage between meeting course objectives and incorporating culturally relevant materials consisted of having to engage in some research.

> How can I be culturally responsive to my students? Before... teaching white students, they needed to be aware of multicultural literature and how to work with students. This is the opposite, in a sense, it was kind of a different perspective of: How am I culturally relevant? So, the course focuses on how to use nonfiction texts. How do I make this engaging for my students? How do I integrate their language, knowledge, and experiences into my course? Some of the things that I've been struggling with myself is the nonfiction authors. I need to figure out who they are, specifically, Latinos or authors of color.

It is important to note that while white teachers make up 83% of the teaching force of the U.S. and white women at 63% encompass the largest group (Coopersmith, 2009), Latinx teachers encompass only about 7% for both women and men combined with women making just over 5% and Latino men accounting for 1.7% (Lara & Fránquiz, 2015). In PWIs, as María stated, the majority of the work encompasses exposing the majority white teaching force to CSP. In our case, the context of the university in which we taught was 90% Latino (UTRGV, 2019b), far from what is common in the rest of the U.S. In a sense, the demographic imperative implored us to seek ways in which we could center Latinx culture and language in our courses. The majority Latinx student population in our university courses would eventually teach a predominantly Latinx PK-12 student population. Gilberto shared how he initially seized on the opportunity to incorporate readings in Spanish including a reading from a nationally renowned author from the region (Anzaldúa, 1987) that problematized the different linguistic registers of the region and the power dynamics between Spanish and English.

> I guess my biggest challenge was to find documents or readings in Spanish first, but that were timely, and that was a challenge because there's…different works from Spain, and maybe South America but I wanted it to be relevant to the Valley. What I did find was done in the context of Spain and bilingual education. I felt conflicted because it's written in a different context. For example, they're talking about how parents are helping their children be bilingual. But the language they're trying to learn is English, and English is the one that they're pushing for. So, it's a different context because in Spain and the U.S. the languages are opposite. Here, the struggle is to keep Spanish…there was a difference, and how the languages have different powers and that's what I was trying to think and bring out. With what I was able to find, I don't think it does justice to any of that. I ended up finding readings that were in Spanish about bilingualism, which was the point of the course, but I still feel, as far as it being culturally relevant to them, it's hard to find. The only one that is from here, I used Anzaldúa, she wrote the book *Borderlands* where she has "*How to Tame a Wild Tongue.*"

Here, Gilberto illustrated the complexity of incorporating culturally relevant literature in an area that is demographically, culturally, and linguistically unique as opposed to other contexts such as the rest of the U.S. The readings written in Spanish tend to privilege a different context where Spanish is not in danger of being subsumed by English. In the context of the borderlands, parents often make a cost-benefit analysis toward the maintenance of Spanish and it still tends to lag behind English in status (Achugar & Pessoa, 2009; Rangel, Loureíro-Rodriguez, & Moyna, 2015; Velázquez, 2009). Centering the Spanish language is complicated by the lack of contemporary academic writing in Spanish in the specific content areas. It would behoove those of us who can write in other languages to take up these issues and publish in languages other than English in order to privilege those languages. Rogers (2018), in her presidential address at the Literacy Research Association (LRA) conference, candidly illustrated the propensity for social science scholarship to be published in English and in places like the U.S. and Europe, while the scholarship that is considered non-Western is largely ignored. Often, this is compounded by the fact that even in Latin America, readings at the graduate level take place mostly in English and it is often required to have a certain level of English competence as a prerequisite to engage in graduate studies (Bohn, 2003; Nielsen, 2003; Velez-Rendon, 2003). Not to be lost on the readers is the ironic twist that Gilberto did use Anzaldúa's (1987) chronicle of attending Pan American University (which later became UTRGV) where she describes how she and other Latinxs had to attend two compulsory speech classes. It seems that even in places where bilingualism is widely practiced, there are mechanisms to ensure that folks are reminded which language has privilege.

Discussion

What does this mean in the context of one of the largest HSIs? Garcia (2017) asks us to examine what it means to be a Latinx-serving institution beyond enrollment and graduation rates, one that "...enacts a culture that is educationally enhancing and welcoming" (p. 122S). We propose that we examine ways in which we help to perpetuate mechanisms that may do the opposite of welcoming, but instead engage in practices that de-center the white notions of the academy to create a version of the academy by the community and for the community. Heeding that notion of careful analysis of what it means to "serve," we should note that the students have made it through the "leaky educational pipeline" (Yosso, 2006) and now they must deal with the deficit rationales faculty may have toward them. As an act of refusal, we can choose to engage in pedagogical practices that challenge majoritarian tales and privilege our students' cultural and linguistic assets.

Just as Nuñez et al. (2010) who as first-year tenure-track professors worked collaboratively at UTSA (The University of Texas at San Antonio), an HSI, our HSI SIRG also provided a space for us as first-year tenure-track assistant professors to engage with one another, be vulnerable in sharing our thoughts, experiences, worries, fears, and uncertainties as we engaged with our students and learned from and with them in hopes of creating a positive learning environment that honored who they are and where they came from. Our work took us on a journey that involved being open to learning in and about a new setting and adopting a willingness to engage in pedagogical innovation. This process entailed us identifying the master narratives that are woven into the fabric of post-secondary institutions. Upon being conferred with our degrees we are encouraged to go forth and spread our knowledge to other places. However, hidden deep within our practices we have the potential to also introduce institutional practices that act as gatekeeping mechanisms and deficit-laden legitimization-minded practices to push out folks of color from our universities, done in the name of rigor. Scholars like Antrop-González and De Jesús (2006) remind us that with high academic expectations must also come, "caring characterized by supportive instrumental relationships" (p. 413). Anything less puts us at risk of color blindness and power blindness (Irizarry & Antrop-González, 2007). These scholars propose a form of "hard caring" (Antrop-González & De Jesús, 2006) that takes the individual and community into account, not of paternalism but of respect for people's dignity and individuality (Valenzuela, 1999), especially toward students' language and culture.

Implications for HSCOEs

While the conversation on HSIs has largely focused on graduation and enrollment, we propose that our work goes beyond retention and granting degrees. Our work seeks to explore how we, as teacher educators, can lay the foundation for academic success through our pedagogies and pedagogical practices. Just as Ladson-Billings (2009) had shown that great teachers engaged in culturally relevant pedagogy, our task as teacher educators is to go beyond just presenting connections to our students' lives. Paris and Alim (2014) remind us that "CSP must resist static, unidirectional notions of culture and race that reinforce traditional versions of difference and (in)equality without attending to shifting and evolving ones" (p. 95). The CSP framework is incredibly apt when considering the diverse preservice Latinx populations we serve at HSIs. Part of this work has meant recognizing the heterogeneity of our Latinx population and actively making space for students' linguistic repertoires, the histories, and ways of knowing outside of traditionally Western philosophies (e.g. *curandera* and *yerbatero* traditional knowledge our students bring that are quickly dismissed in academic knowledge settings).

As teacher educators (regardless of race or ethnicity) within an HSCOE, it is vital to engage in critical reflection about our pedagogies and pedagogical practices in order to understand how they support or hinder the academic success of our preservice teachers in sustaining and reclaiming their linguistic and cultural assets. As teacher educators, we are role models for the kind of work we encourage our preservice teachers to engage in. Ultimately, our pedagogies and practices are likely to influence the ways in which our preservice teachers will interact with their future students. Therefore, it is crucial for HSI teacher educators who work with Latinx preservice teachers to learn about their students and engage in introspection on the ways in which they model how to sustain bilingualism, biliteracy, and biculturalism. Essentially, by exploring our socialization, ideologies, and humanity we can gain the tools to develop our preservice teacher's capacity to foster and cultivate the next generation of university enrollees.

Note

1 María and Gilberto chose to self-identify as Chicana and Chicano, respectively. "The name Chicana is not a name that women (or men) are born to or with, as it is often the case with "Mexican," but rather it is consciously and critically assumed" (Alarcón, 1990, p. 250). Urrieta adds that Chicana and Chicano activist educators consciously undertake community-centered activism. Embodying Chicanismo "implies taking on a strong political orientation and a commitment to struggle against white supremacy to work toward individual and collective self-determination" (2009, p. 69).

References

Achugar, M., & Pessoa, S. (2009). Power and place: Language attitudes towards Spanish in a bilingual academic community in Southwest Texas. *Spanish in Context, 6*(2), 199–223.

Alarcón, N. (1990). Chicana feminism: In the tracks of 'the' native woman. *Cultural Studies, 4*(3), 248–256.

Antrop-González, R., & De Jesús, A. (2006). Toward a theory of critical care in urban small school reform: Examining structures and pedagogies of caring in two Latino community-based schools. *International Journal of Qualitative Studies in Education, 19*(4), 409–433.

Anzaldúa, G. (1987). *Borderlands/La Frontera: The new mestiza.* San Francisco, CA: Spinsters/Aunt Lute.

Arbelo-Marrero, F., & Milacci, F. (2016). A phenomenological investigation of the academic persistence of undergraduate hispanic nontraditional students at hispanic serving institutions. *Journal of Hispanic Higher Education, 15*(1), 22–40.

Astin, A. W., & Oseguera, L. (2003). *Degree attainment rates at American colleges and universities.* Los Angeles, CA: Higher Education Research Institute.

Bensimon, E. M., Hao, L., & Bustillos, L. T. (2006). Measuring the state of equity in public higher education. In P. Gándara, G. Orfield, & C. L. Horn (Eds.), *Expanding opportunity in higher education: Leveraging promise* (pp. 143–165). Albany, NY: SUNY Press.

Bernal, D. D. (2001). Learning and living pedagogies of the home: The mestiza consciousness of chicana students. *International Journal of Qualitative Studies in Education, 14*(5), 623–639.

Bohn, H. I. (2003). The educational role and status of English in Brazil. *World Englishes, 22*(2), 159–172.

Bucholtz, M., Casillas, D. I., & Lee, J. S. (2017). Language and culture as sustenance. In D. Paris & H. S. Alim (Eds.), *Culturally sustaining pedagogies: Teaching and learning for justice in a changing world* (pp. 43–60). New York, NY: Teachers College Press.

Coopersmith, J. (2009). Characteristics of public, private, and bureau of Indian education elementary and secondary school teachers in the United States: Results from the 2007–2008 schools and staffing survey. First Look. NCES 2009–324. *National Center for Education Statistics.*

Elenes, C. A., Gonzalez, F. E., Bernal, D. D., & Villenas, S. (2001). Introduction: Chicana/Mexicana feminist pedagogies: Consejos, respeto, y educación in everyday life. *International Journal of Qualitative Studies in Education, 14*(5), 595–602.

Espinoza, P. P., & Espinoza, C. C. (2012). Supporting the 7th-year undergraduate: Responsive leadership at a Hispanic-Serving Institution. *Journal of Cases in Educational Leadership, 15*(1), 32–50.

Excelencia in Education. (2019). *Hispanic-Serving Institutions (HSIs): 2017–2018 Infographic.* Retrieved from https://www.edexcelencia.org/research/infographics/hispanic-serving-institutions-hsis-2017-18-infographic

Flores, S. M., & Park, T. J. (2013). Race, ethnicity, and college success: Examining the continued significance of the minority-serving institution. *Educational Researcher, 42*(3), 115–128.

Fránquiz, M. E., Salazar, M., & DeNicolo, C. P. (2011) Challenging majoritarian tales: Portraits of bilingual teachers deconstructing deficit views of bilingual learners. *Bilingual Research Journal, 34*(3), 279–300.

Garcia, G. A. (2013). Does the percentage of Latinas/os affect graduation rates at four-year Hispanic Serving Institutions (HSIs), emerging HSIs, and non-HSIs? *Journal of Hispanic Higher Education, 12*(3), 256–268.

Garcia, G. A. (2017). Defined by outcomes or culture? Constructing an organizational identity for Hispanic-Serving Institutions. *American Educational Research Journal, 54*(1_suppl), 111S–134S.

Garcia, G. A., & Okhidoi, O. (2015). Culturally relevant practices that "serve" students at a Hispanic Serving Institution. *Innovative Higher Education, 40*(4), 345–357.

Garcia, G. A., Patrón, O. E., Ramirez, J. J., & Hudson, L. T. (2016). Identity salience for Latino male collegians at Hispanic Serving Institutions (HSIs), emerging HSIs, and non-HSIs. *Journal of Hispanic Higher Education, 17,* 171–186. Advance online publication.

Glaser, B. G., & Strauss, A. L. (1967). *The discovery of grounded theory: Strategies for qualitative research.* Chicago, IL: Aldire.

Harro, B. (2013). The cycle of socialization. In M. Adams, W.J. Blumenfeld, C. Castaneda, H.W. Hackman, M.L. Peters, & X. Zuniga, (Eds.), *Readings for diversity and social justice*, 3rd ed., (pp. 45–51). New York, NY: Routledge.

Irizarry, J. G., & Antrop-González, R. (2007). RicanStructing the discourse and promoting school success: Extending a theory of culturally responsive pedagogy for diasporicans. *Centro Journal, 19*(2), 37–59.

Jang, B. G. (2017). Am I a qualified literacy researcher and educator? A counterstory of a Professional journey of one Asian male literacy scholar in the United States. *Journal of Literacy Research, 49*(4), 559–581.

Ladson-Billings, G. (2009). *The dreamkeepers: Successful teachers of African American children.* Chichester, England: John Wiley & Sons.

Lara, G. P., & Fránquiz, M. E. (2015). Latino bilingual teachers: Negotiating the figured world of masculinity. *Bilingual Research Journal, 38*(2), 207–227.

Lee, S. M. (2002). Do Asian American faculty face a glass ceiling in higher education? *American Educational Research Journal, 39*(3), 695–724.

Maestas, R., Vaquera, G. S., & Zehr, L. M. (2007). Factors impacting sense of belonging at a Hispanic-Serving Institution. *Journal of Hispanic Higher Education, 6*(3), 237–256.

Malcom, L. E. (2010, April). *Hispanic-serving or Hispanic-enrolling? Assessing the institutional performance of public 4-year HSIs and emerging HSIs.* Paper presented at the annual meeting of the American Educational Research Association, Denver, CO.

Merriam, S. B., & Tisdell, E. J. (2016). *Qualitative research: A guide to design and implementation* (4th ed.). San Francisco, CA: John Wiley & Sons.

Muñoz, E., Jaime, A. M., McGrill, D. L., & Molina, A. H. (2012). Assessment of student learning: Estudios Chicano/s cultivating critical cultural thinking. *Teaching Sociology, 40*(1), 34–49.

Nielsen, P. M. (2003). English in Argentina: A sociolinguistic profile. *World Englishes, 22*(2), 199–209.

Núñez, A. M., & Bowers, A. J. (2011). Exploring what leads high school students to enroll in Hispanic-Serving Institutions: A multilevel analysis. *American Educational Research Journal, 48*(6), 1286–1313.

Núñez, A. M., Ramalho, E. M., & Cuero, K. K. (2010). Pedagogy for equity: Teaching in a Hispanic-Serving institution. *Innovative Higher Education, 35*(3), 177–190.

Oboler, S. (1995). *Ethnic labels, Latino lives: Identity and the politics of (re)presentation in the United States.* Minneapolis: University of Minnesota Press.

Paris, D., & Alim, H. S. (2014). What are we seeking to sustain through culturally sustaining pedagogy? A loving critique forward. *Harvard Educational Review, 84*(1), 85–100.

Paris, D., & Alim, H. S. (2017). *Culturally sustaining pedagogies: Teaching and learning for justice in a changing world.* New York, NY: Teachers College Press.

Perea, J. F. (1997). The Black/White binary paradigm of race: The "normal science" of American racial thought. *California Law Review, 85*, 1213–1258.

Rangel, N., Loureiro-Rodríguez, V., & Moyna, M. I. (2015). "Is that what I sound like when I speak?": Attitudes towards Spanish, English, and code-switching in two Texas border towns. *Spanish in Context, 12*(2), 177–198.

Reyes, R. (2007). A collective pursuit of learning the possibility to be: The CAMP experience assisting situationally marginalized Mexican-American students to a successful student identity. *Journal of Advanced Academics, 18*(4), 618–659.

Rogers, R. (2018). Literacy research, racial consciousness, and equitable flows of knowledge. *Literacy Research: Theory, Method, and Practice, 67*(1), 24–43.

Santiago, D. A. (2012). Public policy and the Hispanic-Serving Institutions: From invention to accountability. *Journal of Latinos and Education, 11*(3), 163–167.

Sebanc, A. M., Hernandez, M. D., & Alvarado, M. (2009). Understanding, connection, and identification: Friendship features of bilingual Spanish-English speaking undergraduates. *Journal of Adolescent Research, 24*(2), 194–217.

Seidman, A. (2005). *College student retention: Formula for student success.* Westport, CT: Praeger.

Shannon, S. M. (1995). The hegemony of English: A case study of one bilingual classroom as a site of resistance. *Linguistics and Education, 7*(3), 175–200.

Sleeter, C. E. (2001). Preparing teachers for culturally diverse schools: Research and the overwhelming presence of whiteness. *Journal of Teacher Education, 52*(2), 94–106.

Solorzano, D. G., & Bernal, D. D. (2001). Examining transformational resistance through a critical race and Latcrit theory framework: Chicana and Chicano students in an urban context. *Urban Education, 36*(3), 308–342.

Stanley, C. A. (2006). Coloring the academic landscape: Faculty of color breaking the silence in predominantly White colleges and universities. *American Educational Research Journal, 43*(4), 701–736.

Toshalis, E. (2015). *Make me! Understanding and engaging student resistance in school.* Cambridge, MA: Harvard Publishing Group.

Tuan, M. (1998). *Forever foreigners or honorary whites? The Asian ethnic experience today.* New Brunswick, NJ: Rutgers University Press.

UTRGV. (2019a). *Fast Facts 2018.* Retrieved from https://www.utrgv.edu/sair/fact-book/2018_fast-facts.pdf

UTRGV. (2019b). *UTRGV Enrollment Profile Fall 2019. Strategic Analysis Institutional Reporting (SAIR).* Retrieved from https://www.utrgv.edu/sair/_files/documents/fall-2019-student-profile.pdf

Urrieta, Jr. L. (2005). Playing the game" versus "selling out": Chicanas and Chicanos relationship to whitestream schools. In B. K. Alexander, G. L. Anderson, & B. Gallegos (Eds.), *Performance theories in education: Power, pedagogy, and the politics of identity* (pp. 173–196). Mahwah, NJ: Lawrence Erlbaum Associates.

Urrieta, Jr. L. (2009). *Working from within: Chicana and Chicano activist educators in whitestream schools.* Tucson: University of Arizona Press.

Valdes, F. (1996). Latina/o ethnicities, critical race theory, and post-identity politics in postmodern legal culture: From practices to possibilities. *La Raza Law Journal, 9,* 1–31.

Valdes, F., Culp, J. M., & Harris, A. (Eds.). (2002). *Crossroads, directions and a new critical race theory.* Philadelphia, PA: Temple University Press.

Valencia, R. R. (2002). "Mexican Americans don't value education!" On the basis of the myth, mythmaking, and debunking. *Journal of Latinos and Education, 1*(2), 81–103.

Valenzuela, A. (1999). *Subtractive schooling: US-Mexican youth and the politics of caring.* Albany, NY: State University of New York Press.

Velázquez, I. (2009). Intergenerational Spanish transmission in El Paso, Texas: Parental perceptions of cost/benefit. *Spanish in Context, 6*(1), 69–84.

Velez-Rendon, G. (2003). English in Colombia: A sociolinguistic profile. *World Englishes, 22*(2), 185–98.

Yosso, T. J. (2005). Whose culture has capital? A critical race theory discussion of community cultural wealth. *Race Ethnicity and Education, 8*(1), 69–91.

Yosso, T. J. (2006). *Critical race counterstories along the Chicana/Chicano educational pipeline.* New York, NY: Routledge.

Zeichner, K. M., & Noffke, S. E. (2001). Practitioner research. In V. Richardson (Ed.), *Handbook of research on teaching* (4th ed., pp. 298–330). Washington, DC: American Educational Research Association.

4 Cultivating an Ethic of Care at a Hispanic-Serving College of Education

Individual Stories and a Collective Narrative

Karin Ann Lewis, Miryam Espinosa-Dulanto, Jacqueline B. Koonce and Vejoya Viren

In this chapter, we examine how diverse, non-Hispanic faculty members cultivate and enact an ethic of care in critical pedagogy at our Hispanic-Serving College of Education (HSCOE), where we are transplanted outsiders within this predominantly Hispanic university, community, and culture. Through collective autoethnographic study, we interrogated how we endeavor to transcend boundaries, bridge insider-outsider beliefs, engender trust, develop mutual understanding, and cultivate empathic teaching/learning relationships. We each found our place and voice in understanding where we belong within a 21st-century HSCOE in the borderlands of the U.S./Mexican *frontera* making meaning of our roles in *serving* the Hispanic learners who comprise the majority of our student population. This included exploring the multiplicities of non-Hispanic faculty perceptions and experiences among predominantly Hispanic students, colleagues, and community to inform our understanding of what it means to be an HSCOE in contemporary higher education. We discuss our realizations regarding our disparate experiences, multiple voices used for articulating these experiences, and diverse ways these manifest in classroom practices and interactions.

Methodology

We leverage collective autoethnography as a process of inquiry—as a "genre of writing research that displays multiple layers of consciousness connecting the personal to the cultural" (Patton, 2002, p. 86). Recursively, we first reflect and write individually, including exploring various forms such as poetry, and then collectively interpret our moments/experiences depicting our di-verse, different voices/verses of our story (Chang, 2008). As researcher-educators, we engage in reflexive self-examination and relational ethical plurality as elements for collectively understanding and interpreting our individual autoethnographic inquiries (Ellis, Adams, & Bochner, 2011). We bring our different life experiences, perspectives, interpretations, and ways of knowing to the shared phenomena of our experiences at our HSCOE, the context and catalyst for our inquiry. Collectively, we interrogate our reflections and interpretations as lived curricula and layer our different voices/verses in a collective narrative (Hughes & Pennington, 2017). The central themes that emerged connect and resonate with *an ethic of care, an ethic of community, an ethic of agency, and an ethic of inquiry.*

Our Realizations

Karin's Voice

Care

We four authors of this chapter hold different frames of reference for what *care* means. We struggled, often fought with this term. To my surprise, I discovered the following definition:

> Care (noun): 1) suffering of mind; 2) a disquieted state of mixed uncertainty, apprehension, and responsibility; cause for such anxiety; 3) painstaking or watchful attention; 4) regard coming from desire or esteem; 5) charge, supervision; 6) a person or thing that is an object of attention, anxiety, or solicitude; (verb) 1) to feel trouble or anxiety; 2) to give care; 3) to have a liking, fondness, or taste; to have an inclination; (intransitive verb) 1) to be concerned about.
> (Merriam-Webster, 2019)

Every morning I sip my coffee from a vibrant orange mug printed with a personal challenge for my day ahead, "It starts HERE." The mug was a gift for participants in a convening of educators from across the U.S. charged with the question, "what does it mean to be an HSI?"—extending the HSCOE's Special Interest Research Group (SIRG) initiative to a national conversation. Again, I am challenged to contemplate my place in this conversation, as a white, non-Hispanic/non-Latina woman. Through collective autoethnography, I have come to realize, "My expertise is in knowing *not* to be an expert" (Horton & Freire, 1990, p. 128).

The context surrounding our HSCOE—the tropical climate, long stretches of white sand beaches, perpetually churning Gulf waves, a haven for butterflies, hummingbirds, wildlife, sea turtles, dolphins, bright pink fish, and myriad exotic birds—compels me to reevaluate my original, naïve attraction to come here juxtaposed with the reason I stay, despite my *disquieted state of mixed uncertainty, apprehension, and responsibility.* I am from the Northeast U.S., New England. My ancestry is indeed *Anglo-Saxon*, which makes the reference to me as an *Anglo* in this place valid, literally. However, it is a new label for me—one received upon arrival. Growing up, the rich history of the Rio Grande Valley (RGV) was not in the textbooks I read. It had not occurred to me that I was coming to work at an HSCOE, nor had I ever explored what that meant, nor my place in it. I had not anticipated the complexity of the U.S.-Mexico borderlands, the *frontera*. With my colleagues, I have become acutely aware of plurality, socioeconomic challenges, the proliferation of ever-present homeland security, border patrol, and the amplified political rhetoric propelling people into daily convulsions of emotion, fear, and angst, as well as solidarity, empathy, and collective resistance. As an outsider transplant, very different from my colleagues and students, daily I face the query, what *does* it mean to be a white woman from the Northeast teaching, researching, and *serving* in this HSCOE? What do I offer? How may *I* serve?

Why *care*? If care is defined as *suffering of mind*, then why do I/we invest in care? Investing conscious, reflexive meaning-making centered on an *ethic of care* unearthed a plethora of feelings, intentions, interpretations, reflection, vignettes of disparate experiences. Though sound questions for collective exploration, in what ways do I manifest care? In my view, it's more than a superficial sentiment or a glib expression; the meaning extends beyond the definition of the verb, *to feel trouble or anxiety* or even the alternative, *to have a liking, fondness, or taste*. Care is an ethical, conscious choice, a commitment, an action. Care enacted is an investment of time, inward- and outward-directed actions, and a metacognitive evolution with an ebb and flow of intensity. There are moments of acute attentiveness, intense feelings, and conscientious acts of kindness and compassion in the face of pain, particularly when I cannot possibly fully understand, although I seek to understand my colleagues and students—understand their experiences, hopes, dreams, and fears.

Community

Within this HSCOE community, the Golden Rule is a reasonable place to begin. I am an *Other* here. Treat *Others* as I wish to be treated. This fundamental principle drives what I think of as *care*—mutual respect—making the effort, being genuine, co-creating an affirming space where difference is respected and valued, including my own in our HSCOE. Albeit new for me, I now live and work among people who have lived as the *Other*, not by choice or relocation, who have been *othered* throughout their lives. Difficult discussions emerge, stereotypes are challenged; I openly acknowledge my misunderstandings and assumptions, and consciously excavate my vulnerability—together we navigate experiences of being *Other* compassionately.

I share stories of my experiences as a learner, teacher, mother, person—my human-ness, myself. As my colleagues and students share their stories, I seek to understand. Though not an easy task, the challenge to

"...dethrone ourselves from the centre of our world and put the other there and to honour the inviolable sanctity of every single human being..." (Armstrong, 2008) resonates. It starts here.

Initially seeking the comforts of a warm climate on the water, I now embrace discomfort and vulnerability. I am learning Spanish. Where everyone seems to speak Spanish, I struggle with understanding, attempting to join the conversation, awkward in my efforts to speak a new language—the tables are turned. Humbled, I appreciate my emergent bilingual students and my colleagues who navigate academe in English, not their heritage language. Indeed, it requires *painstaking attention.* I value and welcome the unfamiliar-to-me, hoping my colleagues and students will welcome the unfamiliar-to-them. Difference becomes the currency of growth. I/we do not teach/learn in a tropical vacuum. I/we need space for understanding, both individually and collectively, as I/we cannot afford to become stagnant, obtuse, nor succumb to hostile rhetoric in divisive times.

I recognize that within this community I am one encounter, one teacher, one colleague, one *Anglo,* with whom others relate, or not. My presence may or may not leave an impression, yet the *frontera* and our HSCOE community has made an indelible impression on me. If people I encounter take something from their interaction with me, an *Anglo,* I want it to be positive.

Inquiry

Begin with *why.* Beyond my role and responsibilities, I approach my life in education with conscious intention to cultivate the growth and development of others concurrently with my own—to co-create learning. For me, change is the purpose of education, lifelong mutual learning, and growth. Within the context of our HSCOE, I am compelled to check my assumptions, interrogate my biases, and acknowledge my privilege and opportunities. My experiences are my experiences, and I recognize that my colleagues and students, and subsequently their students, have had and will have different perspectives by the very nature of varying origins, backgrounds, sociocultural, political, and historical differences; teaching/learning encounters with diverse beliefs, perspectives, and motivations is the mutual gift. I practice appreciation, not assuming or taking for granted the richness of our diversity. It is a vulnerable space yet brimming with courage. To care about teaching/learning demands embracing an inquiry stance, a learning stance, and a compassionate stance toward those with whom I interact and myself. I seek to really understand my colleagues and students, before seeking to be understood—my first inclination. I share stories, harvested from 27 years of teaching in predominantly white Massachusetts, Upstate New York, and rural Kentucky, very selectively highlighting hopefully relatable stories, yet emphasizing these stories are from my experience. I encourage others to share their stories. I consciously listen—sustain a space for sharing and understanding. We all want to be heard. I strive to remain open, mindful of my responses and interpretations of what others say and do. Here, in this HSCOE context and the Hispanic community, I recognize I am an *other*. To *care* means I must empathize—we cohabitate this humanity. Engaging in an ethic of inquiry, it is incumbent upon me to inquire within and beyond myself.

Agency

It seems simple to say, "I care." Yet, it is daunting. Engaging in discomfort, vulnerability, holding myself accountable, being an *other* is exhausting! It requires effort, commitment, deep thought, authenticity, attitude adjustments, humility, hard work, and action. It is worthwhile work. Every morning, I reset my intentions; read inspiring authors; and reflect, write, and choose to invest in learning. I need to fill back up when I am depleted and create spaces for others to do the same. I choose not to interfere or invade but to cultivate agency.

> How is it possible for us to work in a community without feeling the *spirit* of the culture that has been there for *many* years, without trying to understand the soul of the culture? We cannot interfere in this culture. Without understanding the soul of the culture we just invade the culture.
>
> (Horton & Freire, 1990, p. 131)

Amidst crowded days, being an *Anglo* at our HSCOE prompted a personal, albeit unanticipated transformation. Nurturing relationships with colleagues and students requires investing time, energy, and showing up—showing up with intentions of being open, even when I feel like retreating. There are days when I am exhausted. This work is a marathon, not a sprint, along long stretches of the road ahead. I need to center myself, so that I can show up with patience and appreciation, with an attitude of reverence for what I may never fully understand, yet I seek to understand. Being *different* is exhausting. I deeply appreciate those around me who live day in and day out as *Other*. The exploration of being *Other*, empathy for *Others*, provides a new perspective. Showing up, I discovered a space for connecting through our shared humanity. Perhaps beyond an HSCOE, we are a community of *Others*, co-creating a collective consciousness of a *Humanity*-Serving Institution. A common expression attributed to Paulo Freire asserts, "Education changes people. People change the world." Indeed, to leverage our own agency as educators and inspire agency among our students, It starts HERE.

Miryam's Voice

Ethics of Care and Agency

> For to survive in the mouth of this dragon we call america, we have had to learn this first and most vital lesson – that we were never meant to survive. Not as human beings. And neither were most of you here today, Black or [Brown]. And that visibility which makes us most vulnerable is that which also is the source of our greatest strength.
>
> (Lorde, 2007, p. 33)

It has been only five years from the time I started working at this HS-COE located on the U.S./Mexican border, and at this point of my life I can't imagine being in a different location. Why is living/working at the border and in an HSCOE so important? In my case, it is the people, the community, the environment, the liminal space, the in-betweenness, and the ever-changing limit/less that offers/denies openings and creations.

In the U.S., I'm primarily a foreigner/outsider/immigrant, a Mestiza, and a South American Latina. At the HSCOE where I work, I may be seen as a walking contradiction as I had categorically rejected the Hispanic label embraced by the Mexican-American majority. Officially—demographically—I still am counted as a Hispanic/[1]... yet... my upbringing made me reject that designation. I reached adulthood outside the U.S.—in Peru, a country highly politicized, where I became aware of the practices and oppression imposed by neo-colonialist governments. There, "Hispanic" was understood by the majority as a term directly related to Spanish colonialization and its consequences: annihilation of indigenous populations, prohibition to follow cultural traditions, prohibition to speak any indigenous languages—but Quechua—and prohibition to practice indigenous rituals and learnings. However, officially, the same Spanish colonization was considered, welcomed, and taught as the "origin of civilization" adding total support to the highly regarded widespread use of the Spanish language, Western culture, and Catholic religion together with denying the historical facts. As such, growing up in the double standards of this paradox was not easy. As a Mestiza, I have both Western and Indigenous heritages. I'm both and I'm neither. In the Peruvian social paradox, anything related to the Western world and cultures is identified with economic and social power, yet 27.2% of the population identifies as Amerindian—belonging to indigenous, non-Western groups with their own languages and cultural heritages—plus 59.2%, the majority, also identifies as Mestizo (Amerindian mixed with different races), and only 4.9% as White (European/Western ancestry).[2]

It is the Latin American's racial and cultural history that makes my rejection of the term Hispanic almost physical. I deeply reject it. In all my time in the U.S., I had no conflicts while choosing the Latina/o/x label instead of Hispanic, until I moved to South Texas. Here, *Hispanic* is embraced not only as the term that includes the majority of the Mexican-American population—93.9% as estimated by the 2017 Census Bureau (U.S. Census Bureau, 2017)—but also reflects pride, resilience, and resistance. Here, in the border community, *Hispanic* denotes a way of life where a colonial trait such as the Spanish language has mutated to become "indigenous" and helps celebrate people's "otherness," their "Mexicaness," and their cultural traditions. The South Texas community has reclaimed the Hispanic label and has adopted it as an empowering tool—a totally new way to understand the label that is otherwise offensive to me.

As an academic who proposes decoloniality as emancipation and freedom, I have to humbly accept that, while at the border and at this HSCOE, I must understand and respect the "Hispanic" label as reclaimed by the community. Moreover, as a professional social sciences educator, I will continue teaching the historical facts of the Spanish and British colonization that support my previous experience. It is in the social context of the border, the connections within the community we serve and where we are located, that I locate my narrative.

Ethic of Care and Community

As a foreigner/outsider/immigrant and as a South American Latina/ *Hispanic* faculty at the HSCOE, I *do* care profoundly for my students. Given my background, my chosen role is one of a catalyst, an agitator, maybe a builder of disarray, a provocateur... a person whose "weirdness" is present to show the tools of the master...

> For those of us who write, it is necessary to scrutinize not only the truth of what we speak, but the truth of that language by which we speak it. For others, it is to share and spread also those words that are meaningful to us. But primarily for us all, it is necessary to teach by living and speaking those truths which we believe and know beyond understanding. Because in this way alone we can survive, by taking part in a process of life that is creative and continuing, that is growth.
>
> (Lorde, 2007, p. 44)

Our HSCOE serves a large Hispanic community with strong ties to their Mexican and indigeneous (Apache Carrizo-Comecrudo) ancestry powered by its closeness to Mexico, its desire to protect the Spanish/ Tex-Mex language and culture, and its own local-regional building/creation. The HSCOE is an integral part of this community; it feeds it and feeds from it. From the historical, traditional institutions (museums to confederate groups), to community/worker's union (La Union del Pueblo Entero—LUPE), to environmentalists opposing the building of a border wall (Sierra Club Borderlands, the Carrizo/Comecrudo Tribe of Texas), to gender rights and affordable health care and sex education (Planned Parenthood, Valley AIDS Council), and to social justice champions (Catholic Charities of the RGV/Respite Center, Angry Tias & Abuelas of RGV, Beatrix Lestrange/Drag-show), there is synergy. Through collaboration, education, and capacity building we individually and collectively as an HSCOE serve and are an integral part of the community of the RGV.

For example, I participate in a community effort that involves many diverse communities and HSCOE members. There, we have current and former students, instructors, and staff involved in an effort to dream about a "Better Brownsville." *A Right to Dream* is the motto for a group convened by the *Imaginistas*. The *Imaginistas* are local residents, UTRGV/HSCOE workers/professors/students, and community activists. Its purpose is to dream about the future with *"dreamers, visionaries, creatives, punk historians and passionate activists of the Rio Grande Valley"* (Imaginistas, 2019). This group is using art, performances, focus groups, interviews, workshops, art installations as opportunities to learn, and *invitations to reflect, react, give input, and take it with you and socially networking.* The communal goal is to *imagine a decolonized civic landscape and infrastructure* for the city/community surrounding one of our university's campuses.

As a caring member of our HSCOE, I'm committed to offering these different educative perspectives and decolonializing opportunities to every student who comes to my classroom. My hope is for all the HSCOE members to understand and to discover their right to dream and their/our power and agency to design and to build those dreams. Examples are many, and the power is in the community. The following is a poem that I offer as my reflection and understanding of an ethic of care.

Care at the HSCOE

Carnival
  Reform
    Holocaust

Difference is togetherness
Paradox to find logic
Logic to accept ignorance
Ignorance to bear injustice
Beauty to enjoy life
Strength to give up

I can't measure learning
I can't evaluate responsibility
I can't define process
> Just hear the voices
>> The themes
> All sensitivity
> All responsibility
>> Joy   pain   beauty   monstrosity

Understanding is not needed
Awareness is required
Togetherness and loneliness are accepted
Where we all are welcome
One and all together
To re-learn
To care

Jacqueline's Voice

Cultivating Care, Agency, and Community

Culturally relevant caring has helped me transcend racial, cultural, and linguistic boundaries with my students. That is why this topic is so meaningful to me. Another part of my motivation for this research on caring revolves around my undergraduate background. I attended an Historically Black University (HBCU), and that experience, in part, informs how I approach cultivating care, agency, and community in my own courses. My HBCU, North Carolina Agricultural & Technical State University, not only provided a quality education, but the professors, administrators, and staff fostered a nurturing atmosphere of care, love, and agency. I want my students in our HSCOE to have that experience. Cultivating a classroom environment where students feel valued, cared for, and empowered through agentive teaching is important to me. However, as I have learned over my approximately 13 years in teaching, critically caring for students is foundational to everything else that happens in a classroom. Though it might seem cliché, the oft-quoted sentiment, "they don't care how much you know until they know how much you care," rings true for me.

Noddings (2003) talks about the reciprocity that happens when the student (cared-for) perceives that the teacher (one-caring) cares about his or her well-being and success. My students have, on several occasions, reciprocated my care, and it has literally brought me to tears and taken my breath away. They express care for me just as much as I express care for them. However, through my conversations with the other authors of this chapter, I learned the importance of culturally relevant caring and agentive teaching, and that caring and love alone are not enough. Although I am a person of color, I did not perceive that Noddings was missing that important aspect until my colleagues challenged me to think more deeply. I read Nodding's work after a colleague recommended it to me and her work resonated with my own thinking. However, it was through dialogue with my SIRG colleagues that I became aware of the need to contextualize caring within a culturally and linguistically diverse framework particularly in relation to its applicability to people of color and indigenous peoples. Hearing their arguments for culturally relevant care as well as researching other authors (e.g., Bartolomé, 2008; Beauboeuf-Lafontant, 2008; Garad, 2013; Rojas & Liou, 2017; Valenzuela, 1999), I learned that it is not enough to love or care for our students because even love can be oppressive (Bartolomé, 2008):

> [M]any teachers of liberal persuasion claim to love and care for minority students; however, their love is often condescending and very much informed by deficit views of their students. In such situations, teachers often "lovingly" coddle their students and shelter them from having to learn dominant academic discourses because of their erroneous belief that their students already have a culture and should not have the dominant culture imposed on them.
>
> (pp. 2–3)

Consequently, it is "armed love" (Freire, 1998) that we need. Armed love is "...the fighting love of those convinced of the right and the duty to fight, to denounce, and to announce. It is this form of love that is indispensable to the progressive educator and that we must all learn" (p. 41). I strive to implement this armed love in my classes by providing the tools for my students to enhance their academic discourses so that they can also fight against oppression. This helps them as educators in that they can prepare their students to understand the sociopolitical climate of this country and how it plays out in the RGV and beyond so that they can take action when necessary thereby becoming agents of change. We are not only preparing our students to teach content but also how to facilitate student empowerment. I believe that empowerment is foundational to a positive classroom climate conducive for learning.

Part of this armed love and empowerment through culturally relevant care is the development of agentic educators who are able to move into the classroom and nurture student agency. In fostering agency, it is ideal that professors and students co-construct "teaching and learning opportunities ...as they cause each group to question and reject long-established roles in favor of new ways of engaging proactively with critical, voiced involvement at every stage of teaching and learning" (Rodriguez, 2013, p. 108). In teaching, I strive to co-construct knowledge with my students and provide them with opportunities to express their thoughts on content and pedagogy in dialogic discussions. Lipponen and Kumpulainen

(2011) state that in discussion-based classrooms, the possibilities for student agency abound, because students are encouraged to ask questions and participate in meaning-making.

I have found that cultivating a caring and agentive classroom ecology is foundational for students' success. By positioning myself as both teacher and learner and by providing opportunities for students to become the leaders of different learning experiences, I hope to arm my students with the ability to take ownership of their own learning. Through this, students sense the professor's care for their success. When we model culturally relevant caring and agentive teaching, students are more prepared to create this atmosphere in their own future classrooms.

Vejoya's Voice

Three years ago, during the first cycle of the SIRG initiative, we sat and mulled over our role at an HSCOE. "Like the *United Colors of Benetton*" (Levi, 2011) we joked, as we took in the diversity we represented. All of us were transplants from other states/nations. All of us spoke English with varying lilts and twangs, and our life experiences were different. We had one thing in common: our presence at an HSCOE on the U.S./Mexico border. While exchanging stories of our experiences in and out of the classroom, our search for similarities and patterns seemed to no avail. Ideas, concepts, and themes were interpreted in four different ways and scrutinized through four different lenses. It was frustrating and exhilarating at the same time. I felt a tremendous sense of liberation when we recognized the strength in our plurality. The university was not some inchoate space at the periphery of two nations; instead, the possibilities of exchange and growth seemed infinite. We began by looking into our interactions with our students as an "ethic of care." This is my version.

Ethic of Care

The "ethic of care," according to Sander-Staudt (2016), is built on the "motivation to care for those who are dependent and vulnerable, and is inspired by both memories of being cared for and the idealizations of self" (n.p.). This idea of dependency and vulnerability contradicts my view of my students as independent and empowered and my interactions with them neither merely evokes my past memories of caring nor extols my virtues. My Indian middle-class experience of academia is founded on the premise that a student is primarily and exclusively a student, with no other responsibilities except studying and maintaining grades that will eventually get one out of school and into a profession. In India, most parents bear the expense of educating offspring from cradle to career. In contrast, the students I teach in our HSCOE wear multiple hats and juggle complex personal and professional lives while attending to academics, and more often than not, bear the cost of education. These complexities find their way into my classroom and instead of adding them to the list of unusual excuses for late assignments and poor performance, I find myself marveling at the tenacity of students to continue toward a goal against such odds. In the process, I realize how little my orderly progression through the academic system in India prepared me in offering adequate support to students struggling with hectic personal lives and responsibilities. Finding creative and flexible solutions that support students to maneuver the demands of academia and personal lives have often been more influenced by the pragmatist in me than by the "motivation to care for those who are dependent and vulnerable" (Sander-Staudt, 2016).

As part of our SIRG work I wrote the following poem.

> They sat quite still
> and turned their eyes, not meeting mine
> I had ranted and raved (or so I thought)
> On how ill prepared and disinterested
> their grades showed they were!
> I waved my hands and shook my head
> And as they sat
> diminished...
> I found myself saying
> "then please tell me how
> I should teach, inspire, or preach
> because if you fail
> this test and the next and the next, next, next,
> it's not your fault, it is Mine".
> Some years later while visiting a public school
> A preschool teacher rushed up to me.
> "Doctora, I hope you still teach
> I was your student once"
> She grinned and reminded me of my rant
> and thanked me for taking the guilt of failed test
> away from her and making it mine,
> "Your English is so nice, but not mine.
> I know you tried," she said
> And I replied, "So did you"
> And remembered then
> This mother of two, who sat her children
> Outside the door
> With coloring books and food.
> Till I asked them to come in
> And her 10 year old listened and took notes for her mom!
> Caring as a virtue, I am not sure I possess
> But common grounds and common good
> Can always be found and counted on

My experience at this HSCOE is a continuous journey of discovery and reinvention of self as I teach and learn in a reciprocal exchange with my students, the institution, and the community. I recall, vividly, my first-day teaching at the *frontera*; I walked into a classroom packed with women in their 40s and 50s, who appeared unsure, uncertain, and out of place. My first-day jitters as a new professor were mirrored back and magnified by them. They were the displaced workers from the recently closed Levi's and Hagar factory in Brownsville, and I was the young, novice, Asian professor. They were terrified at the prospect of learning, and I was daunted by the task of teaching students older than me. The *Guru-Shishya parampara* (teacher-student tradition) of my Indian up-bringing had, to me, always been about the teacher's age and wisdom and the students' youth and enthusiasm. I remember asking my first set of students what they found most daunting about being in a classroom and they replied, "learning and retaining this information" tapping their heavy textbooks. I asked if it would help to know that within the next 45 minutes, they would be able memorize the names and one detail of all their classmates. They were skeptical even as I introduced the name-chain game. Once the game gained momentum, they helped each other out, they cheered and laughed, and at the end of the class, each one got up and introduced everyone else in the class (there were 44 students). One of them exclaimed, "That was easy!" and I said the rest would be just as easy, and they believed me for that moment.

Research on teaching behaviors that make a difference to student learning (Prosser, 2013) implies that good relationships with students and the ethics of care are important practices of teaching. However, these are not overtly stated, "possibly because the concepts are nebulous and more philosophical than pragmatic" (Scott, 2015, p. 3). I frequently wonder about this and my relevance to my students and the institution. I followed my husband to a location and clime that "felt more like home". After spending ten years with cold winters in Upstate New York and Virginia, here I find the climate, food, and the vivacity and warmth of the people, familiar and comforting. I was moved when an elderly lady at the grocery store touched my infant's head and blessed her, just like a grandparent back in India would. I was thrilled when our new neighbor handed a plate of barbecued chicken over the wooden fence and advised us on the sprinkler system. This sense of familiarity from stangers felt like home. I am delighted by the title of "Maestra" and "Professora" and that my students take pleasure in introducing me to their family when I meet them in public spaces. Personally, I feel at peace with my surroundings. Professionally, I am continuously seeking relevance as a transnational, in an institution that is also in the process of finding and redefining itself as it endeavors to find relevance and identity as an HSI.

Perhaps the greatest challenge and most meaningful breakthrough in my teaching is in creating a safe space in my classroom. A space in which we can afford to make mistakes, question our beliefs, share our perspectives, and be respected. I know from personal experience that when your language has systemically been devalued during school, when the strength of your accent has been mistaken for ineptitude, and when you fail to see the wealth of your culture represented adequately in textbooks, then a classroom cannot be presumed to be a safe space. It has to be deliberately created. The first week of class is dedicated to relationship-building through shared stories—through celebrations of personal joys and sorrows. We exchange phone numbers, find weekend community events to participate in, and share food and celebrations. The students I teach are non-traditional. They work full time, they often have families with young children and/or aging parents, and they have consciously decided to get an education. I am constantly amazed and in awe of their determination. My students rarely ask for special accommodations because of personal matters. My decision on how I accommodate these infrequent requests is based on practicality and what works best for the student to be successful. As a teacher, it is my duty (dharma) to teach and encourage success, and how I do it (karma) has the potential to impact me and the student in the present and the future. Care as an act is often perceived differently by the recipient and the provider.

Often, the impact of one's teaching practice on students is revealed through meetings with former students who remember interactions, unrelated to content, that left an impression on them. Or when an older couple stops by my table at a restaurant and asks if I teach at the university, because their child gave them a vivid description of "their professor."

My students are capable wo/men, strong advocates for themselves, often bilingual, they are rich, they are poor, they are single, they support families, they are privileged, they are marginalized, they struggle, they are documented, they are undocumented, they are citizens, and they are transnationals ... and THEY afford this HSCOE at the border a sense of relevance and agency. This was most pronounced when I traveled with my graduate students to a conference in Virginia. They presented their action research on *Opportunity, Accessibility, and Potential for Play for Children with Special Needs in Our Community* to an audience of experts and advocates of play. Their voices as agents of change were recognized and applauded. They were invited to share their experiences and stories with names they had read only in their textbooks. They all came back strengthened by the knowledge that their voices made a significant contribution to important discourses. The trip to Virginia to present at the joint conference of The Association for the Study of Play (TASP) and International Play Association (IPA) was at first, for many of my students, a quest to find cultural relevance in a national/international arena. What they found was that they gave relevance to the current discourse on the subject. Our role as an HSCOE is in getting their voices heard and their presence felt.

Implications for HSCOE

The insights we derive from the findings of our collective autoethnographic study reveal potent lessons learned for what it means to be a member of an HSCOE. Our unique, di-verse stories, perspectives, and lenses through which we collectively reflect on and interpret our lived experiences provide pieces of meaning-making at our HSCOE. Each of us is like the prisms that form a kaleidoscope for us, our colleagues, and our students to glimpse through—we are constantly reflecting, shifting, and creating a beautiful, colorful, intricately dancing view of the meaning we make in this place and space.

Under the auspices of our ethnic/cultural identities and being situated at an HSCOE on the U.S./Mexico *frontera,* we each live, work, create, and reinvent ourselves and our world. Yet, clearly the dynamic experiences of what it means to be Hispanic-*Serving* are not one-size-fits-all. Gratefully, we are not all the same, and neither are our colleagues and students, regardless of the label(s) applied to categorize us. From our di-verse stories, myriad fascinating verses and voices reveal, individually and collectively, we all consciously contribute vibrant, uniquely textured pieces in the grand *tapetes* mosaic of our HSCOE. As we endeavor to define/discover what it means to be an HSCOE, we evolve while enacting *an ethic of care, an ethic of community, an ethic of agency, and an ethic of inquiry* to assert our collective identity.

Notes

1 The U.S. Office of Management and Budget (OMB) defines "Hispanic or Latino" as a person of Cuban, Mexican, Puerto Rican, South or Central American, or other Spanish culture or origin regardless of race.
  From: US Census Bureau. (2018) Webpage. Downloaded https://www.census.gov/topics/population/hispanic-origin/about.html on 2/16/2019.
2 In 2006, a survey from the Instituto Nacional de Estadística e Informática (INEI), Peruvians self-identified as Mestizo (59.5%), Quechua (22.7%), Aymara (2.7%), Amazonian (1.8%), Black/Mulatto (1.6%), white (4.9%), and other (6.7%). Downloaded from https://www1.inei.gob.pe/ on 2/16/2019.

References

Armstrong, K. (2008). My wish: The charter for compassion. *TED Talk.* Retrieved March 18, 2019, from https://www.ted.com/talks/karen_armstrong_makes_her_ted_prize_wish_the_charter_for_compassion

Bartolomé, L. I. (2008). Authentic cariño and respect in minority education: The political and ideological dimensions of love. *International Journal of Critical Pedagogy, 1*(1), 1–17.

Beauboeuf-Lafontant, T. (2008). Politicized mothering: Authentic caring among African American women teachers. In L. I Bartolome (Ed.), *Counterpoints: Ideologies in Education* (Vol. 319, pp. 251–264). New York, NY: Peter Lang.

Chang, H. (2008). *Autoethnography as method.* New York, NY: Routledge.

Ellis, C., Adams, T., & Bochner, A. (2011). Autoethnography: An overview. *Forum: Qualitative Social Research, 12*(1). Retrieved from http://www. qualitative-research.net/index.php/fqs/article/view/1589/3095

Freire, P. (1998). *Teachers as cultural workers: Letters to those who dare teach.* Boulder, CO: Westview Press.

Garad, B. H. (2013). Spiritually centered caring: An approach for teaching and reaching Black students in suburbia. In C. Dillard (Ed.), *Engaging culture, race and spirituality: New visions* (pp. 66–80). New York, NY: Peter Lang.

Horton, M., & Freire, P. (1990). *We make the road by walking: Conversations on education and social change.* Philadelphia, PA: Temple University Press.

Hughes, S., & Pennington, J. (2017). *Autoethnography: Process, product, and possibility for critical social research.* Los Angeles, CA: Sage.

Imaginistas. (2019). Informative webpage. Retrieved March 05, 2019 from https://www.lasimaginistas.com

Levi, J. (2011). *United colors. Now with more benetton.* Retrieved from https:// www.underconsideration.com/brandnew/archives/united_colors_now_with_ more_benetton.php

Lipponen, L., & Kumpulainen, K. (2011). Acting as accountable authors: Creating interactional spaces for agency work in teacher education. *Teaching and Teacher Education, 27,* 812–819.

Lorde, A. (2007). *The transformation of silence into language and action. Sister Outsider: Essays and Speeches.* New York, NY: Ten Speed Press, 40–44.

Merriam-Webster. (2019). Retrieved from https://www.merriam-webster.com/ dictionary/care

Noddings, N. (2003). *Caring: A feminine approach to ethics and moral education.* Berkeley: University of California Press.

Patton, M. (2002). *Qualitative research & evaluation methods.*Thousand Oaks, CA: Sage Publications.

Prosser, M. (2013). Quality teaching quality learning. In D. J. Salter (Ed.), *Cases on quality teaching practices in higher education* (pp. 26–37). Hershey, PA: IGI Global.

Rodriguez, G. (2013). Power and agency in education: Exploring the pedagogical dimensions of funds of knowledge. *Review of Research in Education, 37*(1), 87–120. doi:10.3102/0091732X12462686

Rojas, L., & Liou, D. D. (2017). Social justice teaching through the sympathetic touch of caring and high expectations for students of color. *Journal of Teacher Education, 68*(1), 28–40.

Sander-Staudt, M. (2016). Care ethics. *The Internet Encyclopaedia of Philosophy.* Retrieved from https://www.iep.utm.edu/care-eth/

Scott, D. E. (2015). The nebulous, essential dimensions in effective university teaching: The ethic of care and relational acumen. *Journal of University Teaching & Learning Practice, 12*(2), 9.

United States Census Bureau. (2017). QuickFacts. Brownsville city, Texas. March 6, 2019. Retrieved from https://www.census.gov/quickfacts/fact/table/ brownsvillecitytexas/PST045217

Valenzuela, A. (1999). *Subtractive schooling: U.S.-Mexican youth and the politics of caring.* Albany: State University of New York Press.

5 Conducting Research through the Eyes of Chican@ Researchers at a Borderlands HSCOE

Cinthya M. Saavedra, J. Joy Esquierdo,
Dagoberto E. Ramirez and Isela Almaguer

Necesitamos teorías that will rewrite history using race, class, gender and ethnicity as categories of analysis, theories that cross borders, that blur boundaries...

~Gloria Anzaldúa (1990), p. xxv

Anzaldúa's words provided a call to action as our research team thought deeply about what it means to do research in a college of education at one Hispanic-Serving Institution (HSI) and explored the tensions and possibilities of our own research project. As we conceptualized, performed, wrote, and presented about our research, uppermost in our mind was the question: what does it mean for Latinx researchers to decolonize community research in one HSI's local borderland community? Four researchers from different fields and positionalities determined that this question would help us be more mindful, intentional, and critical about our project. This chapter speaks to the journey we engaged in and consejos or implications we have for other Latinx[1] researchers. This should not be seen as a "how to" but more so as a starting point for contemplation, with hopes that doing so will provoke additional questions that could be important for decolonizing research at HSIs.

Briefly, literature on HSIs can be summarized in four categories: (1) the designation of the HSI name, (2) the demographic trends, (3) the history of its development, (4) and its ties to other minority-serving institutions (Gasman, 2008; Santiago, 2006). Through this literature, a foundation and history can be appreciated and explored. Within the literature on Minority-Serving Institutions, several issues emerge. What, if any, commonalities exist between HSIs, Historically Black Colleges and Universities (HBCUs), Tribal Colleges and Universities (TCUs), and Asian American and Native American Pacific Islander-Serving Institution (AANAPISI)? To what extent are the challenges and complexities faced by these institutions consistent across these institutions? Furthermore, are these challenges and complexities consistent with those faced in mainstream or Predominantly White Institutions (PWIs)? Additionally, what are the logistics, infrastructures, and support systems that enhance or limit the positive experiences of diverse students in general and Latinx students specifically attending HSIs (Bridges, Kinzie, Nelson, & Kuh, 2008; Crisp, Nora, & Taggart, 2009; De Los Santos & De Los Santos, 2003; Núñez & Bowers, 2011)? Lacking is literature that addresses the positionality of Latinx researchers and how they intentionally and purposely engage and conduct their research at HSIs.

Service/Research Project Context

Our project began with an invitation from the executive director of the Edinburg Housing Authority to address the low levels of literacy in one of its housing units. Latinos have a high rate of below-basics literacy skills, and historically South Texas has one of the lowest literacy rates in the state (National Center for Education Statistics, 2006; South Texas Literacy Coalition, 2015). Informed by these studies, the executive director asked us to create a literacy center/space that would help increase literacy skills for its community members. We decided to conceptualize this project as a way to engage and examine the organic literacies of immigrant and Latinx women living in the South Texas borderlands as a starting point to address literacy skills.

After we came together to think of the best approach to engage the community in literacy skill building activities, we agreed that a space for storytelling was a culturally relevant way to begin our project. We held twice a month pláticas and coffee to have a more inviting approach for our participants. At these convivios, we all shared stories and testimonios about our lives and experiences which we collected via audio recordings and field notes. As researchers, we met often to discuss the progress of the research where we had many conversations about our own positionalities and experiences and discussed ways our positionalities were informing our views of research, methodologies, and theories. It is out of our conversations during these peer debriefing sessions that the discussion for this chapter was born. Our conversations prompted us to ask deeper questions of the research process: What does it mean for Latinx researchers to decolonize community literacy research in one Hispanic-Serving College of Education's (HSCOE)'s local borderland community? The following sub-questions helped us to address our overarching question:

1   How is the recognition of our complex positionality an important first step in critical qualitative research?
2   What does it mean to seek theoretically/methodologically relevant framings in research?
3   How is critical reflexivity important and necessary for doing research in an HSI?

Below we first discuss the colonial roots of research and the need to incorporate decolonizing methodologies (Smith, 1999) to situate our conversation in this chapter within a broader discussion of decolonial methodologies and research. The rest of chapter is organized in sections that address the three research questions. We end with implications or consejos for other Latinx researchers at HSCOEs, other universities, and PWIs.

De/colonizing Research

> ...research is not an innocent act or distant academic exercise but an activity that has something at stake and that occurs in a set of political and social conditions.
>
> Linda T. Smith (1999) p. 5

For many indigenous and minoritized people, research has served to reproduce unequal power relations through defining them as culturally and intellectually deficient Other (Bhattacharya, 2009; Denzin, Lincoln, & Smith, 2008; Smith, 1999; Visweswaran, 1994). We know that research is not a neutral act but a politically charged activity that is situated in the onto-epistemological embodied performance and world views of researchers (Denzin & Lincoln, 2005; Smith, 1999). Denzin and Lincoln (2005) assert that "qualitative research, in many if not all of its forms (observation, participation, interviewing, ethnography), serves as a metaphor for colonial knowledge" (p. 1). Research indeed can be a trojan horse harboring Western hidden assumptions like white supremacy, colonial imaginaries, and heteronormative and patriarchal tendencies— even when carried out by researchers of color. Smith (1999), speaking of indigenous researchers, but applicable to other racial ethnic minority researchers, captures the tensions present for indigenous researchers when she states,

> There are a number of ethical, cultural, political and personal issues that can present special difficulties for indigenous researchers who, in their own communities, work partially as insiders, and are often employed for this purpose, and partially as outsiders, because of their Western education...
>
> (p. 5)

Qualitative researchers, then, must employ critical methodologies to advance decolonial aims. In discussions of critical methodologies (Bhattacharya, 2009; Delgado Bernal, 1998; Denzin, et al., 2008; Mutua & Swadener, 2004; Pillow, 2003; Saavedra, 2011; Villenas, 1996), community/context relevant theories, research positionality, and critical reflexivity matter and in combination are perhaps the most important aspects of the inquiry process. We contend that when all three are intentionally centered in research, neither research nor the researchers are neutral. In fact, the opposite is true. Situating the researcher positionality and explicating the theoretical framework and critical reflection become necessary research activities in order to exhume biases and contexualize data analysis and interpretations. We want to emphasize that we do not believe that critical reflections get rid of biases, they only bring them out to light so that one can become aware of them. Further, these activities enable us to 'see' our participants and our own involvement differently—a process we call decolonial framing.

In order to construct a decolonial framing we must understand what frames are "seeing." Lather (1993) discusses this "seeing" in terms of research validity after the influence of postmodernism. She compels us to consider deeply and situate what "frames our seeing" (p. 675) as a way to better understand the dynamic and political tensions being played in our study and in our own selves as researchers. "What frames our seeing" goes beyond just pointing out theoretical orientations, it's also recognizing one's (research) positionality (Fine, 1994) through the development of critical reflexive practices and methodologies (Denzin, et al., 2008; Pillow, 2003).

Villena's (1996) ethnographic study as a Chicana/Latina offers us such an example of the kinds of decolonial research that offers critical awareness of theories, positionality, and reflexive methodologies needed in our research projects. She documents well the struggles between being trained in dominant research paradigms and educational theories in academia that recreate deficit perspectives of the Latinx community through research. Villenas situates her positionality as an insider/outsider in the Latinx community contexts. Drawing from Rosaldo (1989) and Fine (1994), Villenas points out that while researchers continue to advocate for an understanding of their multiple and political identities, they still write from "unidirectional manner as imperialist researchers and colonizers in relation to research participants" (1996, p. 714). She further notes that in many ways she's colonized in the larger society but simultaneously can act as colonizer because she's an "educated, 'marginalized' researcher, recruited and sanctioned by privileged dominant institutions to write for and about Latino communities" (p. 714). This is a powerful observation that is crucial for any Latinx researcher, perhaps even more so at an HSCOE. For us, it was important to turn the gaze back on ourselves and examine the methodological and theoretical assumptions that lurk in the corners of our being. What follows is our attempt to address and discuss our research conceptualization in the context of advancing decolonizing inquiry in our surrounding community.

Understanding Research Positionalities in HSI Research

> ...become the subjects and look at and analyze our own experiences, a danger arises that we may look through the master's gaze, speak through his tongue, use his methodology...
>
> Gloria Anzaldúa (1990), p. xxiii

How is the recognition of our complex positionality an important first step in decolonizing research? Though our different and intersecting work has consistently included a social justice agenda, our research questions helped us to frame our research more intentionally with the goal of creating critical frameworks for engaging in research with Latinx communities, especially as we work in a designated HSI. Many scholars engage in meaningful research with minoritized populations around the U.S. However, how conscious are we of who we are, and how that plays out in research? Do we carry such awareness into the research process? These questions led us to reflect, both internally and externally, on our research design, collection and analysis of data, and the more critical conscious interpretation of the interviews and the group pláticas. We were mindful of our respective political tendencies, our cultural experiences in the frontera, and our own linguistic practices.

Paramount in our work is the reality that even though we are "Chican@s" we come from very distinct backgrounds and experiences that include immigration, generational levels, various levels of bilingualism, and different class upbringing. Something we all had in common was our use of English and Spanish and the concept of translanguaging (Garcia, 2009)—the natural, mixing of languages that stems from the lived realities of bilingual and bicultural world views. We regularly use some form of translanguaging in our personal and professional lives. Translanguaging helped us to relate to our participants use of translanguaging during our pláticas and interviews.

Because we knew our positionality mattered in how we viewed, connected to, and related to the experiences of our participants, we spent time thinking and writing about our own positionality and discussed it during a research meeting. We shared our unique experiences as Chican@s living and working in the borderlands and acknowledged our differences as Latinx researchers, much like we acknowledged the different life experiences of our Latina research participants. Below we share our positionality and lessons learned from our reflections.

Cinthya was very aware of her own immigration status throughout the project, because she came from Nicaragua to Texas with her family when she was a little girl. This experience is central to how she might read the experiences of the immigrant mujeres who participanted in the research study. She could relate to the experiences of being in a new land, and new language and culture. She struggled with her parents not understanding her new double life, a hybrid life that is somewhere in between U.S. American, nicargüense, and tejana cultures. Many of the participants were experiencing how their children were developing a bicultural experience that sometimes the mothers were not exactly understanding. Yet, at the same time, Cinthya had to recognize her privileged border crossing experience that was unlike many of the mujeres.

Reflecting on her positionality enabled Cinthya to acknowledge how complex the "who we are" is in any research endeavor. She is not one identity label all the time, therefore her research positionality must take into account the intersectionality of who she is. Just calling oneself "Latina" or "Chicana" is not enough to have immediate entry into or understanding of Latinx communities. As researchers, we must unpack the multitude of ways we are similar to and different from our participants. The connections she has or does not have are not clean or neat. For example, because Cinthya is an immigrant does not mean she's like her immigrant participants, far from it. Positionalities are complicated and must be critically reflected on so as to not ascribe sameness or equal experiences but in fact experiences that are intersecting or parallel and not at all relatable at other times. Understanding this complexity helped Cinthya see our participants as not unitary, always victims and/or always resilient or always immigrant, or always low income.

Joy's experience was different. She is a fourth-generation Tejana with almost a non-existent connection to Mexico. She grew up in a strong bilingual community in deep South Texas, an area that is culturally rich and that celebrates the unique transborder culture found in the borderlands between the tip of Texas and *la frontera* with Mexico. Her perspective is highly influenced by deeply rooted pride in her Mexican heritage and strong relation to the *Tejano* experience. Although her home was mostly English-dominant, her bilingualism, biliteracy, and biculturalism was fostered by attending a Spanish-dominant church in her bilingual community. Falcón (2013) describes these types of transfronteriz@ experiences as living and navigating the international borderlands in distinctive, ingenious, and (re)mixed ways. While her upbringing didn't include much physical border crossing, her environment was rich with transfronteriz@ experiences that provide cultural wealth. She inherited cultural experiences that varied from her maternal World War II veteran grandfather to her paternal migrant labor worker grandmother. These experiences have provided a unique perspective to her research positionality.

Reflecting on Joy's positionality helped her gain a deeper appreciation of students' home language, experiences, culture, knowledge, and literacy practices that may not be traditionally recognized by the schools. Acknowledging that her own home experiences closely aligned to the "conventional" school culture, she realized the true complexity of the home-school relationship. The concept of home and school cultures can be so deeply rooted in their expectations of one another that the relationship can become unidirectional, mainly from school to home. Additionally, her positionality as a K-16 student in the borderlands, elementary bilingual teacher, university faculty, and researcher provided an opportunity to better connect the richness of the authentic transfronteriz@ literacies shared by the mujeres in the study. Therefore, as a bilingual teacher and professor in a teacher preparation program in an HSCOE, she better understood how transfronteriz@

literacies are developed and fostered in a variety of ways, outside from traditional methodological approaches taught to her and other bilingual teachers at the university.

Isela's positionality was genuinely impacted by engaging in this project, which helped her recognize the magnitude of her own personal lived experiences. Her perspective is one that crosses cultural, linguistic, and physical borders as her experiences positioned her to view, become part of, and connect to two different worlds—Mexico and the U.S.—each with its own defined cultural and social norms. Isela was born in California and raised by parents with strongly grounded Mexican roots. Regular travel across the U.S./Mexico border, with expectations of adapting to both worlds depending on her geographic location, was pivotal in fortifying her transnational culturally empowering experiences. These transnational life experiences cultivated an ability to connect with and embrace both cultures. The privilege of this experience came with expectations of using both the socially defined appropriate languages: within the correct context, and within its differing cultural and social norms. Her literacy experiences and perspectives as a Latina resonate from her rich cultural upbringing. What emerged was a newfound understanding of the significance life experiences have on one's *being* and one's *becoming* in life through an enriched understanding of her own strength and resiliency embodied in a bilingual, biliterate, and bicultural Latina.

Dagoberto is also from the Rio Grande Valley, where he was born and grew up in a border town named Roma. He lived his first 13 years half a block from the Rio Grande River, *El Rio Bravo del Norte*. Dagoberto lived a mixed dual-language experience, growing up initially in a Spanish-dominant home those first 13 years, as his family lived with his recently widowed maternal grandmother. Out of respect for her, Dagoberto's parents used mostly Spanish while living in her home. English became his language at school, and he mastered it quickly once he entered first grade. Dagoberto learned that his life experiences of weaving back and forth between Spanish and English on the southern border in deep South Texas, as well as his recognition of his male privilege, inform his positionality. This was important as the only male researcher among the Latina researchers and participants.

Theories in the Borderlands: Being Epistemologically and Theoretically Relevant

> What is considered theory in the dominant academic community is not necessarily what counts as theory for women of color.
>
> ~Gloria Anzaldúa (1990) p. xxv

Life on *la frontera* has a richness that is rarely captured in schools and much less in society. As a result, most educational studies miss the richness and position Latinx families as deficit (Licona, 2013; Valencia, 1997). As we began to conceptualize the project, Cinthya invited us to consider centering a Chicana feminist epistemology in our research project (Anzaldúa, 1987; Delgado Bernal, 1998; Moraga & Anzaldúa, 1983, Saavedra & Nymark, 2008; Villenas, 1996). Chicana feminist educational research has been central in reimagining deficit perspectives of Chicanxs and Latinxs in and outside formal educational experiences (Calderon, Delgado Bernal, Pérez Huber, Malagón, & Vélez, 2012; Cruz, 2001; Delgado Bernal, 1998; Delgado Bernal, Elenes, Godinez, & Villenas, 2006; Saavedra, 2011; Villenas, 1996). What dominant researchers define as a deficit, such as missing school because a child's parents are migrant workers, could be seen as source of strength and resilience for students, parents, and the community. Educators could then ponder the important lessons learned in those community contexts that children could use to draw from and connect to school knowledge, therefore constructing a bridge between the home and school (Moll, Amanti, Neff, & Gonzalez, 1992). This is why it's important to center methodologies that address the "unique social and cultural history and demonstrates that our experiences as Mexican [and Latina] women are legitimate, appropriate, and effective in designing, conducting, and analyzing educational research" (Delgado Bernal, 1998, p. 563).

Chicana feminist educational research pushed us to think of our methodologies differently, moving away from sterile and clinical views of research tools and incorporating critical methodologies of testimonios (Delgado Bernal, Burciaga, & Flores Carmona, 2012) and pláticas (Fierros & Delgado Bernal, 2016; Preuss & Saavedra, 2014) as ways to honor participant herstories, cuentos, and the everyday navigations of the life of the mujeres (Galván, 2011). Testimonios and pláticas become necessary tools to gather data. The use of testimonios and pláticas afforded our participants an authentic and culturally responsive process to share memories and experiences, either pleasant or painful, that have been silenced for far too long. It is through these methodologies that our participants found ways to voice experiences that allowed them to desahogarse con nosotros and through that find some healing (Pérez & Saavedra, 2020). In other words, what we noticed was that women's sharing of stories and telling their testimonios were helping them have more agency, perhaps even more power than they realized they had. That was healing—an unplanned, unexpected outcome in our project.

Another important aspect we learned from our attempt at decolonizing our HSI research was to undertand the socio-historical and political context of our participants in South Texas. For example, because we were exploring the literacies of immigrant families, we had to seek different theories, in particularly literacy. Critical sociocultural theories of literacies (Lewis, Enciso, & Moje, 2007) allowed us to see literacy as beyond the confines of the formal print, vocabulary, and reading comprehension (typically taught in school environments) and into literacies happening in the fabric of people's everyday experiences. These critical sociocultural theories of literacies recognize the importance of the power dynamics and the role of language, culture, and context in shaping each other (Luke, 2003; Perry, 2012). This prevented us from starting with the stereotype of Latinxs lacking "basic" reading skills and that we can measure literacy through narrow interpretations of what counts as literacy. It pushed us to acknowledge how language and literacy are used in a variety of ways: in the homes, communities, and schools. Thus, we went from a conceptualization of how to "increase" literacy to how Latinas navigate, engage, and make sense of their literate lives and what is meaningful to them (Perry, 2012).

Thinking deeply about the social context of living in the borderlands also compelled us to grapple with the complex relations we have with this very borderland we inhabit. Critical understanding of the land is part of the decolonizing attempts for Chicana feminists (Pendleton-Jimenez, 2006). Our geopolitical location also necessitated that we think deeply about the contentions and artificial construction of the border and how geography and context shape our identities both for the participants and ourselves (Anzaldúa, 2015). To describe the border, we turn to Rio Grande Valley native philosopher and queer feminist scholar Gloria Anzaldúa (2012), "[t]he U.S.-Mexican border es una herida abierta where the third world grates against the first and bleeds. And before a scab forms it hemorrhages again, the lifeblood of two worlds merging to form a third country—a border culture" (p. 25). This open wound that Anzaldúa portrays is the sociopolitical and historical conditions and lived reality of transfronteriz@s. As researchers in an HSI, how can we ignore that history and politics that surround the people in the borderlands?

We learned that taking into consideration the land and context matter in decolonizing research. Ignoring the land suppresses the more nuanced understanding of the sociopolitical nature of cultures, languages, and history. Therefore, the recognition of our geopolitical border location led us to center transnational and transfronteriz@ experiences and why we turned to transnational and border/fronteriza literacies (Brochin, 2012; de los Rios, De la Piedra, & Guerra, 2012; Hornberger & Link, 2012; López & Brochin, 2014; Fránquiz & Ortiz, 2017; Smith & Murillo, 2012). This body of literature examines how transfronteriz@s engage with language and literacy and focuses on the fluid movement of bodies, languages, and literacies of the metaphorical and literal Mexico/U.S. border. Fránquiz and Ortiz (2017) describe transfronteriz@s as having a "unique perspective of traversing different cultures in order to navigate and assimilate into systems that were not built for their transnationally mobile realities in mind" (p. 111). For de la Piedra and Guerra (2012) "the border is prime space to observe the fluidity of languages, literacy practices and knowledge across national borders" (p. 628). Our project benefited from this lens because it was a strong reminder of the importance of capturing the language and literacy practices of our participants within these amazing skills rarely recognized in traditional literacy education and research. It is in this way that we can highlight and document the organic, unique, and powerful everyday literacies of our participants—their borderland literacies.

Critical Reflexivity in the Borderlands: Challenge and possibilities

> I lack imagination you say.
> No. I lack the language.
> The language to clarify
> My resistance to the literate
>
> Cherrie Moraga, (1993) p. 62

Understanding how we had to seek theories and methodologies that were relevant to our geo/socio-historical and political context and for our participants also meant that we had to critically reflect on the challenges and possibilities for doing this kind of work in the borderlands with marginalized populations. In our peer debriefing conversations, we discussed our experiences and how it shaped what we were seeing or not seeing not only for ourselves but for our overall project. For example, we wanted to focus on how these mujeres were using literacy in their everyday lives, but ultimately more pressing concerns arose for us, specifically methodological challenges. We also learned that we had to let go of any outcome or result we had expected. We decided to write about these because they are timely in our current sociopolitical context.

For example, one of the challenges that we could not ignore dealt with participants who freely and openly insisted that they be named in their stories by their given names and not with an identity-masking pseudonym. Yet, most participants in this study are not documented citizens of the U.S. With the exception of one, all of the mujeres came to the U.S. crossing the South Texas border (the Rio Grande River) as an undocumented immigrant, a perilous journey that in reality is not yet over.

We struggled with trying to help the participants determine for themselves just what they *ought* to and *ought not* to share, so that their un/documented status, as well as their general well-being, would not be jeopardized. How can we tell their stories or how can they fully represent themselves, if we have to silence part of their vidas for fear of their lives? As researchers on the southern border of the U.S., we are fully cognizant of the current political and legal landscape when it comes to citizenship status. We are all too familiar with the anti-immigrant border rhetoric and realities we live with here in deep South Texas. The mujeres in our study could very easily put their current residency in South Texas (whether documented or not) and physical well-being at risk by openly exposing their true identities and border-crossing stories with the world at large.

At the same time, this kind of research if performed with respeto and critical reflexivity is encouraging, to say the least. We learned that our participants were eager to share their historias, sus vidas, logros y luchas. Sharing their border-crossing stories (read as multiple and metaphorical as well) in many ways was a healing process (Pérez & Saavedra, 2020). They began to re-read their experiences differently. They began to see themselves with more agency and power—a power that they had not recognized before in their lives. Furthermore, the mujeres would encourage one another with words of support and admiration for each other's journey. These experiences are counter-examples of what dominant research would have us see as people with "low income" and having "basic" literacy skills. In actuality, if we can dismantle deficit research methodologies, these mujeres can be "seen" to live rich literate lives in strong bilingual communities.

Our participants discussed how they live/d with struggles yet also have/had rich experiencias to share with the world. They read their world and lives with spirituality, reflexivity, and hope (Freire, 2000; Pérez & Saavedra, 2020). Their experiences and journeys can teach the world about navigating tough circumstances while redefining survival and embodying supervivencia—beyond mere survival (Galván, 2011). If we dare unshackle the term literacy and research, our participants can be read as living rich literate lives.

Thus, through this kind of research we can "see" our participants differently. We can acknowledge that they are agentic and reflective human beings capable of understanding, analyzing, and reading their worlds. They are not just victims. As Pérez (1999) illuminates, "[o]ne is not simply oppressed or victimized; nor is one only oppressor or victimizer. Rather, one negotiates within the imaginary to decolonize otherness where all identities are at work in one way or another" (p. 7). Of course, we know that all of us still need to work to make our world a better place, but we must recognize the power of humans to navigate through and theorize their worlds. Equally important is the recognition of the fluid identities we all possess. It is in this space that we found wisdom and richness from the borderlands (Saavedra, Esquierdo, Almaguer & Ramirez, 2018).

Implications: Consejos for HSCOEs

> How educational research is conducted significantly contributes to what and whose history, community, and knowledge is legitimated.
> ~Dolores Delgado Bernal (1998), p. 574

This chapter speaks to the need for Latinx researchers to decolonize research. We tried to be respectful to and honor different ways of knowing, especially given the frontera where our university is positioned. As we consider how language and literacy is inherently political, emotionally charged, and not ever neutral (Freire, 2000), an approach with reflection and reflexivity to this type of organic study was necessary.

Consejo 1: Positionality matters. Reflection is interpreted through the lens of one's research positionality. Engaging in this research project with Latinas who have lived language and literacy experiences that differ in scope and sequence but form the realities of their lives was a lesson for us and forced us as researchers to analyze our own theoretical and personal perspectives, biases, and attitudes. We must ask, would an attempt to separate from our own positionalities and still analyze using a critical lens be possible? We think not, as we had to keep turning back to Villenas (1996) work and remind ourselves how we embody the insider, outsider, and all in between positionality during our project.

Consejo 2: Culturally relevant theories matter. We encourage researchers to find theories and methodologies (Denzin, et al., 2008) that help us "see" participants and ourselves as researchers differently. Because as Pérez (1999) reminds us, "...women's activities are unseen, unthought, merely a shadow in the background of the colonial mind. Yet, Chicana, Mexicana, India, mestiza actions, words spoken and unspoken, survive and persist whether acknowledged or not" (p. 7). Dominant frameworks and methodologies negate the socio-historical context or even the geographical location that certainly impacts not only our participants but even ourselves as researchers. We create here a decolonial Latinx framing for conducting research with Latinx populations. Though some of these ideas and concepts are not new to the field, centering Latinx experiences as a starting point for creating decolonial Latinx framework is a more situated and nuanced approach to research that we believe can be helpful for other researchers.

Consejo 3: Critical reflexivity matters. We advise other HSI researchers to incorporate critical reflexivity that is mindful of research. Even qualitative research methods courses and university training that highlights nuance and complexity may not prepare us to think critically about the legacy of colonialism, racism, sexism, and other conditions that impact our participants and ourselves as the researchers in intricate ways (Smith, 1999). Furthermore, our training may actually prevent us from seeing the agentic ways people navigate systems of oppression. Let us then unearth the unacknowledged actions, and unspoken and spoken words of our participants. In this way, we find new her/stories, vocabularies and possibly new realities that can catapult us out of the coloniality of power coma. Consequently the view of our research participants can be transformed from using a deficit lens to an asset-based lens. Let's add to the collective decolonial experience with important diverse knowing (Delgado Bernal, 1998). New theories and methodologies can be found in the everyday lives of women (Gálvan, 2011). It is in this way that research can be rethought, redesigned, and remapped in the aims of creating decolonial imaginaries (Pérez, 1999) for the communities HSIs serve.

Note

1 The term Latinx will be used when we are ascribing the identity and speaking broadly of anyone who could be of Mexican and Latin American descent. For ourselves, we self-identify as Chicanas and Chicano, hence the title using Chican@s. The scholars or studies we quote might use any variaton of Latinx, Latina/o, Latin@, or Chicanx; Hispanic and we will honor their identification. For our participants, we used Latinas or Mexicanas interchangeably as that's how they self-identify.

References

Anzaldúa G. E. (1987/2012). *Borderlands/La frontera: The new mestiza*. San Francisco, CA: Aunt Lute Books.

Anzaldúa G. E. (1990). Haciendo caras, una entrada. In G. E. (Ed), *Making face, making soul, haciendo caras: Creative and critical perspectives by women of color*, (pp. xv–xxviii). San Francisco, CA: Aunt Lute Books.

Anzaldúa, G. E. (2015). *Light in the dark/luz en lo oscuro*. In A. Keating (Ed.), *Light in the dark/luz en los oscuro: Rewriting identity, spirituality, reality* (pp. 1–257). Durham, NC: Duke University Press.

Bhattacharya, K. (2009). Othering research, researching the other: De/colonizing approaches to qualitative inquiry. In J. C. Smart (Ed.), *Higher education: Handbook of theory and research* (pp. 105–150). Dordrecht, Netherlands: Springer.

Bridges, B. K., Kinzie, J., Nelson Laird, T., & Kuh, G. D. (2008). Student engagement and student success at historically black and Hispanic-Serving Institutions. In M. Gasman, B. Baez, & C. S. V. Turner (Eds.), *Understanding minority-serving institutions* (pp. 217–236). Albany: SUNY Press.

Brochin, C. (2012). Literacies at the border: Transnationalism and the biliteracy practices of teachers across the US–Mexico border. *International Journal of Bilingual Education and Bilingualism, 15*(6), 687–703.

Calderon, D., Delgado Bernal, D., Huber, L., Malagón, M. C., & Vélez, V. N. (2012). A Chicana feminist epistemology revisited: Cultivating ideas a generation later. *Harvard Educational Review, 88*(4), 513–539. doi:doi:10.17763/haer.82.4.l518621577461p68

Crisp, G., Nora, A., & Taggart, A. (2009). Student characteristics, pre-college, college, and environmental factors as predictors of majoring in and earning a STEM degree: An analysis of students attending a Hispanic-Serving Institution. *American Educational Research Journal, 46*, 924–942.

Cruz, C. (2001). Towards an epistemology of the brown body. *Qualitative Studies in Education, 14*(5), 657–669.

De la Piedra, M. T. & Guerra, J. C. (2012). The literacy practices of tranfronterizos in a multilingual world. *International Journal of Bilingual Education and Bilingualism, 15*(6), 627–634.

Delgado Bernal, D. (1998). Using a Chicana feminist epistemology in educational research. *Harvard Educational Review, 68*(4), 555–579.

Delgado Bernal, D., Burciaga, R., & Flores Carmona, J. (2012). Chicana/Latina testimonios: Mapping the methodological, pedagogical, and political. *Equity & Excellence in Education, 45*(3), 363–372.

Delgado Bernal, D., Elenes, C. A., Godinez, F. E., & Villenas, S. (Eds.). (2006). *Chicana/Latina education in everyday life: Feminista perspectives on pedagogy and epistemology.* Albany: State University of New York Press.

Denzin, N., & Lincoln, Y. S. (Eds). (2005). *The sage handbook of qualitative research.* London, England: SAGE.

Denzin, N., Lincoln, Y., & Smith, L. T. (Eds). (2008). *Handbook of critical and indigenous methodologies.* Los Angeles, CA: SAGE

De Los Santos, A. G., & De Los Santos, G. E. (2003). Hispanic-Serving Institutions in the 21st century: Overview, challenges, and opportunities. *Journal of Hispanic Higher Education, 2*(4), 377–391.

Falcón, V. (2013). *The hybrid identity development process of college students who live a cross-border lifestyle in the San Diego, California and Tijuana, Mexico border region. Masters Thesis.* California State University Long Beach.

Fierros, C., & Delgado Bernal, D. (2016). Vamos a platicar: The contours of pláticas as Chicana/Latina feminist methodology. *Chicana/Latina Studies, 15*, 98–121.

Fine, M. (1994). Working the hyphens: Reinventing self and other in qualitative research. In N. Denzin & Y. Lincoln (Eds.), *Handbook of qualitative research* (pp. 70–82). Thousand Oaks, CA: Sage.

Fránquiz, M. E., & Ortiz, A. A. (2017). Co-editors' introduction: Who are the transfronterizos and what can we learn from them? *Bilingual Research Journal, 40*(2), 111–115, doi:10.1080/15235882.2017.1329378

Freire, P. (2000). *Pedagogy of the oppressed.* New York, NY: Continuum.

Galván, R. T. (2011). Chicana transborder vivencias and autoherteorías: Reflections from the field. *Qualitative Inquiry, 17*(6), 552–557. doi:10.1177/1077800411409888

Garcia, O. (2009). Education, multilingualism and translanguaging in the 21st century. In A. K. Mohanty, M. Panda, R. Phillipson, & T. Skutnabb-Kangas (Eds.), *Multilingual education for social justice: Globalising the local* (pp. 128–145). New Delhi, India: Orient Blackswan.

Gasman, M. (2008). Minority-Serving Institutions: A historical backdrop. In M. Gasman, B. Baez, & C. S. V. Turner (Eds.), *Understanding minority-serving institutions* (pp. 18–27). Albany: SUNY Press.

Hornberger, N., & Link, H. (2012). Translanguaging and transnational literacies in multilingual classrooms: A biliteracy lens. *International Journal of Bilingual Education and Bilingualism, 15*(3), 261–278. doi:10.1080/136700 50.2012.658016

Lather, P. (1993). Fertile obsession: Validity after poststructuralism. *Sociological Quarterly, 34*(4), 673–693.

Lewis, C. J., Enciso, P., & Moje, E. B. (Eds). (2007). *Reframing sociocultural research on literacy: Identity, agency and power.* Mahwah, NJ: Lawrence Earlbaum Associates.

Licona, M. (2013). Mexican and Mexican-American children's funds of knowledge as interventions into deficit thinking: Opportunities for praxis in science education. *Cultural Studies of Science Education, 8*(4), 859–872.

López, M. M., & Brochin, C. (2014). Transnational preservice teachers' literate lives and writing pedagogy in a digital era. In R. Ferdig & K. Pytash (Eds.), *Exploring multimodal composition and digital writing* (pp. 1282–1299). Hershey, PA: IGI Global.

Luke, A. (2003). Literacy and the other: A sociological approach to literacy research and policy in multilingual societies. *Reading Research Quarterly, 38*, 132–141.

Moll, L., Amanti, C., Neff, D., & Gonzalez, N. (1992). Funds of knowledge for teaching: Using a qualitative approach to connect to homes and classrooms. *Theory into Practice, XXXI*(2), 132–141.

Moraga, C. (1993). *The last generation*. Boston, MA: South End Press.

Moraga, C., & Anzaldúa, G. (1983). *This bridge called my back: Writings by radical women of color*. Watertown, MA: Persephone Press.

Mutua, K., & Swadener, B. B. (Eds.). (2004). *Decolonizing research in cross-cultural contexts*. Albany: State University of New York Press.

National Center for Education Statistics (2006). U.S Department of Education Sciences, National Assessment of Adult Literacy. Retrieved on December 1, 2016 from http://nces.ed.gov/NAAL/PDF/2006470.PDF

Núñez, A. M., & Bowers, A. J. (2011). Exploring what leads high school students to enroll in Hispanic-Serving Institutions: A multilevel analysis. *American Educational Research Journal, 48*(6), 1286–1313. doi:10.3102/0002831211408061

Pendleton Jiménez, K. (2006). 'Start with the land': Groundwork for Chicana pedagogy. In D. D. Bernal, C. A. Elenes, F. E. Godinez, & S. Villenas (Eds.), *Chicana/Latina feminist pedagogies and epistemologies for everyday life: Educación en la familia, comunidad y escuela* (pp. 219–230). Albany: SUNY Press.

Pérez, E. (1999). *Decolonial imaginary: Writing Chicanas into history*. Bloomington: Indiana University Press.

Pérez, M., & Saavedra, C. M. (2020). Womanist and Chicana/Latina feminist methodologies: Contemplations on the spiritual dimensions of research. In C. Taylor, C. Hughes, & J. Ulmer (Eds.), *Transdisciplinary feminist research practices*. New York, NY: Routledge.

Perry, K. (2012). What is literacy? –A critical overview of sociocultural perspectives. *Journal of Language and Literacy Education [Online], 8*(1), 50–71.

Pillow, W. S. (2003). Confession, catharsis, or cure? Rethinking the uses of reflexity as methodological power in qualitative research. *Qualitative Studies in Education, 16*(2), 175–196.

Preuss, C. L., & Saavedra, C. M. (2014). Revealing, reinterpreting, rewriting mujeres. *International Journal of Qualitative Studies, 24*(7), 901–921.

Rosaldo, R. (1989). *Culture and truth: The making of social analysis*. Boston, MA: Beacon Press.

Saavedra, C. M. (2011): De-Academizing early childhood research: Wanderings of a Chicana/Latina feminist researcher, *Journal of Latinos and Education, 10*(4), 286–298.

Saavedra, C. M., Esquierdo, J., Almaguer, I., & Ramirez, D. (2018). *(Re)reading Mujeres in the borderlands: Centering Chicana feminist epistemology in Literacy Studies*. Paper presented at the Annual conference of the Literacy Research Association. Indian Wells, CA.

Saavedra, C. M., & Nymark, E. D. (2008). Borderland-mestizaje feminism: The new tribalism. In N. K. Denzin, Y. S. Lincoln, & L. Tuhiwai-Smith's (Eds.), *Handbook of critical and indigenous methodologies* (pp. 255–276). Thousand Oaks, CA: SAGE.

Santiago, D. (2006). *Inventing Hispanic Serving Institutions (HSIs): The basics*. Washington, DC: Excelencia in Education.

Smith, L. T. (1999/2002). *Decolonizing methodologies: Research and indigenous peoples*. London, England: Zed Books.

Smith, P. H., & Murillo, L. A (2012). Researching transfronterizo literacies in Texas border colonias. *International Journal of Bilingual Education and Bilingualism, 15*(6), 635–651.

South Texas Literacy Coalition (2015). Annual Report. Retrieved December 1, 2016 from http://www.southtexaslitcoalition.org/2015%20Annual%20 Report.pdf

Valencia, R. R. (Ed.). (1997). *The evolution of deficit thinking: Educational thought and practice*. Washington, DC: Falmer Press.

Villenas, S. (1996). The colonizer/colonized Chicana ethnographer: Identity marginalization, and cooptation in the field. *Harvard Educational Review, 66*, 711–731.

Visweswaran, K. (1994). *Fictions of feminist ethnography*. Minneapolis: University of Minnesota Press.

6 Embracing a Translanguaging Stance and Redefining Teacher Preparation Practices in a Hispanic-Serving Institution

Sandra I. Musanti, Alyssa G. Cavazos and Alma D. Rodríguez

In the Rio Grande Valley (RGV), our bilingual community, we hear, see, and experience the fluidity of languages in everyday situations, from academic classroom discussions to social interactions in the community. Translanguaging is a natural occurring phenomenon and an identity marker in bilingual and multilingual communities (Mazak & Caroll, 2017) that has been defined as "the ability of multilingual speakers to shuttle between languages, treating the diverse languages that form their repertoire as an integrated system" (Canagarajah, 2011, p. 401). The natural fluidity of languages in our region provides teacher educators and preservice teachers with opportune learning moments that challenge monolingual and standardized views of language. This is important to afford our students their complex linguistic repertoires as tools for learning, thereby creating more equitable spaces for teaching and learning. The University of Texas Rio Grande Valley (UTRGV), a Hispanic-Serving Institution (HSI), is primed to fully engage bilingual education and English Language Arts (ELA) preservice teachers in linguistically inclusive and diverse approaches to teaching. UTRGV is engaged in revisiting and amplifying its role serving a predominantly Latinx student population, to become a leader among the increasing number of institutions federally identified as HSI (HACU, 2018; Nuñez, Hurtado & Calderón, 2015).

Recently, translanguaging pedagogies have been defined as a political act because they leverage students' linguistic repertoire while challenging traditional monolingual views of bilingual education that privilege English as the language of instruction and knowledge (García & Wei, 2014; Mazak & Caroll, 2017; Palmer, Mateus, Martínez, & Henderson, 2014). This chapter aspires to contribute to emerging conversations and pedagogical innovations that tap into Latinx preservice teachers' full linguistic repertoire arguing for a translanguaging stance (García, Ibarra Johnson, & Seltzer, 2016) to designing undergraduate teacher preparation courses. This is especially relevant in an HSI like UTRGV where 88% of the student body identifies as

Hispanic or Latinx, 81% are low income, 59% are first-generation students, and 65% identify as bilingual, speaking Spanish and English (UTRGV, 2019).

The purpose of this chapter is to explore the impact translanguaging pedagogies have on preservice teachers' translingual dispositions. Translingual dispositions can be defined by both openness to language diversity and the different ways in which people use language and embrace language difference (Horner & Tetreault, 2017; Lee & Jenks, 2016). This matters because embracing translingual dispositions encompasses pedagogical choices that integrate different languages to promote learning as a socially just approach to education. Specifically, informed by recent explorations on translanguaging practices in higher education (Canagarajah, 2011, 2013; Horner & Tetreault, 2017; Mazak & Caroll, 2017; Mazak & Herbas-Donoso, 2015; Van der Walt & Dornbrack, 2011), this chapter explores preservice teachers' translingual dispositions in two undergraduate courses at our institution: one in the bilingual education teacher preparation program and one in the ELA teacher preparation program. Sandra and Alyssa, the faculty members teaching these courses, embrace a translanguaging stance and attempt to move from a language-compartmentalized instructional approach to a dynamic approach that leverages students' bilingualism (García & Wei, 2014).

Literature Review

In this chapter, we draw from literature on teacher education in HSIs and research on bilingual education and language teacher preparation. Our study is framed from the perspective of a holistic and dynamic understanding of bilingualism. We ground our study in translanguaging pedagogies in higher education institutions.

Teacher Preparation in HSIs for a Linguistically Diverse Population

Amidst the growth of the Latinx student population (HACU, 2018), the fact that most students classified as English language learners (77%) speak Spanish at home (McFarland et al., 2018), and the reality that most—if not all—teachers in the 21st century will teach in a bilingual or multilingual classroom (García & Woodley, 2014); it is imperative that HSIs research how to better prepare teachers to serve Latinx students. There is a growing body of research on bilingual education and language education and what teachers should know to effectively teach in culturally and linguistically diverse contexts (Oleksak, 2009; Woodley, 2016; Wright, Boun, & García, 2015). However, research that explores the pedagogy of preparing teachers for multilingual contexts is still scarce, especially in what relates to embracing and enacting a holistic and dynamic view of bilingualism and the bilingual learner. Clark and Flores (2001) highlight that most teachers are still not prepared to understand and embrace cultural and linguistic differences. As García and Kleyn (2013) state, "...*all* teachers must be prepared both to advance the plurilingual competencies of students, as well as teach students with different home language practices and bilingual abilities" (p. 5543). This is particularly relevant in HSIs with a genuine commitment to provide equitable educational opportunities for Latinx students, and to model how to provide education that is not alienating students by denying access to their cultural and linguistic assets following an "Anglo" and "assimilationist" model (Olivos & Quintana De Valladolid, 2005). De Mejía and Hélot (2015) contend that teacher education programs should foster "a change of mindset" in preservice teachers regarding how to teach in a multilingual classroom by learning to use the appropriate tools.

Traditionally, language learning has been divorced from the learning of teaching (Tedick, 2009), and learning about the role of language in teaching and learning has been restricted to the preparation of English as a second language (ESL) or bilingual education teachers (Burns & Richards, 2009). The literature on language teacher preparation shows that most programs focus on language-as-object, or language as an isolated content area of study, thus emphasizing methods of language teaching and failing to reflect the connection between language and culture and language and content (Salvatori, 2009; Tedick, 2009). For instance, the bifurcation of language and content instruction is still prevalent in language departments by developing content-based programs designed to prepare teachers (Salvatori, 2009). To overcome this disconnect, it is important to consider that "the classrooms we create as academics, researchers, and activists in teacher preparation programs must mirror the spaces we advocate for our students to create as teachers themselves" (Woodley, 2016, p. 572). In this sense, in the RGV, it is critical that our teacher preparation courses model a dynamic approach that leverages the learners' bilingual or multilingual repertoire for learning language and content (García & Wei, 2014; Musanti & Rodríguez, 2017). We contend that we need to prepare all teachers to understand the role of language as a resource for learning and to embrace a positive stance toward language diversity so that they can design instruction that leverages students' linguistic repertoires.

Translanguaging Pedagogies in a HSI

García and Wei (2014) remind us that "translanguaging is the discursive norm in bilingual families and communities" (p. 23). This means that teachers need to understand translanguaging practices as part of the linguistic repertoire of their students (Alvarez, 2014; García & Wei, 2014; Horner, NeCamp, & Donahue, 2011). Translanguaging refers to the fluid, dynamic, and interconnected ways in which bilinguals use their linguistic repertoire integrated by two or more named languages to communicate and make meaning (García et al., 2016; García & Wei, 2014; Lewis, Jones & Baker, 2012; Mazak & Caroll, 2017). The term translanguaging is grounded on research in the field of bilingual education (Mazak & Caroll, 2017), in particular, exploration of the different ways in which language was used in teaching and learning in bilingual contexts (Lewis et al., 2012). Important research investigating languaging in the context of teaching and learning took place in Wales with the pioneering work of Williams (2002) who concluded that translanguaging was a central practice to develop both languages successfully while learning content. Mazak (2017) provides a comprehensive definition of translanguaging as a language ideology that defines bilingualism as the norm, a theory of bilingualism that understands bilinguals as possessing an integrated linguistic repertoire, a pedagogical stance that embraces bilingual students' linguistic repertoire as a resource, and a set of practices that go beyond what traditionally has been defined as code-switching.

Translanguaging approaches have been contested and questioned in the fields of bilingual studies, second language writing, linguistics, and writing studies (Cummins, 2017; Donahue, 2016; Matsuda, 2014; Shapiro, Cox, Shuck & Simnitt, 2016). Although disagreements exist in the scholarship, we can argue that all scholars across disciplines have one critical factor in common: they all care for multilingual students' academic success. From this perspective, translanguaging pedagogies present teachers with opportunities to teach all students, not only bilingual students, through a holistic and fluid approach to language. Therefore, it is important that we approach research and pedagogies with a focus on the impact translanguaging pedagogies have on students' learning and especially on future educators. One of the central objectives of translanguaging pedagogies is that educators deliberately challenge monolingual ideologies in spaces of learning by recognizing the linguistic realities of the students in academic classrooms and sociocultural communities (Horner & Tetreault, 2017). Scholarship in translingual and translanguaging pedagogies has explored translanguaging within instructional space (Cavazos, Hebbard, Hernandez, Rodriguez & Schwarz, 2018; García & Wei, 2014), translanguaging as resources for learning and knowledge making (Alvarez, 2014; García and Wei, 2014; Horner et al., 2011), and translingual approaches as building rhetorical and reflective awareness (Bommarito & Cooney, 2016; Canagarajah, 2011, 2013; Cavazos, 2015; Guerra, 2016). Most of the scholarship addresses translanguaging in public education spaces, and few studies have focused on bilingual education teacher preparation programs (Musanti & Rodríguez, 2017). The scholarship in higher education has explored instructors' experiences in diverse disciplines and institutional contexts (Mazak & Caroll, 2017), students' bilingual/multilingual translingual abilities (Cavazos, 2019; Guerra, 2016), and instructors' pedagogical strategies and the impact on students' language use for learning (Musanti & Cavazos, 2018; Musanti & Rodríguez, 2017). Research on translanguaging practices and pedagogies is limited in HSIs. We do not yet know to what extent translanguaging pedagogies at an HSI impact preservice teachers' translingual dispositions, both their openness to language difference and their enactment of language difference (Lee & Jenks, 2016), which is one of the central components our study explores in this chapter.

Context of the Study and Methods

In fall 2017, we joined efforts to apply for an HSI Special Interest Research Group (SIRG) seeking to investigate how translanguaging pedagogies at an HSI impact bilingual education and ELA preservice teachers' perceptions of linguistically inclusive literacy instruction in order to improve teacher preparation. Each of us in our respective teaching disciplines has been previously exploring the implications of taking a more open and fluid stance toward language in teaching our respective courses (see Cavazos et al., 2018; Musanti & Rodríguez, 2017). We envisioned this collaboration as a twofold opportunity: (1) explore how to create translanguaging spaces in teaching undergraduate level courses with preservice bilingual education and ELA preservice teachers, and (2) delineate the theoretical underpinnings grounding a translanguaging pedagogy for teacher preparation in an HSI.

Our shared journey exploring and reflecting on our translanguaging stance (see Musanti & Cavazos, 2018) and the implications for a translanguaging pedagogy at an HSI included regular meetings to discuss translanguaging events that occurred in our classes, peer observations of our teaching, and developing and implementing a faculty learning community to engage in a transdisciplinary exploration of translingual and community-engaged pedagogy (Cavazos, Musanti, Rodriguez, Cavazos, & Dibrell, 2017). We use a case study approach (Dyson & Genishi, 2005) to explore how two HSI faculty members implement a translanguaging pedagogy while inquiring about preservice teachers' translingual dispositions. We identify our respective courses as cases of a specific phenomenon considering that a case "is not the phenomenon itself ... that phenomenon may look and sound different in different social and cultural circumstances, that is different cases" (Dyson & Genishi, 2005, p. 4). In this chapter, we analyze data collected during fall 2018 from two undergraduate courses taught by Sandra and Alyssa, respectively, that involved joint planning of a translingual self-assessment reflective activity for participating preservice teachers.

During fall 2018, Sandra taught EDBE 3324 Early Biliteracy, a course taught in Spanish in the elementary bilingual education teacher preparation program. Being bilingual (Spanish-English) is a requirement to be part of this program given that it prepares teachers to teach in bilingual education and dual language programs. Most of the preservice teachers in this program speak Spanish at home and completed their schooling in South Texas where bilingual instruction is offered predominantly through early-exit transitional programs (Hinton, 2015; Musanti, 2014; Musanti & Rodríguez, 2017). In Sandra's class, there were 26 Latina female preservice teachers, most of them in their early 20s, with the exception of four preservice teachers in their late 20s or early 30s.

The course focused on principles and foundations of biliteracy development and how bilingual children learn to read and write in both the minority and majority languages. Even though the major language of instruction for this course was Spanish, Sandra infused the course design with a translanguaging approach that acknowledges how preservice teachers engage in reading both Spanish and English and how the use of language during instruction is fluid. At times, Sandra followed a preview-view format presenting a topic in one of the target languages (preview), and then developing the topic in the other language (view). For instance, if the reading for the day was in English, Sandra would start by introducing the topic in English, activating prior knowledge related to the topic, and then transitioning to Spanish as the main language of instruction. Occasionally, Sandra would go back to English to connect academic vocabulary or to refer to specific experiences or knowledge previously built in English. In addition, Sandra might allow preservice teachers to explain an idea in English when they encountered challenges in Spanish, then revoicing the idea in Spanish. These are some of the translanguaging practices embedded in the course to favor cross-linguistic connections and to model ways to approach instruction in bilingual classrooms. The goal was to provide multiple opportunities for preservice teachers to strengthen their understanding of the content as they negotiated meaning in Spanish and English while supporting their development of Spanish academic language. In order to privilege Spanish as the language of instruction, all assignments were written in Spanish. The only assignment that did not include a language requirement, but that opened the space for language choice was a translingual questionnaire and self-reflection, which was a common assignment for the two courses in this study. The course included several activities that involved reflecting orally and in writing given that becoming a reflective practitioner is an important trait of effective teachers.

Alyssa taught ENGL 4343 Composition Theory and Pedagogy, a course in the secondary ELA teacher preparation program. Alyssa's class included 24 preservice teachers, 11 males and 13 females. Even though information on students' ethnicity was not collected for this class, the majority of students were Latinx as indicated in their writing topics. The preservice teachers in the course possessed varied linguistic backgrounds as some self-identified as bilingual and biliterate in English and Spanish while others noted they felt more confident in the English language. All preservice teachers expressed interest in becoming ELA teachers, and some also expressed interest in pursuing graduate education as well as careers in writing and editing. The purpose of the course was for ELA preservice teachers to learn about and apply diverse composition theories and pedagogies. Alyssa's goal for this class was to challenge traditional approaches to teaching writing, especially monolingual ideologies to create linguistically inclusive teaching spaces and a sense of openness to language difference. The main objective of the course was for preservice teachers to develop a sense of agency in the teaching of writing as they explored new theories and pedagogies and make the case for their respective approaches through linguistically inclusive pedagogies. In order to accomplish these objectives, ELA preservice teachers engaged in a series of assignments that consisted of rhetorical responses, a research project, and a teaching portfolio. Preservice teachers in the course were expected to critically respond to readings by challenging, analyzing and synthesizing arguments, and exploring new perspectives through personal and academic experiences. Informed by course readings and their own inquiries as future educators, ELA preservice teachers conducted research on a question of their choice about the teaching of writing. Finally, preservice teachers designed a Teaching Writing Portfolio that consisted of a teaching philosophy, a writing assignment design that was linguistically inclusive, and they provided feedback to a student from one of Alyssa's lower level courses. Ultimately, they wrote a reflection articulating how course readings and their research influenced their choices for how they wrote and designed each of the elements in the portfolio. To achieve the learning objectives of the course, Alyssa's translanguaging pedagogy consisted of deliberate readings that challenged monolingual ideologies in writing instruction and encouraging preservice teachers to compose rhetorical responses and their research project by drawing on their full linguistic repertoire. Alyssa's translanguaging pedagogy also included a teaching portfolio that was linguistically inclusive in writing instruction. ELA preservice teachers could use the language that was both most natural to them and more appropriate for their audience and purpose.

Procedures

We decided to design a common reflective activity to provide a space for bilingual education and ELA preservice teachers to self-assess their openness to language difference and to identify any shifts in their consideration to language at the end of the semester. As instructors and researchers, this assignment afforded us the opportunity to gauge how our translanguaging approach to instruction might influence how preservice teachers envision language in the classroom. We used a validated translingual dispositions' questionnaire (Cavazos & Karaman, 2018) as springboard for reflection on language. After questionnaire validation, Cavazos and Karaman (2018) determined that the questionnaire assesses three dimensions of translingual disposition to language difference: negotiation of language practices, resistance to language standards, and exploration through questioning language usage. The authors described the survey as consisting of 27 Likert scale questions from strongly agree to strongly disagree. The statements asked participants to indicate their level of agreement on each statement that asked them about their experiences reading, writing, and communicating by drawing on their knowledge of different languages. For each of the three dimensions, examples of statements are as follows: (a) negotiation of language practices ($N = 16$) "I create meaning through my knowledge of different languages;" (b) resistance to language standards ($N = 7$) "I mix languages, dialects, symbols, and/or visuals when I write;" (c) exploration through questioning language usage ($N = 4$) "I question the use of language when I write."

The preservice teachers in each of our respective courses completed the questionnaire and wrote a reflection about their responses at the beginning (pre-reflection) and at the end of the semester (post-reflection). The activity asked preservice teachers to reflect on their responses to the questionnaire by drawing on their personal, academic, and professional experiences as students and future educators. Preservice teachers were asked to reflect on how their language experiences influenced their responses to the questionnaire, and they were also asked to share additional insights about their perceptions of language in education. When preservice teachers completed the questionnaire at the end of the semester, Sandra asked her bilingual education preservice teachers to consider their responses to the questionnaire and reflect on their experience learning during the semester while trying to make sense of their present and past experiences with language and biliteracy and their future role as a bilingual education teachers. Similarly, Alyssa asked her ELA preservice teachers to focus their reflection on changes or shifts they noticed in their responses and their perceptions about how their experiences during the semester influenced those shifts. Additionally, preservice teachers were provided with minimal guidance and feedback on these reflections in order for them to represent their genuine and natural perspectives toward language diversity in the classroom.

Data Analysis

For the purpose of this chapter, we focused on analyzing preservice teachers' written reflections after completing the pre- and post-questionnaires. To identify and gain analytic insight into our students' translingual dispositions as represented in their reflections, we followed an inductive process through which we individually coded each reflection and then engaged in examining the interrelationships within and between courses (Dyson & Genishi, 2005). In order to accomplish this, each of the three researchers read through the reflections for each course and open coded each sample looking for references to openness to language difference, language awareness, enactment of language difference, language negotiation, and resistance to language standards. After completing the open coding of each writing sample, individually we worked on identifying patterns within each code, and we met during this process to discuss commonalities and differences and reach a consensus regarding overarching themes. As a result of assessing the interrelationships in our coding results, we decided to collapse the data for each course into the three dimensions that the questionnaire assesses in relation to language dispositions: exploration, negotiation, and resistance. After comparing and contrasting the data for both courses, we identified common patterns and differences for each course in terms of openness to language differences—how they see language—and the enacting or "doing" of translingual dispositions, or how they envision using language (Lee & Jenks, 2016). To respect our students' linguistic experiences, we chose to represent their words in the original language they wrote them. Instead of providing a direct translation, we provide context for readers to understand the meaning.

Findings

We describe preservice teachers' translingual dispositions in each course and the shifts we noticed in the pre- and post-reflections. We highlight how preservice teachers engaged in exploring and negotiating their dispositions to language differences and a more dynamic understanding of bilingualism while still showing some resistance to embracing translanguaging.

Bilingual Education Preservice Teachers' Translingual Dispositions

Pre- and post-reflections written by bilingual education preservice teachers focused on exploring their self as bilinguals and how they use language in fluid ways. Specifically, they described experiences of language loss and resistance, and how they experienced the language fluidity that surrounds them in a context that privileges English as the language of learning.

We noticed how in their reflections preservice teachers engaged in exploring their bilingual self, the personal significance of being bilingual and being part of a bilingual community. While acknowledging Spanish as the language of emotions and the language they use to build relationships, they recognized the scarce opportunities to use Spanish as a resource for learning. Most preservice teachers identified Spanish as the language of home and family, and English as the language of school and education. Nevertheless, they acknowledged a shift toward English in their households with the younger generations, mostly influenced by the predominance of English at school, as one of the preservice teachers expressed: "Con mis padres, yo use el Español y con mis hermanos, hable el Ingles y en Español. En mi infancia mi primer lengua fue el Español pero mis hermanos llegaban de la escuela y hablaban en Ingles [sic]." The hegemony of English as the language of school is evident in that most preservice teachers chose to write the reflection in English (13 out of 24 for the pre-reflection and 11 out of 24 for post-reflection).

Bilingual education preservice teachers participating in this study had taken at least one or two courses offered in the bilingual education course sequence, and they had engaged in reading, learning, and thinking about bilingualism, and being bilingual prior to this study. This might help to explain how their pre-reflections referred to the benefits of bilingualism from an asset perspective rather than from a deficit one. A clear shift was evident in the post-reflection that showed a more nuanced way to reflect on their dispositions toward language. For instance, in her post-reflection, a bilingual education teacher candidate explained the value of being bilingual as language brokers helping to translate for others, especially family members, and the value of communicating to different audiences by using their bilingual repertoire depending on the context (e.g., friends, family members, social places, and school):

> Las experiencias que me llevaron a contestar de esta manera son las que vivo a diario ya sea en casa con mi familia, amigos, en la Universidad o simplemente una salida a la tienda o un restauran [sic]. El vivir aquí en la frontera me ha expuesto a comunicarme en inglés y español en diferentes ocasiones dependiendo de como me contesten las personas, yo adapto mi lenguaje a eso. Una de las grandes ventajas de ser bilingüe es precisamente eso.

They expressed awareness of language choices and how they used it in different ways. For instance, a bilingual education teacher candidate explained translanguaging as a cognitive tool to express her thoughts in two languages: "busco la manera de expresar ese mismo pensamiento lo mas parecido posible pero en inglés."

Bilingual education preservice teachers' initial reflections revealed general openness to language diversity. Their ability to negotiate languages as they engage with different audiences seemed to be acknowledged as a natural part of their self as bilingual individuals. They demonstrated their awareness and openness to embrace opportunities to capitalize on their already natural abilities as bilingual language users as they identified approaches for students in the classroom. Their shifts focused on approaches that can be enacted to negotiate languages in the classroom with their students.

At the end of the semester, they expressed the importance of understanding the power, value, and significance of bilingualism and biliteracy. In her post-reflection, one bilingual education preservice teacher reflected on her learning about biliteracy during the semester:

> I've learned so much regarding the importance of biliteracy instruction and how it embraces an extensive range of teaching and learning activities involving reading and writing in both languages. This helped me understand how essential it is to embrace both languages to the max instead of excluding one or the other.

An important shift involved acknowledging language fluidity as an asset. For instance, a bilingual preservice teacher explained how translanguaging would help her as a future teacher to support bilingual learners:

> [Antes] no me gustaba usar lo que se llama "translanguaging." En este curso aprendí que es totalmente aceptable expresarse usando tu conocimiento en su totalidad y aun mas aceptable dejar que los estudiantes lo hagan.

In addition, the post-reflection demonstrated the realization of exploring the self as a model for students. One candidate explained,

> Something I am taking with me to my future classroom is allowing the students to express in the language they are comfortable with, and let the students think-pair-share as much as possible to allow all students to develop their speech.

Preservice teachers' sense of exploration focused on what translanguaging meant for them as bilingual language users and how they would enact it in the classroom.

Post-reflections highlighted preservice teachers' sense of pride in being bilingual that shifted from their previous tendency to apologize or feel ashamed of their way of speaking using both languages. Still most preservice teachers understood bilingualism from a sequential perspective, defining a first and second language, or positioning Spanish as the language of home and English as the language of school, required for learning or to demonstrate learning. Still persistent was the idea of speaking two languages as two monolinguals as illustrated by the comment, "I am a simultaneous bilingual and have never felt that I have fully been able to dominate one of the languages like a monolingual." While they valued bilingualism and biliteracy, a tension remained between a standard or "correct" view of language that aligns with a monolingual perspective versus a more dynamic and holistic perception of being bilingual.

ELA Preservice Teachers' Translingual Dispositions

After analyzing the pre- and post-reflections written by ELA preservice teachers, we noticed that there was a continued need to challenge monolingual ideologies in educational spaces. Because English-only perspectives permeate throughout public school education as well as in higher education, this view has been engrained in our students' literacy experiences. As Alyssa intentionally challenged monolingual views toward language in her course, ELA preservice teachers demonstrated a sense of openness to explore what it means to teach English from a translanguaging lens. ELA preservice teachers' pre-reflections aligned more with dominant and standard writing expectations, such as a "correct" or "right" way to write, and even questioned the need for language fluidity in an ELA secondary class. For instance, one teacher candidate shared,

> I do believe that it is important to use and understand more than one language, however, I do not believe that we should encourage students to write in languages other than English unless the course is specifically in that language.

The statement assumes that named languages should be separated for written communication purposes rather than naturally integrated to achieve certain aims.

As the semester progressed, ELA preservice teachers' post-reflections demonstrated a significant shift in resisting monolingual ideologies in the classroom. In fact, many ELA preservice teachers reflected on negotiating the ELA classroom space to one where teachers and students explore other languages as they think about linguistic and rhetorical choices, such as audience, purpose, and context. For instance, an ELA preservice teacher who had previously questioned the presence of other languages in English class reflected in her post-reflection,

> I have changed my mind when it comes to English as a subject. The required readings and the research I conducted for this class, especially those that speak about teaching for agency, have truly opened my eyes to the many benefits of allowing students to exert agency in their own learning. In an English class, exerting agency means being able to make your own decisions on what will be more effective with your audience, and in those decisions, I believe that students should also consider their native languages/slang/dialects.

This shift from language separation to language negotiation informed by audience and context created more of a sense of openness to different perspectives and people's experiences with language. For many ELA preservice teachers in that course, this shift was attributed to specific experiences writing that semester where they were placed in the position to navigate their linguistic choices for specific purposes and contexts by drawing on their linguistic background as a positive rhetorical tool, which even led to a sense of pride in their linguistic background. For instance, one preservice teacher reflected on his linguistic experience writing a song for his bisabuela the same semester he took English 4343:

> I noticed that I had to first write out what it is that I wanted to express in the song in English. Then, in Spanish I went ahead and tried to find the words that would fit that idea [...] I hadn't really noticed that I did that before, but it helped me to mix the languages when writing song lyrics.

The fact that the preservice teacher became aware of how he negotiated language choices in the act of writing for a specific audience, his great-grandmother in this case, illustrates the impact a course infused with translanguaging pedagogies had on building his openness to language difference and enactment of language difference.

While not all preservice teachers shifted their linguistic mindset toward a translingual disposition, they did demonstrate a sense of openness to explore these arguments through research as most of them chose to research issues of language diversity and second language writing. For instance, one preservice teacher shared

> I don't necessarily believe [students] should be encouraged [to use languages other than English]. I just think they should be allowed to if they want, but not for real assignments. Maybe like brainstorming and such but not a real assignment.

This preservice teacher demonstrated a shift in thinking about the presence of languages other than English as he moved from a strict standard writing perspective to a sense of openness to invite students to explore languages other than English in less formal assignments. Although the preservice teacher placed value on standard writing practices in "real assignments," his willingness to consider the learning benefits of engaging languages other than English in informal assignments illustrates an important initial move toward translingual dispositions.

The majority of the ELA preservice teachers were committed to posing questions about the role of different languages in the English classroom and conducting research on how languages relate to each other. Many of the preservice teachers reflected on the need to continue exploring translanguaging pedagogies, especially in the assessment of student learning. As a result, they also noted the need for teachers to "advocate for their class and their students" on issues of diversity and inclusivity as well as the need to explore how to "create opportunities for students to feel comfortable with their linguistic knowledge, as it is a reflection of their identity as people." When future educators were exposed to translanguaging pedagogies, their sense of openness was revealed in their willingness to learn about others' experiences, languaging, and even exploring their own variations of language in the learning and writing process.

Discussion and Conclusions

This chapter aims to explore the impact of a translanguaging pedagogy in teacher preparation on preservice teachers' translingual dispositions. Inasmuch as preservice teachers in this HSI were predominantly Latinx, it was evident that not all preservice teachers arrived in our classrooms with translingual dispositions. Moreover, both groups, ELA and bilingual education preservice teachers, initially engaged in self-assessing their language development using a monolingual view of bilingualism, where languages are seen as independent and separate from each other (García & Woodley, 2014). Following Lee and Jenks' (2016) conceptualization of translingual dispositions, the reflective assignment, embedded in courses where the instructors used a translanguaging approach to instruction, created spaces for preservice teachers to reflect on two key traits of their dispositions toward language: openness to language differences and enactment of a translingual stance. Specifically, preservice teachers were prompted to reflect on their openness to language differences, which is understood as awareness of linguistic diversity and the role of language as a resource for learning, and their enactment of translingual dispositions defined as the possibility to plan for and/or engage in actions to support linguistic diversity and translanguaging in teaching and learning (Lee & Jenks, 2016).

Openness to Language Difference

Living in a bilingual community influenced preservice teachers' awareness of the importance of context when negotiating language use. In particular, preservice teachers who identified as bilingual displayed an awareness of how context influenced their language choices naturally, knowing how and when to switch. There was an increased awareness of and sense of pride in their own bilingualism. The translanguaging approach to instruction afforded preservice teachers an opportunity to shift from openness to language differences in the community to openness to language differences in their future classrooms for teaching and learning. Preservice teachers recognized the role of language in teaching and learning, breaking away from the traditional separation between language learning and learning to teach (Tedick, 2009). Preservice teachers recognized language as a right, indicating students should be allowed to use all their linguistic resources for learning. This openness to language difference is essential in today's classrooms to teach students from diverse language backgrounds (García & Kleyn, 2013).

In their post-reflections, preservice teachers displayed a greater degree of openness toward translanguaging and translingual practices, especially in relation to instructional settings. They acknowledged these were new concepts for them and they recognized their usefulness in classrooms. Moreover, as they reflected on these translanguaging pedagogies for their future classrooms, they displayed a more nuanced and sophisticated academic discourse. The translanguaging stance adopted by Sandra and Alyssa fostered a shift in mindset regarding teaching in multilingual classrooms.

Enacting Translingual Dispositions

Early in the semester, preservice teachers elaborated on the ways they enact bilingualism, especially in their jobs and communities. They emphasized bilingualism as an asset that brings opportunities for advancement. Toward the end of the semester, many preservice teachers acknowledged a change in their mindset regarding language. The majority of preservice teachers displayed an understanding of the significance and uses of language beyond communication. Language was recognized as a way for people to represent or define themselves. They recognized the connections between culture and language as advocated by Tedick (2009) and Salvatori (2009) and the role of language in identity.

These two groups of preservice teachers were encouraged to do translingual dispositions at an HSI. In Sandra's class, the translanguaging approach to instruction validated these preservice teachers' linguistic resources allowing them to enact translingual dispositions through the understanding and verbalizing of translanguaging pedagogies while moving away from traditional models of bilingual education based on strict separation of languages (García & Wei, 2014). In Alyssa's class, ELA preservice teachers engaged in doing translingual dispositions through the incorporation of languages in their writing as a powerful rhetorical tool to convey meaning (Canagarajah, 2011, 2013). Some ELA preservice teachers began exploring writing in different languages or integrating languages in their writing. Translingual dispositions were also enacted by both groups when they described translation as a resource for themselves and for others. Based on the insights gained from this study, we contend that translanguaging pedagogies can indeed create spaces where preservice teachers can experience the type of instruction we expect them to replicate (Woodley, 2016, p. 572).

Implications for a Hispanic-Serving College of Education

Teacher preparation at HSIs should equip all preservice teachers with the translingual dispositions necessary to teach culturally and linguistically diverse students. As educators in an HSI, it was critical to foster an openness to language difference in the ELA preservice teachers who participated in this study, given that learning about the role of language in teaching is often reserved for bilingual education and ESL teachers. We should not assume that at an HSI, by default, students and faculty hold translingual dispositions, such as openness to language diversity. Still, we can affirm that this is an area where HSIs have a lot to contribute, especially when committed to honor the linguistic and cultural roots of the community of which they are part.

First, an important implication of this study indicates that preparing preservice teachers to serve an increasingly culturally and linguistically diverse student population requires considering the criticality of fostering translingual dispositions as content in teacher preparation programs. To accomplish this, teacher educators need to understand language as a resource for learning and value the linguistic repertoire preservice teachers bring to counteract deficit views, still predominant in higher education, of those who speak languages other than English or language varieties. In addition, our findings suggest that teacher educators need to embrace and enact purposefully designed linguistically dynamic practices. A way to approach this is by engaging preservice teachers in using reflection as a rhetorical tool to develop language awareness, which involves understanding and challenging the tensions that arise around integrating translanguaging by embracing a fluid use of language for teaching and learning and/or writing purposes. Creating spaces where preservice teachers self-reflect on their language negotiation practices can lead to exploration of how to create similar spaces with their future students.

Second, to foster translingual dispositions, all faculty across disciplines who collaborate with the College of Education in the preparation of teachers in an HSI should embrace openness to language diversity and a translanguaging stance. This means that teacher educators need to create spaces where language becomes the learning content, the resource for learning, and the focus of ongoing reflection. The result should be working toward language difference as the norm in teacher preparation as opposed to continue to mirror and perpetuate language separation trends still evident in public education.

As a result of our interdisciplinary undertaking for this research project, we highlight that teacher preparation is not solely the responsibility of colleges of education, but it is and should be an interdisciplinary endeavor. Interdisciplinary work on how to promote openness to language diversity and linguistic awareness can inform and pave the way to the development of a Hispanic-Serving College of Education identity aimed at transforming teacher preparation by drawing from diverse views of language and how instructional design should reflect these views. Ultimately, we assert the importance of all teacher educators enacting, validating, and modeling translanguaging as a resource for learning and as a matter of social justice, embracing the natural ways of doing language in the community.

References

Alvarez, S. (2014). Translanguaging tareas: Emergent bilingual youth as language brokers for homework in immigrant families. *Language Arts, 91*(5), 326–339.

Bommarito, D. V., & Cooney, E. (2016). Cultivating a reflective approach to language difference in composition pedagogy. *Composition Studies, 44*(2), 39–57.

Burns, A., & Richards, J. C. (Eds). (2009). *The Cambridge guide to second language teacher education*. New York, NY: Cambridge University Press.

Canagarajah, S. (2011). Codemeshing in academic writing. Identifying teachable strategies of translanguaging. *The Modern Language Journal, 95*(3), 401–417.

Canagarajah, S. (Ed). (2013). *Literacy as translingual practice: Between communities and classrooms*. New York, NY: Routledge.

Cavazos, A. G. (2015). Multilingual faculty across academic disciplines: Language difference in scholarship. *Language and Education, 29*, 317–331.

Cavazos, A. G. (2019). Encouraging languages other than English in first-year writing courses: Experiences from linguistically diverse writers. *Composition Studies, 47*(1), 38–56.

Cavazos, A. G., Hebbard, M., Hernandez, E., Rodriguez, C., & Schwarz, G. (2018). Advancing a transnational, transdisciplinary and translingual framework: A professional development series for teaching assistants in writing and Spanish programs. *Across the Disciplines: Interdisciplinary Perspectives on Language, Learning, and Academic Writing, 15*(3), 11–27.

Cavazos, A. G., & Karaman, M. (2018, March). *Development and validation of a translingual disposition questionnaire: Implications for teaching and learning*. Paper presented at the Linguistics Seminar Series, the University of Texas Rio Grande Valley, Edinburg, TX.

Cavazos, A. G., Musanti, S. I., Rodriguez, A. D., Cavazos, L. J., & Dibrell, N. D. (2017). *Proyecto Transformar: Transcending language boundaries by fostering a translingual-community engaged pedagogy for all*. Edinburg, TX: Transforming Our World Strategic Plan, The University of Texas Rio Grande Valley

Clark, E., & Flores, B. (2001). Who am I? The social construction of ethnic identity and self-perceptions in Latino preservice teachers. *Urban Review, 33*(2), 69–86.

Cummins, J. (2017). Teaching minoritized students: Are additive approaches legitimate? *Harvard Educational Review, 87*(3), 404–425.

De Mejía, A., & Hélot, C. (2015). Teacher education and support. In W. E. Wright, S. Boun, & O. García (Eds.), *The handbook of bilingual and multilingual education* (pp. 270–281). Oxford, UK: John Willey & Sons, Inc.

Donahue, C. (2016). The "trans" in transnational-translingual: Rhetorical and linguistic flexibility as new norms. *Composition Studies, 441,* 147–150.

Dyson, A. H., & Genishi, C. (2005). *On the case: approaches to language and literacy research.* New York, NY: Teachers College Press/NCRLL.

García, O., Ibarra Johnson, S., & Seltzer, K. (2016). *The translanguaging classroom: Leveraging student bilingualism for learning.* Philadelphia, PA: Caslon Publishing.

García, O., & Kleyn, T. (2013). Teacher education for multilingual education. In C. A. Chapelle (Ed.), *The encyclopedia of applied linguistics* (pp. 5543–5548). Oxford, UK: Wiley-Blackwell.

García, O., & Wei, L. (2014). *Translanguaging: Language, bilingualism and education.* New York, NY: Palgrave Macmillan.

García, O., & Woodley, H. (2014). Bilingual education. In M. Bigelow & J. Ennser-Kananen (Eds.), *The Routledge handbook of educational linguistics* (pp. 132–144). New York, NY: Routledge.

Guerra, J. C. (2016). Cultivating a rhetorical sensibility in the translingual writing classroom. *College English, 78*(3), 228–233.

HACU Office of Policy Analysis and Information. (2018). *Fact sheet Hispanic higher education and HSIs.* Washington, DC: Author.

Hinton, K. A. (2015). "We only teach in English": An examination of bilingual-in-name-only classrooms. In D. Freeman & Y. Freeman (Eds.), *Research on preparing inservice teachers to work effectively with emergent bilinguals. Advances in research on teaching* (vol. 24, pp. 265–289). London, UK: Emerald Group Publishing Limited.

Horner, B., NeCamp, S., & Donahue, C. (2011). Toward a multilingual composition scholarship: From English only to a translingual norm. *College Composition and Communication, 63*(2), 269–300.

Horner, B., & Tetreault, L. (Eds.) (2017). *Crossing divides: Exploring translingual writing pedagogies and programs.* Logan, UT: Utah State University Press.

Lee, J. W., & Jenks, C. (2016). Doing translingual dispositions. *College Composition and Communication, 68*(2), 317–344.

Lewis, G., Jones, B., & Baker, C. (2012). Translanguaging: Origins and development from school to street and beyond. *Educational Research and Evaluation: An International Journal on Theory and Practice, 18*(7): 641–654. doi:10.1080/13803611.2012.718488

Matsuda, P. K. (2014). The lure of translingual writing. *PMLA, 129*(3), 478–483.

Mazak, C. (2017). Introduction: Theorizing translanguaging practices in higher education. In C. M. Mazak & K. S. Caroll (Eds.), *Translanguaging in higher education. Beyond monolingual ideologies*s (pp. 1–10). Bristol, UK: Multilingual Matters.

Mazak, C. M., & Caroll, K. S. (2017). *Translanguaging in higher education. Beyond monolingual ideologies.* Bristol, UK: Multilingual Matters.

Mazak, C. M., & Herbas-Donoso, C. (2015). Translanguaging practices at a bilingual university: A case study of a science classroom. *International Journal of Bilingual Education and Bilingualism, 18*(6), 698–714.

McFarland, J., Hussar, B., Wang, X., Zhang, J., Wang, K., Rathbun, A., Barmer, A., Forrest Cataldi, E., & Bullock Mann, F. (2018). *Condition of Education*

2018 (NCES 2018–144). U.S. Department of Education. Washington, DC: National Center for Education Statistics.

Musanti, S. I. (2014). *"Porque sé los dos idiomas."* Biliteracy beliefs and bilingual preservice teacher identity. In Y. Freeman & D. Freeman (Eds). *Research on preparing preservice teachers to work effectively with emergent bilinguals (advances in research on teaching, Volume 21)* (pp. 59–87). London, UK: Emerald Group Publishing Limited.

Musanti, S. I., & Cavazos, A. (2018). "Siento que siempre tengo que regresar al inglés." Embracing a translanguaging stance in a Hispanic higher education institution. *EuroAmerican Journal of Applied Linguistics and Languages, 5*(2), 44–61.

Musanti, S. I., & Rodríguez, A. (2017). Translanguaging in bilingual teacher preparation: Exploring pre-service bilingual teachers' academic writing. *Bilingual Research Journal, 40*(1), 38–54.

Nuñez, A., Hurtado, S., & Calderón, E. C. (Eds.) (2015). *Hispanic-serving institutions: Advancing research and transformative practice.* New York, NY: Routledge.

Oleksak, R. (2009). Building capacity, shaping the Future. *Modern Language Journal, 93*(2), 278–280.

Olivos, E., & Quintana De Valladolid, C. (2005). Entre la espada y la pared: Critical educators, bilingual education, and education reform. *Journal of Latinos and Education, 4*(4), 283–293.

Palmer, D. K., Mateus, S. G., Martínez, R. A., & Henderson, K. (2014). Reframing the debate on language separation: Toward a vision for translanguaging pedagogies in the dual language classroom. *The Modern Language Journal, 98*(3), 757–772.

Salvatori, M. (2009). A Canadian perspective on language teacher education: Challenges and opportunities. *The Modern Language Journal, 93*(2), 287–291.

Shapiro, S., Cox, M., Shuck, G., & Simnitt, E. (2016). Teaching for agency: From appreciating linguistic diversity to empowering student writers. *Composition Studies, 44*(1), 31–52.

Tedick, D. (2009). K-12 language teacher preparation: Problems and possibilities. *The Modern Language Journal, 93*(2), 263–267.

UTRGV Office of Strategic Analysis and Institutional Reporting. (2019). *Data and reports.* Edinburg, TX: Author. Retrieved from: https://www.utrgv.edu/sair/fact-book/index.htm

Van der Walt, C., & Dornbrack, J. (2011). Academic biliteracy in South African higher education: Strategies and practices of successful students. *Language, Culture and Curriculum, 24*(1), 89–104.

Williams, C. (2002). A language gained: A study of language immersion at 11–16 years of age. Bangor, UK: School of Education, University of Wales.

Woodley, H. (2016). From pain to healing in language teacher education. *The Modern Language Journal, 100*(2), 570–572.

Wright, W. E., Boun, S., & García, O. (2015). *The handbook of bilingual and multilingual education.* Oxford, UK: John Willey & Sons, Inc.

7 Language and Literacy Practices of Bilingual Education Preservice Teachers at a Hispanic-Serving College of Education

Elena M. Venegas, Veronica L. Estrada, Janine M. Schall and Leticia De Leon

In the U.S. today, nearly 22% of the population age five and older speak a language other than English at home. Findings from the American Community Survey show that Spanish is the largest non-English language by far, spoken by 13% of the population age five and older (U.S. Census, 2017). As the bilingual population rises, so too does the demand for teachers who can serve this population. In Texas, with over one-third of Texas public school students speaking a language other than English at home, 18.8% are classified as English Learners, 9.73% as bilingual, and 9.01% are serviced by English as a second language (ESL) programs (Texas Education Agency, 2018b). Yet recruiting bilingual certified teachers within the state of Texas and beyond is difficult for various reasons including a rigorous certification process and additional workload demands such as translating English curriculum into Spanish (Swaby, 2017). The number of bilingual and/or English Learner students coupled with low numbers of certified bilingual teachers, and a difficult recruitment process suggests that colleges of education must be proactive in recruiting, retaining, and supporting bilingual preservice teachers.

The teacher preparation program where we work is in a Hispanic-Serving Institution (HSI) on the U.S./Mexico border in South Texas. We primarily enroll students from the Rio Grande Valley (RGV), a highly Spanish/English bilingual region where most of the population is of Mexican heritage. While the HSI designation means that an institution of higher education has an enrollment of at least 25% Hispanic students, in our college approximately 92% of the students identify as Hispanic. Many are also first-generation college students from immigrant families. While our bilingual education program is the largest elementary certification program in the college, we do not produce enough bilingual teachers to meet the demand of the local and state public schools. As teacher educators who care deeply about the education of Latinx students and who understand the need to produce more highly qualified and competent Latinx teachers, we believe that a preparation program built upon preservice teachers' cultural, linguistic, and community assets will help us recruit, retain, and graduate teachers who not only possess content and pedagogical knowledge, but who also understand and value their own culture and that of their future students. Given our context, we have the unique opportunity to access and affirm the rich linguistic and cultural resources of our students.

As a Hispanic-Serving College of Education (HSCOE), it is imperative that we better understand the assets and needs of our preservice teachers. The research presented in this chapter centered on an exploratory study of the language and literacy practices of undergraduate students within our HSCOE. Although all undergraduate students were invited to participate in the survey, here we present only those findings related to the language and literacy practices of bilingual education preservice teachers, as they were the largest group of participants. Furthermore, understanding the language and literacy practices of bilingual education preservice teachers is an essential step in affirming biculturalism for Latinx students not only within P-12 schooling but also in teacher education. To achieve this goal, HSCOEs must first understand and approach the language and literacy practices of bilingual education preservice teachers from an asset-based perspective.

Theoretical Framework

Two theoretical perspectives informed our study: asset-based education and an ecological view of literacy. Historically, the institution of education in the U.S. has viewed students from marginalized populations, such as the preservice teachers at our college, in negative terms since they diverge from white, middle-class population norms. These divergences are seen as problems, or deficits, that inhibit the academic success of students and communities of color. As Paris and Alim (2014) wrote, deficit approaches view the "languages, literacies and cultural ways of being of many students and communities of color as deficiencies to be overcome" (p. 87). Yosso (2005) stated, "One of the most prevalent forms of contemporary racism in US schools is deficit thinking" (p. 75) as it ignores or devalues the many strengths found in communities of color. Rather than focusing on the so-called deficits of marginalized populations, many educators today believe that culturally sustaining pedagogies in asset-based education are the best way to affirm the language, literacy, and cultural practices of students and access their strengths for academic success. Beginning in the 1990s, asset pedagogies "repositioned the linguistic, literate, and cultural practices of working-class communities—specifically poor communities of color—as resources and assets to honor, explore, and extend" (Paris & Alim, 2014, p. 87).

The assets that students of color bring with them include a set of literacy practices that help communities of color navigate personal, professional, and academic worlds. Literacy is far more than the ability to write and comprehend printed text. The ecology of literacy perspective explains that literacy is a set of social practices embedded within specific historical, linguistic, economic, and political contexts (Barton, 2007). This perspective allows for attending to sociocultural aspects of literacy without excluding cognitive dimensions inherent to reading and writing (Hall, Smith, & Wicaksono, 2011). This means that what counts as literacy, what types of literacy practices are valued or devalued, who is given access to literacy, and in what ways, are not fixed points in the universe, but instead emerge from socially constructed contexts.

Review of Literature

Language and literacy practices shape people's identities and how they exist in the world (Jimenez, 2000; Moll, 2014). Language and literacy development also have an essential role in adult success since reading allows people to access, analyze, synthesize, and use knowledge to understand the world and learn new things (Murnane, Sawhill, & Snow, 2012).

Much of the literature related to language and literacy practices at the postsecondary level focuses on academic literacy, especially the particular language of higher education and academia (Maloney, 2003). All undergraduates are expected to enter college with academic literacy skills, yet research suggests that professors and students believe that these skills are underdeveloped. Burrell, Tao, Simpson, and Mendez-Berrueta (1997) found that faculty at a Predominantly White Institution (PWI) worried that their students did not enter postsecondary education with the writing, reading, critical thinking, and problem-solving skills needed for success in college. Some students also feel their PK-12 schooling inadequately prepared them for the rigor of higher education. First-generation college students rated themselves lower than their peers on a self-assessment of their oral and written communication (Penrose, 2002), and Latinx students reported difficulty meeting the academic literacy demands of college (Murillo & Schall, 2016). Similarly, African American college students reported being held to lowered academic expectations by their high school teachers, which resulted in them feeling underprepared for college (Banks, 2005). In addition, the academic literacy demands of college may be greater for students whose first language is not English (Berman & Cheng, 2001).

Upon entering college, many students undergo a process of "reacculturation" (Elmborg, 2006, p. 196) as they learn the literacy conventions of the academy and their respective disciplines. Reacculturation may be painful for students of color, "because the academy is itself so imbued with white western culture...as an outsider to that culture these students [of color] were not even aware that they lacked the requisite literacy they needed for survival in the system" (White, 2005, p. 377). Thus, students of color may feel alienated from the academic community, especially if their cultural and/or linguistic backgrounds are not respected.

Yet, despite the potential difficulties of adapting to academic literacy at the postsecondary level, students from marginalized populations are as successful as their peers. Penrose (2002) found no differences between the academic performance of first-generation college students and their peers. Banks (2005) noted that "despite the frustration of limited high school preparation, once experienced in the college English setting, the students developed a variety of academic and personal strategies to compensate for lack of literacy preparation" (p. 31) while Berman and Cheng (2001) saw that the academic performance, as measured by grade point average (GPA), of non-native speakers of English mirrored that of their peers. In fact, research indicates that for bilingual Latinx students, their bilingualism is not a deficit but a positive predictor of academic success (Jang & Brutt-Griffler, 2018; Lutz & Crist, 2009).

The intersection of language and academic preparedness and performance for bilingual Latinx students is particularly noteworthy. First, language literacy proficiency of Latinx students is a positive predictor of four-year college attendance (Jang & Brutt-Griffler, 2018). Arguably, the literacy and cognitive skills of bilingual students are greater than those of their Spanish monolingual and their English monolingual peers (Roosa et al., 2012). Lutz and Crist (2009), for example, found that biliterate Latinx students had a higher high school GPA than their Latinx peers whose Spanish proficiency was limited. García, Woodley, Flores, and Chu (2012) studied New York City public schools with higher than city average populations of Latinx and emergent bilingual students as well as high graduation rates. A chief contributing factor to their students' success was the utilization of translanguaging and bilingualism (García et al., 2012). Translanguaging involves speakers moving fluidly between linguistic codes—such as English and Spanish—in ways that serve a communicative purpose (Allard, Mortimer, Gallo, Link, & Wortham, 2014).

While translanguaging and bilingualism contributes to academic success, bilingual Latinx students pursuing a teaching career often encounter mixed messages regarding their abilities to speak both Spanish and English. On the one hand, there is a dire need for bilingual teachers as the U.S. school population becomes increasingly racially/ethnically, culturally, and linguistically diverse. On the other hand, bilingual pre-service teachers may have encountered (and internalized) deficit perspectives of their bilingualism not only as PK-12 students but also in their teacher preparation programs.

The U.S. Department of Education (2016) projects that 29% of public school students will be of Hispanic descent by the year 2024. As of 2017–2018, 52.37% of public school students within the state of Texas, where this study occurred, identified as Hispanic, but only 27.2% of their teachers did (Texas Education Agency, 2018a). The disparity between the racial/ethnic composition of U.S. public school students and teachers is likely to continue since U.S. public school students are projected to become increasingly diverse (U.S. Department of Education, 2016), whereas 68% of education majors identify as white (King, 2019).

Thus, within U.S. public school classrooms, there is a plausibility for cultural mismatch. Cultural Mismatch Theory postulates:

> U.S. institutions tend to promote mainstream, independent cultural norms, and exclude interdependent cultural norms that are common among underrepresented groups [and] when institutions promote only mainstream norms, they inadvertently fuel inequality by creating barriers to the performance of underrepresented groups.
>
> (Stephens & Townsend, 2015, p. 1304)

Cultural mismatch in the classroom can lead to students of color being expected to adapt their learning styles and classroom/school behaviors to the cultural norms of their primarily white teachers. Furthermore, cultural mismatch may lead teachers to adopt deficit perspectives of their students, particularly students of color, English Learners, and students from low socioeconomic backgrounds (Milner, 2010).

The need for teachers of color is imperative to the success of students of color since teachers of color are more likely to understand, respect, and advocate for students of color. In addition, teachers of color are more likely to set high expectations and standards and develop strong relationships with students of color (U.S. Department of Education, 2016). As both people of color and speakers of a language in addition to English, bilingual preservice teachers may have encountered deficit perspectives as PK-12 students. Allard et al. (2014) juxtaposed the approaches of one high school and one elementary school toward immigrant students. At the secondary level, students' Spanish language proficiency was viewed as substandard and problematic. This deficit perspective resulted in lowered expectations, including the adoption of a model akin to special education for emergent bilingual students. In fact, the use of Spanish may be viewed as a hindrance to English language acquisition despite research touting the benefits of bilingualism (Tran, 2010). Such deficit perspectives encountered during schooling can be internalized and can influence bilingual preservice teachers as they prepare to become teachers themselves (Miller, 2017).

A survey of presidents and chancellors at HSIs found that nearly 40% of respondents viewed students at their institutions as underprepared for the academic workload required of undergraduates (de los Santos & Cuamea, 2010). In responding to these findings, Garcia and Ramirez (2018) remarked, "These findings suggest that some HSI leaders make decisions influenced by a deficit-based framework—potentially perpetu-ating the marginalization of students, rather than working to transform the campus environment into one that empowers students and recog-nizes their strengths" (p. 359).

A subtractive approach (Valenzuela, 1999)—emphasizing the acqui-sition of the English language at the cost of Spanish—to bilingual ed-ucation pervades U.S. public schools and can inhibit the development of academic Spanish (Guerrero & Guerrero, 2017). This potential lack of academic Spanish can result in deficit perspectives of these preser-vice teachers, even among themselves. As Guerrero and Guerrero stated, "some certified bilingual education teachers enter the classroom unsure of their linguistic abilities, lacking some abilities, and even questioning the very value of academic Spanish" (p. 9).

Monoglossic language ideology, which values only monolingualism and sees language as a decontextualized skill (García & Guevara-Torres, 2010), may persist among both teacher educators and preservice teach-ers through the prevalence, and therefore privileging of, instructional materials produced in English even within bilingual teacher education courses (Guerrero & Guerrero, 2017; Musanti & Rodriguez, 2017). Moreover, bilingual preservice teachers themselves may believe that the language of their homes and communities is unsuitable for academic contexts (Murillo, 2017). However, what happens in K-12 schooling and educator preparation programs can also influence preservice teachers in positive ways. For example, the bilingual preservice teachers who par-ticipated in Miller's (2017) study reported feeling called to teach after having positive experiences with teachers who embraced their culture and languages as assets.

Methodology

This chapter reports on a subsection of results from a larger study that explored language and literacy practices of preservice teachers through an exploratory cross-sectional survey. The question guiding this study was, "What are College of Education & P-16 (CEP) student perceptions regarding the language and literacy practices they use to navigate their personal, work and academic lives?" Sub-questions included the follow-ing: (1) What is the language and literacy knowledge of bilingual pre-service teachers? (2) What language and literacy practices do bilingual preservice teachers use to navigate their personal, work, and academic lives? (3) What are the literate identities of bilingual preservice teachers, and how does language and culture impact these literate identities? (4) What role does the digital literacy of bilingual preservice teachers play in their success, and how do their language and literacy practices play a part in that success? In this chapter, we report specifically on results from the preservice teachers in the bilingual education program.

Data Collection

A primary purpose for collecting data via a survey is to obtain new data that is otherwise not readily available (Calder, 1998). Thus, to learn more about the literacy practices of preservice teachers at an HSCOE, we constructed a survey informed by a systematic review of extant literature (Kelley, Clark, Brown, & Sitzia, 2003). The survey instrument was designed to be anonymous, self-administered, web-based, and cross-sectional. A cross-sectional survey facilitates descriptive research with the intent of "examin[ing] a situation by describing important factors associated with that situation, such as demographic, socio-economic, and health characteristics, events, behaviors, attitudes, experiences, and knowledge" (Kelley et al., 2003, p. 261).

The survey was divided into four sections including the following: demographic information, language and literacy, digital literacies, and literacy identities. The survey consisted of 54 questions and took between 9 and 12 minutes to complete. Questions were formatted as single choice, multiple choice, text entry, Likert single answer, Likert drop-down list, and rank order. In order to validate the survey, we sent it to two literacy experts in the field of teacher education at other institutions of higher education for review, then pre-tested it with five undergraduate students pursuing elementary-level teacher certification (Ruel, Wagner, & Gillespie, 2016). Based on feedback acquired during the pre-testing process, we altered the survey for clarification (e.g., first-generation college student), merged two categories into one regarding language usage (i.e., "Spanglish/Tex-Mex"), and added an "as needed" option for several questions regarding usage of various types of texts.

Participants

After this validation process, we invited 2,053 declared education majors from our HSCOE to participate in our electronic survey, obtaining an overall response rate of 16.37% (n = 336). From this sample, the majority of respondents, 48.7% (n = 162), were bilingual education preservice teachers, followed by 23.4% (n = 78) EC-6 early childhood, 8.71% (n = 29) high school education majors, and considerably lower numbers of students enrolled in special education, middle school, all-level, and ESL teacher preparation programs. We analyze and discuss data from the bilingual education preservice teacher subgroup given they made up almost half of the participants in the survey and it is the largest subgroup in our teacher preparation program.

The bilingual education program is an elementary teacher preparation program that prepares students to work in English/Spanish bilingual classrooms. During the program, the preservice teachers take five education courses, taught in Spanish or bilingually, related to bilingual education content. They also take two courses from the Modern Languages

Table 7.1 Demographics of bilingual education preservice teachers

Question	Yes	No
Were you born in the U.S.?	80.25% (*n* = 130)	19.85% (*n* = 32)
Are you a first-generation college student?	74.07% (*n* = 120)	25.93% (*n* = 42)
Did you do any of your K-12 schooling in another country?	22.22% (*n* = 36)	77.78% (*n* = 126)
Was most or all of your K-12 schooling in the RGV?	83.95% (*n* = 136)	16.05% (*n* = 26)
Was any of your K-12 schooling taught in Spanish?	67.28% (*n* = 109)	32.72% (*n* = 53)

department which are taught in Spanish. One hundred percent of the bilingual education respondents described themselves as 'Hispanic or Latino,' and all but one were female. Table 7.1 provides for basic descriptive demographics of this subgroup.

Data Analysis

Our research questions and sampling procedures were designed to gain insight into language and literacy practices of bilingual education preservice teachers at an HSI. Given that the survey was designed to generate hypotheses and learning, we analyzed survey data through thematic analysis (Gerber, Abrams, Curwood, & Magnifico, 2017; Saldana, 2013). We read through the results of the survey together, generated initial codes, analyzed the codes through reflective discussion, and generated three themes that are discussed below.

Results and Findings

Findings are reported by three themes: *Contextualized Linguistic Flexibility*, *Reflecting a Shift in Literacy*, and *Mixed Perceptions and Attitudes*. Contextualized Linguistic Flexibility refers to our bilingual education preservice teachers' abilities to fully utilize their linguistic resources as well as engage in translanguaging. Reflecting a Shift in Literacy denotes increased usage of multimodal texts and multiliteracies. Mixed Perceptions and Attitudes refers to our bilingual education preservice teachers' self-perceptions of their linguistic and literacy abilities.

Contextualized Linguistic Flexibility

The bilingual education preservice teachers used multiple linguistic codes and engaged in translanguaging in various aspects of their lives. All respondents reported English and Spanish bilingualism. In fact, many reported linguistic abilities in three languages: English, Spanish, and Tex-Mex/Spanglish. The preservice teachers used different languages with different audiences and for different purposes (see Table 7.2).

Given that the research took place in a highly bilingual region, it was not surprising to see large percentages of respondents reporting the use of Spanish across audiences and contexts. Over half (55.97%) of the bilingual education preservice teachers noted that their parents spoke only Spanish, while 43.40% reported that their parents spoke both English and Spanish and only one respondent (0.63%) reported that her parents only spoke English. It makes sense, then, that Spanish is deeply embedded within family contexts, with half of the respondents reporting that they speak only Spanish with their parents and another 33.13% sometimes speaking in Spanish and other times in English. However, even in the family context we see respondents using more English with their siblings than their parents and 20% of the respondents who were parents reported that they used only English to communicate with their children.

Table 7.2 Bilingual education preservice teachers' use of English and Spanish across contexts

Question	English only	Spanish only	Sometimes in English and other times in Spanish	Tex-Mex/ Spanglish	Other language
Communicate with your parents	3.75% ($n = 6$)	50.63% ($n = 81$)	33.13% ($n = 53$)	12.50% ($n = 20$)	0.00% ($n = 0$)
Communicate with your siblings	12.90% ($n = 20$)	8.39% ($n = 13$)	60.65% ($n = 94$)	18.06% ($n = 28$)	0.00% ($n = 0$)
Communicate with your friends	10.63% ($n = 17$)	3.13% ($n = 5$)	65.63% ($n = 105$)	20.63% ($n = 33$)	0.00% ($n = 0$)
Communicate with your professors	51.57% ($n = 82$)	0.00% ($n = 0$)	47.17% ($n = 75$)	1.26% ($n = 2$)	0.00% ($n = 0$)
Communicate with your children	19.61% ($n = 10$)	9.80% ($n = 5$)	66.67% ($n = 34$)	3.92% ($n = 2$)	0.00% ($n = 0$)
Read for pleasure	44.30% ($n = 70$)	4.43% ($n = 7$)	50.00% ($n = 79$)	0.63% ($n = 1$)	0.63% ($n = 1$)
Read for work	53.24% ($n = 74$)	0.72% ($n = 1$)	46.04% ($n = 64$)	0.00% ($n = 0$)	0.00% ($n = 0$)
Read/study for school	33.75% ($n = 54$)	0.63% ($n = 1$)	65.00% ($n = 104$)	0.00% ($n = 0$)	0.63% ($n = 1$)
When using email	50.00% ($n = 79$)	0.00% ($n = 0$)	50.00% ($n = 79$)	0.00% ($n = 0$)	0.00% ($n = 0$)
When texting	9.43% ($n = 15$)	1.26% ($n = 2$)	76.10% ($n = 121$)	13.21% ($n = 21$)	0.00% ($n = 0$)

Respondents were more likely to use Spanish in family and personal contexts, but English was more common in academic and work contexts. Yet, even in academic and work contexts the use of Spanish was reported often, no doubt influenced by the bilingual curriculum in the teacher preparation program and the bilingual nature of the RGV.

Respondents reported relatively low usage of Tex-Mex/Spanglish, which does not seem congruent with our daily experiences living in the RGV. One possible explanation is that speaking in Tex-Mex or Spanglish may be more reflective of academics' view of language. While students may speak in this regional dialect, they may not be familiar or regularly use these descriptors. This is an area we intend to probe in follow-up focus groups.

Reflecting a Shift in Literacy

The large variety in types of texts that respondents reported reading and writing are reflective of a shift away from traditional long-form print texts (e.g., essays, novels, and nonfiction books) to texts reflecting multiliteracies. While over half (51.53%) reported that they often read novels for personal use, 60.74% read magazines, and 30.67% read nonfiction books, online texts dominated, with 87.73% reporting that they often read social media, 85.28% reporting that they often read text messages, and 52.15% reporting that they often read apps. Besides these short, digital texts, respondents reported reading other forms of text: 40.49% often read recipes or cookbooks, 29.45% read religious texts such as the Bible, and 59.50% often read song lyrics or sheet music.

Respondents reported less writing for personal use, but here, too, digital forms dominated with 90.18% often writing text messages, 76.69% often writing posts on social media, and 72.39% often writing emails. Other forms of writing were less popular, but 41.10% of respondents did report often writing a diary or journal and 36.20% reported writing letters. Respondents also produced other texts: 20.86% often wrote prayers or religious texts, 15.34% wrote songs or song lyrics, 15.34% wrote stories, and 11.04% wrote poetry.

Mixed Perceptions and Attitudes

Overall, the bilingual education preservice teachers considered themselves good readers and writers who generally enjoyed reading and writing, yet there were significant numbers who did not have positive attitudes or self-perceptions about their literacy skills. We asked respondents to rate their attitudes toward reading and writing in both print and digital forms. Table 7.3 presents the results from this question.

Respondents had more positive responses toward reading than writing, though reading enjoyment dropped from childhood to present day.

Table 7.3 Reading and writing habits of bilingual education preservice teachers

Question	Always or almost always	Usually	Sometimes	Never or almost never
Did you enjoy reading as a child?	40.63% (*n* = 65)	26.25% (*n* = 42)	24.38% (*n* = 39)	8.75% (*n* = 14)
Do you enjoy reading at this point in your life?	28.75% (*n* = 46)	31.25% (*n* = 50)	32.50% (*n* = 52)	7.50% (*n* = 12)
Think about the reading you do for your classes. Do you consider yourself a good reader of academic text?	19.38% (*n* = 31)	40.63% (*n* = 65)	32.50% (*n* = 52)	7.50% (*n* = 12)
Think about the reading you do for fun. Do you consider yourself a good reader when you read for pleasure?	50.00% (*n* = 80)	33.13% (*n* = 53)	11.88% (*n* = 19)	5.00% (*n* = 8)
Think about the reading you do online. Do you consider yourself a good reader of online text?	33.75% (*n* = 54)	37.50% (*n* = 60)	21.88% (*n* = 35)	6.88% (*n* = 11)
Did you enjoy writing as a child?	32.50% (*n* = 52)	28.13% (*n* = 45)	30.63% (*n* = 49)	8.75% (*n* = 14)
Do you enjoy writing at this point in your life?	28.75% (*n* = 46)	31.87% (*n* = 51)	29.38% (*n* = 47)	10.00% (*n* = 16)
Think about the writing you do for your classes. Do you consider yourself a good academic writer?	20.63% (*n* = 33)	50.00% (*n* = 80)	21.88% (*n* = 35)	7.50% (*n* = 12)
Think about the writing you do for fun. Do you consider yourself a good writer for fun?	33.75% (*n* = 54)	34.38% (*n* = 55)	25.00% (*n* = 40)	6.88% (*n* = 11)

This is possibly because much of their current day reading is related to school, and their self-perceptions of their academic reading lags behind perceptions of reading for enjoyment.

While all respondents were bilingual, they rated their Spanish language proficiency differently across four domains of literacy. Most respondents rated their ability to understand Spanish from *very well*, 31.34% (*n* = 50), to *extremely well*, 63.52% (*n* = 101). The ability to speak Spanish was slightly lower, though still high overall. Forty-three percent (*n* = 70) of the bilingual education preservice teachers rated their ability to speak Spanish as *extremely well*, whereas 37.50% (*n* = 60) rated their ability as *very well*.

The preservice teachers were less confident in their abilities to read Spanish. The percentages of respondents who reported reading Spanish *extremely well* decreased to 46.88% (*n* = 75), *very well* to 34.38%

(n = 55), and *moderately well* to 18.13% (n = 29). Perceptions of Spanish language proficiency declined even further regarding their writing abilities. Overall, 30.82% (n = 49) stated they wrote *extremely well*, 30.82% (n = 49) wrote *very well*, 29.56% (n = 47) *moderately well*, and 8.18% (n = 13) wrote in Spanish *slightly well*.

Respondents also had mixed perceptions of their readiness for college. Of our bilingual education preservice teachers, only 27.63% (n = 42) strongly agreed that their K-12 schooling had prepared them for college, while 45.39% (n = 69) somewhat agreed, 13.16% (n = 20) neither agreed nor disagreed, 10.53% (n = 15) somewhat disagreed, and 3.29% (n = 5) strongly disagreed.

Discussion

Through this survey, bilingual education preservice teachers reported on their literacy and language practices. While people holding deficit views would see the culture and language of these preservice teachers, as well as their status as first-generation college students from immigrant families, as a problem for the teacher preparation program, instead we view these characteristics as potential assets for our program and for their development as successful adults.

Despite high levels of bilingualism within the region, the English language is often privileged within academic settings. English-only curricula is heavily favored by schools within the region (Murillo & Schall, 2016). Therefore, native Spanish speakers are typically identified as English Learners, receive Spanish instruction only within the primary grades, and are speedily transitioned to English-only instruction (Musanti & Rodriguez, 2017). Within academic contexts, the value of the Spanish language is usually limited to its use as a tool for transitioning students to English-only instruction (Murillo & Schall, 2016).

Thus, it is unsurprising even within a highly bilingual community and amidst expectations that they complete coursework taught in Spanish, that the bilingual education preservice teachers who participated in our study reported higher levels of English use within academic contexts. Scanlan, Frattura, Schneider, Capper, and Capper (2012) argued that the term *English Learner* devalues the linguistic assets of bilingual students and contributes to a deficit perspective. According to Elmborg (2006), "school literacies" (p. 195) are a prerequisite for social and economic success although society and thereby school literacies often do not value and/or reflect every community and/or culture. Thus, preservice teachers may internalize messages related to "what it means to be a NNEST [i.e., non-native speaking English teacher] or a speaker of lower-prestige forms of English, or to be racially coded as one" (Motha, Jain, & Tecle, 2012, p. 15). The bilingual elementary students who participated in Allard et al.'s (2014) study, for example, conceived that

"English was the language of power and talked in a way that mirrored tacit school policies in which English was for schooling and Spanish was for home" (p. 349). Thus, Miller (2017) argued that bilingual preservice teachers may readily accept English as the language of schooling. Nevertheless, the primary use of English for academically related purposes is particularly noteworthy as the university's strategic plan is to become a bilingual, bicultural, and biliterate institution.

We also see powerful monoglossic language ideologies in the generational shift toward English as respondents reported using more English with siblings or friends as opposed to parents. Even less Spanish was seen in respondents' communication with their children. Previous research conducted by Rumbaut, Massey, and Bean (2006) found that among third-generation Mexican Americans, only 17% still spoke fluent Spanish and 96% preferred speaking English at home. Nevertheless, our bilingual education preservice teachers successfully navigate the cultural and linguistic resources associated with both the English and Spanish languages.

The language and literacy practices of our bilingual education preservice teachers indicate that many engage in translanguaging. These findings align with those of Tran (2010) whose analysis of data from the Children of Immigrants Longitudinal Survey revealed that the English and Spanish language proficiencies of second-generation Latinx individuals simultaneously increase. Tran (2010) therefore asserted that second language acquisition does not impede retention of one's first language. Instead, Tran recommended frequent use of a language in order to both promote and retain it. For our bilingual preservice teachers, this suggests that they should continue to translanguage in order to maintain their Spanish and English language proficiencies. Second, instead of approaching bilingual education preservice teachers from the perspective of monoglossic language ideology, teacher preparation programs must adopt a heteroglossic language ideology. Allard et al. (2014) describe the heteroglossic approach as "view[ing] bilinguals' languages as interdependent and complementary" (p. 337).

The respondents read and write multiple forms of text for multiple purposes. However, what it means to be literate has clearly changed; multiple literacies and digital forms of text are deeply embedded in the lives of our bilingual education preservice teachers. The continuous evolution of technology has changed learning through its influence on how we communicate and acquire information (Elmborg, 2006). New literacies are beneficial in that they help individuals to identify, synthesize, and critically evaluate important information to solve problems and/or answer questions (Leu, Leu, & Coiro, 2006).

Our bilingual education preservice teachers rated their Spanish language proficiencies highly, particularly in terms of their abilities to comprehend and speak Spanish. The self-reported Spanish language proficiencies of our bilingual preservice teachers juxtapose the call from some bilingual education teacher educators to improve their students' Spanish language skills (Guerrero & Guerrero, 2017). These assertions seem to echo those of Burrell et al. (1997) who found that professors rated their students' academic literacy skills as low. Notably, the Burrell et al. (1997) study was conducted at a PWI with presumably an English-only student speaking population. Nevertheless, Aquino-Sterling (2016) recommended that bilingual education teacher educators recognize, validate, and nurture the linguistic strengths of bilingual preservice teachers while seeking to expand their linguistic repertoires.

The university experience seemed to help our respondents develop a greater sense of self; 64.47% (*n* = 98) of our respondents strongly agreed that since beginning their undergraduate careers, they developed a stronger sense of themselves. Our findings suggest that, in part, the university experience helped our respondents to embrace their bilingualism. On our survey, only about one-third of respondents identified themselves as bilingual students during their PK-12 schooling. However, more than half of our respondents identified themselves as bilingual undergraduates. Perhaps this relates to our institution's strategic initiative to be a bilingual, bicultural, and biliterate institution. In their study of secondary schools who demonstrated success with bilingual Latinx students, García et al. (2012) found that these schools *were* committed to *transculturación*, or "affirm[ing] students' abilities to straddle cultures and to perform features of what might be considered different 'national cultures' as their very own in interaction with each other" (p. 812).

Implications for a HSCOE

The results of our survey suggest that the bilingual education preservice teachers in our program are a heterogeneous group with varied experiences and perspectives. They bring with them linguistic and literate strengths which we are beginning to understand through research such as this. Because the Latinx population is highly diverse and complex (Pertuz, 2018; Torres, 2004) and HSIs themselves are diverse in mission and student characteristics (Núñez, Crisp, & Elizondo, 2016), it is essential that HSCOEs develop processes that help them understand their unique demographics and the lived realities of their students' lives, which will vary across HSCOEs. A better understanding of bilingual education preservice teachers will help HSCOEs adapt programs, policies, and curricula to capitalize on their assets as opposed to approaching these students from a deficit perspective. This is an essential step in preparing future teachers to likewise view Latinx students from an asset-based perspective that affirms bilingual, biliterate, and bicultural identities.

Assets include the rich linguistic knowledge that the bilingual education preservice teachers bring into the teacher preparation program.

Our survey findings revealed that even within our bilingual teacher preparation program which contains seven courses taught bilingually or in Spanish, the English language continues to be privileged. Our bilingual education preservice teachers reported primarily utilizing Spanish to communicate with their parents; however, they translanguage when communicating orally with their siblings, their children, and when using digital tools. Notably, our respondents rated their own Spanish language proficiencies highly and seemed to embrace bilingualism as university students. In order to build on this strength, HSCOEs must deliberately and explicitly consider the role of language within teacher preparation programs. How does a college develop a culture built upon heteroglossic language ideologies? How will translanguaging be integrated into the teacher preparation program as a pedagogical and learning tool? How do we help faculty, staff, and students deconstruct and push back against monoglossic language ideologies? Should we expect some level of Spanish language proficiency from faculty and staff? Do we have a responsibility beyond the bilingual education preparation program to help students develop some level of Spanish language proficiency if they don't already have it? These and many other questions deserve careful consideration.

Our bilingual education preservice teachers reported rich experiences with literacy, including high degrees of comfort with and utilization of information communication technologies in several languages and deep involvement in multiple literacies. These illustrate the changing nature of literacy; HSCOEs must explicitly consider and address this change to take advantage of the strengths and contextualized literacy knowledge that Latinx students have developed through their prior in-school and out-of-school literacy experiences. In addition, the bilingual education preservice teachers will soon be teachers of children who are growing up in this new world of literacy. There are any number of actions HSCOEs might take to address this. For example, they might need to revise their curriculum to incorporate educational technology throughout the program and help preservice teachers be critical consumers and producers of digital texts. HSCOEs should consider other questions as well. How do we help students understand the importance of out-of-school and community forms of literacy (e.g., oral storytelling, religious literacies, and song lyrics) that are traditionally devalued by schools? What professional development do faculty need so that they can use technological and digital resources to transform their teaching in order to better meet the needs of today's students? What role do HSCOEs have in supporting students' English and Spanish language writing skills?

The linguistic, literacy, and cultural strengths of our Latinx students in the bilingual education teacher preparation program provide a strong foundation for a desire and commitment to serve their communities through becoming outstanding teachers. As an HSCOE, that same desire and commitment must be the foundation of everything we do. By building preparation programs upon our preservice teachers' linguistic, literacy, and cultural assets, we will be able to welcome more potential teachers into our college and strengthen retention and graduation rates. These teachers will not only possess content and pedagogical knowledge, but will also understand and affirm their own culture and that of their future students. Given the dire need for bilingual teachers to educate an increasing Latinx student population, HSCOEs must be at the forefront of preparing preservice teachers to meet this need. However, simply being bilingual is not enough. HSCOEs must be intentional in helping preservice teachers to affirm their own language and literacy practices as assets so that they too can celebrate and develop the bilingual and biliterate identities of their P-12 students.

References

Allard, E., Mortimer, K., Gallo, S., Link, H, & Wortham, S. (2014). Immigrant Spanish as liability or asset? Generational diversity in language ideologies at school. *Journal of Language, Identity & Education, 13*(5), 335–353. doi:10.1080/15348458.2014.958040

Aquino-Sterling, C. R. (2016). Responding to the call: Developing and assessing pedagogical Spanish competencies in bilingual teacher education. *Bilingual Research Journal, 39*(1), 50–68. doi:10.1080/15235882.2016.1139519

Banks, J. (2005). African American college students' perceptions of their high school literacy preparation. *Journal of College Reading and Learning, 35*(2), 22–37. doi:10.1080/10790195.2005.10850171

Barton, D. (2007). *Literacy: An introduction to the ecology of written language.* Oxford: Blackwell.

Berman, R., & Cheng, L. (2001). English academic language skills: Perceived difficulties by undergraduate and graduate students, and their academic achievement. *Canadian Journal of Applied Linguistics, 4*(1–2), 25–40.

Burrell, K. I., Tao, L., Simpson, M. L., & Mendez-Berrueta, H. (1997). How do we know what we are preparing our students for? A reality check of one university's academic literacy demands. *Research and Teaching in Developmental Education, 13*(2), 55–70.

Calder, J. (1998). Survey research methods. *Medical Education, 32,* 636–652.

de los Santos Jr., A. G., & Cuamea, K. M. (2010). Challenges facing Hispanic-serving Institutions in the first decade of the 21st century. *Journal of Latinos and Education, 9*(2), 9–107. doi:10.1080/15348431003617798

Elmborg, J. (2006). Critical information literacy: Implications for instructional practice. *Journal of Academic Librarianship, 32*(2), 192–199.

Garcia, G. A., & Ramirez, J. J. (2018). Institutional agents at a Hispanic serving institution: Using social capital to empower students. *Urban Education, 53*(3), 355–381. doi:10.1177/0042085915623341

García, O., & Guevara-Torres, R. (2010). Monoglossic ideologies and language policies in the education of U.S. Latinas/os. In E. G. Murrillo Jr., S. A. Villenas, R. T. Galván, J. S. Muñoz, C. Martínez, & M. Machado-Casas (Eds.), *Handbook of Latinos and education: Research theory and practice* (pp. 182–193). New York, NY: Routledge.

García, O., Woodley, H. H., Flores, N., & Chu, H. (2012). Latino emergent bilingual youth in high schools: Transcaring strategies for academic success. *Urban Education, 48*(6), 798–827. doi: 10.1177/0042085912462708

Gerber, H. R. Abrams, S. S., Curwood, J. S., & Magnifico, A. M. (2017). *Conducting qualitative research of learning in online spaces.* Thousand Oaks, CA: Sage.

Guerrero, M. D., & Guerrero, M. C. (2017). Competing discourses of academic Spanish in the Texas-Mexico borderlands. *Bilingual Research Journal, 40*(1), 5–19. doi:10.1080/15235882.2016.1273150

Hall, C. J., Smith, P. H., & Wicaksono, R. (2011). Literacy. In C. J. Hall, P. H. Smith, & R. Wicaksono (Ed.), *Mapping applied linguistics: A guided for students and practitioners* (pp. 129–153). New York, NY: Routledge.

Jang, E., & Brutt-Griffler, J. (2018). Language as a bridge to higher education: A large-scale empirical study of heritage language proficiency on language minority students' academic success. *Journal of Multilingual and Multicultural Development.* doi:10.1080/01434632.2018.1518451

Jimenez, R. T. (2000). Literacy and identity development of Latino/a students. *American Educational Research Journal, 37*(4), 971–1000.

Kelley, K., Clark, B., Brown, V., & Sitzia, J. (2003). Good practice in the conduct and reporting of survey research. *International Journal for Quality in Health Care, 15*(3), 261–266. doi:10.1093/intqhc/mzg031

King, J. E. (2019). Education students and diversity: A review of new evidence. Washington, DC: American Association of Colleges for Teacher Education. Retrieved from https://secure.aacte.org/apps/rl/res_get.php?fid=4484&ref=rl.

Leu, D. J., Leu, D. D., & Coiro, J. (2006). *Teaching with the Internet K-12: New literacies for new times* (4th ed.). Norwood, MA: Christopher-Gordon.

Lutz, A., & Crist, S. (2009). Why do bilingual boys get better grades in English-only America? The impact of gender, language, and family interaction on academic achievement of Latino/a children of immigrants. *Ethnic and Racial Studies, 32*(2), 346–368. doi:10.1080/01419870801943647

Maloney, W. H. (2003). Connecting the texts of their lives to academic literacy: Creating success for at-risk first-year college students. *Journal of Adolescent & Adult Literacy, 46*(8), 664–673.

Miller, K. (2017). "El pasado refleja el futuro": Pre-service teachers' memories of growing up bilingual. *Bilingual Research Journal, 40*(1), 20–37. doi:10.1080/15235882.2016.1276031

Milner, H. R. (2010). What does teacher education have to do with teaching? Implications for diversity studies. *Journal of Teacher Education, 61*(1–2), 118–131. doi:10.1177/0022487109347670

Moll, L. (2014). *L.S. Vygotsky and education.*New York, NY: Routledge.

Motha, S., Jain, R., & Tecle, T. (2012). Translinguistic identity-as-pedagogy: Implications for language teacher education. *International Journal of Innovation in English Language Teaching and Research, 1*(1), 13–28.

Murnane, R., Sawhill, I., & Snow, C. (2012). Literacy challenges for the twenty-first century: Introducing the issue. *The Future of Children, 22*(2), 3–15.

Murillo, L. A. (2017). Aquí no hay pobrecitos: Decolonizing bilingual teacher education in the U.S.-Mexico Borderlands. *Diaspora, Indigenous, and Minority Education, 11*(4), 163–176. doi:10.1080/15595692.2016.1258694

Murillo, L. A., & Schall, J. M. (2016). "They didn't teach us well": Mexican-origin students speak out about their readiness for college literacy. *Journal of Adolescent & Adult Literacy, 60*(3), 315–323. doi:10.1002/jaal.581

Musanti, S. I. & Rodriguez, A. D. (2017). Translanguaging in bilingual teacher preparation: Exploring pre-service bilingual teachers' academic writing. *Bilingual Research Journal, 40*(1), 38–54. doi:10.1080/15235882.2016.1276028

Núñez, A. M., Crisp, G., & Elizondo, D. (2016). Mapping Hispanic serving institutions: A typology of institutional diversity. *The Journal of Higher Education, 87*(1), 55–83.

Paris, D., & Alim, H. S. (2014). What are we seeking to sustain in culturally sustaining pedagogy? A loving critique forward. *Harvard Educational Review, 84*(1), 85–100.

Penrose, A. M. (2002). Academic literacy perceptions and performance: Comparing first-generation and continuing-generation college students. *Research in the Teaching of English, 36*(4), 437–461.

Pertuz, S. (2018). Exploring Latinx/a/o identity, cultural values, and success in higher education. In A. Bautista, S. Collado, & D. Perez (Eds.), *Latinx/a/os in higher education* (pp. 71–89). Washington, DC: NASPA.

Roosa, M. W., O'Donnell, M., Cham, H., Gonzales, N. A., Zeiders, K. H., Tein, J., Knight, G. P., & Umana-Taylor, A. (2012). A prospective study of Mexican American adolescents' academic success: Considering family and individual factors. *Journal of Youth and Adolescence, 41*, 307–319. doi:10.1007/s10964-011-9707-x

Ruel, E., Wagner, W. E., & Gillespie, B. J. (2016). *The practice of survey research: Theory and applications.* Thousand Oaks, CA: Sage.

Rumbaut, R. G., Massey, D. S., & Bean, F. D. (2006). Linguistic life expectancies: Immigrant language retention in Southern California. *Population and Development Review, 32*(3), 447–460.

Saldana, J. (2013). *The coding manual for qualitative researchers* (2nd ed.). Thousand Oaks: CA: Sage.

Scanlan, M., Frattura, E., Schneider, K., Capper, C., & Capper, C. A. (2012). Bilingual students within integrated comprehensive services: Collaborative strategies. In A. Honigsfeld & M. G. Dove (Eds.), *Coteaching and other collaborative practices in the EFL/ESL classroom: Rationale, research, reflections, and recommendations* (pp. 3–13). Charlotte, NC: Information Age.

Stephens, N. M., & Townsend, S. S. M. (2015). The norms that drive behavior: Implications for cultural mismatch theory. *Journal of Cross-Cultural Psychology, 46*(10), 1304–1306.

Swaby, A. (2017, February 21). Texas school districts struggle to recruit bilingual certified teachers. *The Texas Tribune.* Retrieved from https://www.texastribune.org/2017/02/21/texas-school-districts-struggle-bilingual-certified-teachers/.

Texas Education Agency. (2018a, April 4). PEIMS standard reports: Student enrollment reports. Retrieved from https://rptsvr1.tea.texas.gov/adhocrpt/adste.html

Texas Education Agency. (2018b, April 4). PEIMS standard reports: Student program reports. Retrieved from https://rptsvr1.tea.texas.gov/cgi/sas/broker

Torres, V. (2004). The diversity among us: Puerto Ricans, Cuban Americans, Caribbean Americans, and Central and South Americans. *New Directions for Student Services, 105*, 5–16.

Tran, V. C. (2010). English gain vs. Spanish loss? Language assimilation among second-generation Latinos in young adulthood. *Social Forces, 89*(1), 257–284.

U.S. Census Bureau. (2017, September 14). New American community survey statistics for income, poverty and health insurance available for states and local areas. Press Release Number CB17–157. Retrieved from https://www.census.gov/newsroom/press-releases/2017/acs-single-year.html?CID=CBSM+ACS16

U.S. Department of Education, Office of Planning, Evaluation and Policy, Development, Policy and Program Studies Service. (2016, July). *The state of racial diversity in the educator workforce.* Washington, DC. Retrieved from https://www2.ed.gov/rschstat/eval/highered/racial-diversity/state-racial-diversity-workforce.pdf

Valenzuela, A. (1999). *Subtractive schooling: U.S.-Mexican youth and the politics of caring.* Albany, NY: SUNY Press.

White, J. W. (2005). Sociolinguistic challenges to minority collegiate success: Entering the discourse community of the college. *Journal of College Student Retention, 6*(4), 369–393.

Yosso, T. J. (2005). Whose culture has capital? A critical race theory discussion of community cultural wealth. *Race Ethnicity and Education, 8*(1), 69–91, doi:10.1080/1361332052000341006

8 Counter-Storytelling to Build Teacher Agency in STEM Educators at a Hispanic-Serving College of Education

Ariana Garza Garcia, Felicia Rodriguez and Angela Chapman

> Well, if English isn't your first language then that means you probably aren't from here legally.

This sentiment from a high schooler in Ariana's science classroom resonates with many students throughout the Rio Grande Valley (RGV) who do not belong to the dominant culture.

The statement reflects the mindset of a dominant ideology that is present in many schools and creates shame, fear, and embarrassment in Spanish-speaking and/or immigrant students. Historically, students from nondominant cultures have been silenced and marginalized in school institutions. How can their stories provide voice and awareness to preservice teachers in a Hispanic-Serving College of Education (HSCOE)? How can these stories serve as a foundation to prepare preservice teachers to challenge and disrupt oppressive practices? This chapter shows the journey throughout Ariana and Felicia's preservice years and into the first years of their high school teaching careers. This is a story about an awakening and the development of a critical consciousness about who we are in this context and the responsibility we have as teachers.

Our story draws attention to our cultural factors—native language, immigration status, and being a migrant student. These factors are relevant to many of the teachers and students in the schools where Ariana and Felicia have learned and taught because these systems have reinforced practices that favor white, English-speaking students from the U.S. There is a strong need to provide all preservice science teachers with more substantive preparation that promotes diversity, equity, and inclusion (Hernandez, Morales, & Shroyer, 2013).

Throughout our journey, we examined the prevailing dominant structures that we experienced in our PK-12 education and how Ariana and Felicia now approach teaching students, including those who look and sound like they do. In this journey, Ariana and Felicia not only developed a sense of critical consciousness but also agency.

Teacher Agency

We define teacher agency as a person's ability to act in a way that promotes social justice (Pantić, 2015). Our ability to *do* (our agency) is influenced by *who we are* (our identity) and *where we are* (sociocultural context). Like Pantić, in developing our own sense of agency, we utilize Biesta and Tedder's (2007) conceptualization, which embraces Freire's (1970) notions of *concientización* or critical consciousness, liberation of the oppressed, and social justice. Critical consciousness is a deep understanding or heightened awareness of social, cultural, historical, and political conflicts that exist in society. Critical consciousness also demands action, or agency, to address oppressive practices.

Pantić (2015) conceptualized teacher agency for social justice to include purpose, competence, autonomy, and reflexivity. Teacher agency with purpose means that an educator is mindful and intentional such that his or her actions create a socially just climate. A competent teacher has been conscientized with respect to socially unjust practices that limit or prevent equity and inclusion in the classroom. Autonomy is "how teachers practice their agency...a competent agent will act differently in different contexts and at different times depending, for example, on the ways he or she perceives the locus of power or collective efficacy" (p. 768). Reflexivity allows teachers to reflect and reach a deeper understanding of what they assume to be true about their students and how it impacts their teaching in different contexts (Matthews & Jessel, 1998).

This work is grounded in Latino/a critical theory (LatCrit), a theoretical framework whose goal is eliminating racism by challenging subordinative practices and dominant ideologies with a commitment to social justice (Solórzano & Bernal, 2001; Solórzano & Yasso, 2002). LatCrit supports the use of biographies or narratives of Latino/a students by providing the opportunity for counter-stories from individuals whose voice has been silenced to be heard and analyzed, allowing social injustices and inequitable practices to be exposed.

How We Came to Be a Community of Practice

Angela, a science teacher educator at the University of Texas Rio Grande Valley (UTRGV), worked with Ariana and Felicia, who were students in the secondary science teacher certification program when this project began. One day she asked Ariana and Felicia how they labeled themselves in terms of ethnicity and race – Hispanic? Latinx? Chicano/a? Mexican? This led to a lengthy discussion where Ariana and Felicia realized that they were told by their teachers to check the Hispanic box and as young students did that without thought. What resulted from these initial discussions was a years-long research community of practice (CoP), comprised of Ariana, Felicia, and other undergraduates in which we wrote about growing up in the borderlands as a student in the local PK-12 schools. Wenger (2006) defines a CoP as "groups of people who share a concern or a passion for something they do and learn how to do it better as they interact regularly" (p. 1).

In our CoP, we shared our stories, and asked questions of each other that would often challenge our beliefs and led to the realization of the oppression we experienced or what Freire (1970) coined *concientización*. Our emotional, evocative, and painful experiences emerged through recorded dinner conversations at Angela's home, conversations with family members, and journals, which were written both individually and collectively. Felicia wrote about her experiences growing up in a migrant family, the shame she felt being called the watermelon girl by other children at school, and her tightknit family who shuffled between motels and vacant houses occupied with rattlesnakes. Ariana read Felicia's story and opened up about her own experience of moving to the U.S. as an undocumented immigrant at the age of nine. Our counter-stories emerged as we used autoethnography in this CoP (Toyosaki, Pensoneau-Conway, Wendt, & Leathers, 2009).

According to Ellis, Adams, and Bochner (2011),

> When researchers write autoethnographies, they seek to produce aesthetic and evocative thick descriptions of personal and interpersonal experience. Thus, the autoethnographer not only tries to make personal experience meaningful and cultural experience engaging, but also...she or he may be able to reach wider and more diverse mass audiences that traditional research usually disregards, a move that can make personal and social change possible for more people.
> (p. 277)

Through counter-storytelling we developed a critical consciousness and teacher agency that we feel gave us a voice and empowered us to address and challenge issues of power, race, ethnicity, language, gender, and immigration status in context of our PK-12 education (Hughes & Pennington, 2017).

A Vignette from Ariana's Counter-story

I have been a criminal for 14 years. My surroundings remind me of this every single day. My parents decided to move from Tamaulipas, Mexico when I was nine years old. I remember it was summer and I had no time to say goodbye to my friends. Little did I know back then that I would never see them again. My parents told my brother and I they had asked a friend of theirs to cross over our furniture so the policemen at the bridge wouldn't suspect anything of my family. We brought as few things as possible and my parents asked me to leave behind all my toys. I would like to believe now that my parents felt these were unnecessary items that I did not need in this new life I was about to begin. For a while, my brother and I hated it here and would beg my parents to move back.

In third grade, I was placed in Ms. Casas's (all names are pseudonyms) class, the "bilingual" teacher. Even though that was her title, I remember her not letting me speak Spanish in class. The only thing I had to hold on to, my language, was now taken from me. Carmen, who sat behind me, overheard me say something to myself in Spanish. "Hablas espanol?!", she asked with pure happiness on her face. After some time, Carmen confessed that she too had moved from Mexico illegally. Illegal immigrants placed in a bilingual class. She never had the courage to speak to me until that day because to her I looked American. My light skin and blond curly hair prevented me from making friends that could actually speak to me. Everyone thought I spoke English because I looked the part, but I was desperate for a friend who I could actually talk to someone that also spoke Spanish. Because I looked white, I had a hard time understanding everyone and making other friends. I quickly learned that being able to pass for white was important. It would allow me to look like I belonged with other white students. So, as quickly as possible, I learned to speak English and get rid of my accent in order to pass for white.

My parents always told my brother and I of the dangers of being caught. For example, my parents warned us of the dangers of being pulled over by cops or not having American identification. Every time we would visit our family in Mexico, my mom would tell us not to speak at the bridge when we crossed back into the U.S. My brother and I knew better than to tell anyone we were immigrants. We knew, we just didn't say it out loud to anyone.

I don't remember being aware of the impact of being an illegal immigrant until I started high school. I remember my parents telling me we didn't have papers but I never realized why that mattered until my late teenage years. I had a feeling some of my classmates were also immigrants, but never dared to talk about it. It was my most embarrassing secret, coming to the United States illegally and not being able to do the same things as some of my friends. I had never been past the Falfurrias checkpoint. This checkpoint stops all vehicles and asks all passengers of their citizenship status. If you're a citizen, they let you go through into North Texas. However, if you are not a U.S. citizen, you would be deported (at least this is what I was told by my parents). My family and I would always have less opportunities than my friends. None of us could go to family vacations in Mexico or Houston. I vividly remember my aunt and uncle not taking my brother and I to their ranch to ride bikes because we didn't have papers and they didn't want problems if any border patrol agents were around. Or, friends asking me if I had been certain places past the Falfurrias checkpoint and me having to make up excuses, not that I was undocumented and couldn't pass the checkpoint. This topic was never talked about in school, or anywhere really, so any time it came up I was too embarrassed to say anything.

During my senior year of high school, college tours were coming up and I remember being very scared because I didn't have a green card. To me having a green card was the same as having a social security number. My parents called having a green card having "papeles" (papers). That is, documents proving your legal residency in the U.S. With a green card you can buy a house, your own car, obtain medical aid, and financial aid.

I assumed my teachers had the Falfurrias checkpoint all figured out and I stayed silent. I remember my friends said we were getting near the checkpoint. This was my first time ever crossing. I didn't even know how to act. "Act normal," I thought. "But what is normal, though?" I asked myself. I had never seen this part of the world, so I had no clue what acting normal looked like once you passed Falfurrias. Anxiety overcame me and I would imagine myself getting escorted out of the bus and everyone leaving me behind. I would also fear my family and I being thrown back into Mexico where we no longer had a life. Thank God, this never happened. But in my mind it did every time someone or something reminded me that I was an illegal.

"Can an illegal even go to college?" I asked myself once during my junior year in high school. I applied to the University of Texas at Houston but a familiar voice whispered in my ear. "You're an illegal. You can't go to this school. You can't even cross the checkpoint." As always, I listened to that voice. I deleted the application and only applied to colleges south of the checkpoint. I convinced myself that I was making the right choice. My justification for staying in the Valley was my family. Even if I had found a way to go to school in Houston, my family would never see me until I got my degree. Because of the fears of being separated from my family and not being able to help them if something happened, it was always hard telling my parents I wanted to go away to college. I also knew money was an issue for us and affording college was a big question. But it was much deeper than money, as it wasn't until I suggested going away from home that they told me I couldn't go because I didn't have a social security number. I cancelled my application to the University of Houston and convinced myself it was because I would miss out on all the things I had here, like my mom's goodnight kisses, praying in the car with my dad as he drove me to school, I would even miss dumb fights with my brother over things like chocolate chip cookies. But, although hopeful at first, some part of me always knew it would never be possible for me to be anywhere past the checkpoint.

My autoethnography begins with me coming to the U.S. at the age of nine. I immediately learned that speaking English and passing for white would allow me to be a member of the dominant culture. I worked hard to hide my illegal status. In telling my story through authoethnography, I realized I was wearing many layers of blindfolds, or having *ojos vendados*, which I began to remove to expose my true identity (Garza Garcia, 2018).

Ariana's Teacher Agency

Now that I am a teacher, my agency is enacted in my classroom as I share my story with my students. During my first year teaching high school chemistry, I was at a school with a large population of undocumented students. This apparently subtle shift from illegal to undocumented is deliberate and significant. I had called myself an illegal all my life as that is what I grew up hearing and I always felt ashamed because I felt I was a criminal. I would call others in the same situation illegals as well and felt the term was justified since we were here without legal permission. I was very much aware of the privileges that other legal residents had that I did not. It wasn't until the first year of the HSI Special Interest Research Group (SIRG) research that a professor heard me presenting and challenged my reference to my legal status as illegal. He suggested I use the word undocumented instead. After thinking about it for a while, I realized this was a better way to describe my situation. I practiced calling myself undocumented instead of illegal and realized I didn't feel as ashamed of my story and was more open to sharing it with others. I feel this word is more fitting as I had not done anything wrong to be considered a criminal. Now I am more mindful of how I choose to share my story and the words I use to describe my experiences with being undocumented. For this reason, I now choose to call students with backgrounds similar to mine undocumented instead of illegal. I understand the influence that labels imposed by others can have and have a problem calling other young students illegal as if they're criminals the way I felt.

During my first-year teaching, I had my students read my counter-story about coming to this country as an undocumented immigrant at the age of nine but didn't tell them I was the author until after they had read it. My story reverberated with my students as reflected in their own journals and some reached out to me privately to share their worries about not going to college without a social security number, for the safety and well-being of their family. I realized that I had created a space where students felt safe discussing immigration issues they would not dream of discussing elsewhere.

For the past two years, I have taught at a school with a very different demographic. The majority of students in my chemistry classes have been identified as Hispanic, high socioeconomic status (SES), native English speakers, and are second or subsequent generation immigrants. Since then, I have chosen to have numerous and ongoing discussions of my experience, along with current events, which has created a classroom environment where students are more aware of issues related to immigration. Because these discussions took place throughout the school year, my (documented) students have developed an awareness of the challenges and varied circumstances some students face. For example, one student shared his parent's experience as undocumented immigrants coming to the U.S. from Cuba. I believe my (undocumented) students are more comfortable talking about the subject without fear of being exposed. I encourage my students to talk about these topics because that was never an option when I was in school. Now, I actively work toward creating a classroom culture where students have freedom to talk about their fears, and ask questions without consequence and without worry of judgment. Being a teacher is more than the curriculum. I have strong pedagogical skills and an understanding of the content, but it is just as important to address social and cultural factors that affect student learning.

For me, being a member in a CoP that led to my awakening was necessary to develop a critical awareness of the oppression I faced and how it had shaped who I am today. After analyzing my counter-story, one of my first actions was to remove the blindfolds that masked my identity as an undocumented Mexican-American female whose first language was Spanish. As a teacher, my teacher agency was to share my story with my high school students, offering them the chance to respond. By allowing myself to be vulnerable, I created a safe outlet for students to share their own experiences and help them develop compassion for others.

My agentic purpose is my commitment to creating a safe space for all of my students. I am motivated by personal experience as an undocumented student who navigated the landscape by trying to "pass for white" as soon as possible. That meant speaking English without an accent, and not giving away my immigrant status. I describe my autoethnographic process as *"ojos vendados"* or a removing of the blindfolds. I consider myself a competent teacher agent as I understand the broader social forces that influence the school in which I teach, including an understanding of the administrative culture and power structures in the school. I understand what I am doing and why I am doing it. My autonomy is also seen in that I understand I must act differently in different contexts and in the presence of different people with different levels of power:

> As a chemistry teacher, I often speak Spanish with my high school students. However, there are times when administrators are present, and I default back to English. During my first year of teaching, I taught at a school a few miles from the U.S./Mexico border and spoke Spanish on a daily basis, regardless of whether administrators were present. I am now teaching chemistry in a nearby school district and speak Spanish only to certain students and rarely in the

presence of administrators. I realize now that my teacher agency is influenced by the context—my students, presence of administration, and the school.

(journal entry)

I have developed reflexivity in that I continue to examine and reexamine my actions, have made sense of the school culture and power structures, and am still able to create a safe space for undocumented students. In doing so, I have developed strong relationships based on trust and respect for who my students are and what they bring to the classroom. My teacher agency has transformative potential as it is helping students who have been severely marginalized because of fear of their immigration status being exposed.

A Vignette of Felicia's Counter-story

What does it mean to be a migrant? I remember kids looking at me in class and thinking, "Oh, no! How do I explain to them what it means to be a migrant? Would they even understand?" Almost mumbling, I would tell them, "being a migrant means we go work in the summers." I felt like an outsider in my own predominantly Hispanic hometown and worse I felt shame. How do I explain this? How can I put it into words the struggle that my family and I go through? I could feel the shame for being judged and not accepted. Who was there to tell me that this type of living was wrong? That I had to be ashamed?

As a migrant family, our typical living arrangement was everyone sleeping in one room, each on an individual mattress. We would be out the door at 5:15 AM. My day usually involved placing pallets on a conveyer belt and then stickers on watermelons. My job was to make sure that every watermelon had a sticker. In my mentality, I saw putting every sticker on every watermelon as if I was practicing my stealing skills in basketball. I made it out to be like training for basketball, my favorite sport. By the end of the day, the smell of rotten watermelons was embedded in my clothes and skin. Often, we would slam a watermelon on the floor, wash our hands, and then eat what was left. I remember looking at my arms and pants and seeing all of the dirt, the rotten pieces of watermelon that stuck to me, the slight pinkish hue that would come from washing my hands in pieces of watermelons. I almost felt like I didn't want to clean my arms. I wanted people to see the marks, see the dirt, see the pride in what I did. But even then, there was the other half of me that took a second look at the dirt and would want to make it disappear. I remember licking my thumb and hands and wiping away the smudges in an attempt to completely wipe away a part of my identity, to erase what wouldn't be considered acceptable to society.

One time at school the thing I feared most happened. This white male student asked me what my family did, why I was there, and then called me watermelon girl. I couldn't believe it. I asked him, "what was that?" and he repeated, "watermelon girl." I didn't know how to respond. The students around me didn't say anything. I felt isolated and as if he was mocking not only my entire family's way of living, but also my ancestors. That's how they take care of their families. I remember thinking, was he better than me?

I also remember my first day in Pre-Advanced Placement Chemistry class when my teacher assigned a two-minute nomenclature quiz and I received a 20 out of 100 points. The teacher told me there would be a nomenclature quiz every week. I remember when a new trailer would arrive signaling the work that would begin anew, and my intensity was to make sure the stickers were where they needed to be on the watermelons. I suddenly found that same intensity in the classroom. I was so ashamed of my grade and made it a point that day that I was never going to receive a 20% again. I decided, then and there, that I was going to become one of the students who would excel and serve as a model for the other students. I realized this would be no easy task. Although I was surrounded by female students, it became clear that my teacher wouldn't call on any of us. Rather, he consistently called on the males, along with los machos that would talk without anyone having to call on them.

Through my autoethnography, I developed a critical consciousness with respect to how I was positioned because of gender, language, race, and ethnicity. I learned at a very young age that others saw being a migrant and speaking Spanish as less than. As a female in a high school chemistry class, I saw that male students were called on more often and were considered the smarter students. I also learned at a young age to mask parts of my identity, especially my family's migrant work and speaking Spanish. Most importantly, I learned that there was a dominant culture who defined what was acceptable and what was not.

Felicia's Teacher Agency

During my first semester as a chemistry teacher at a Title I high school, I believed I had a strong foundation on the way I wanted to teach and how I would challenge my students' thinking about what the world is like. As a chemistry teacher, I knew that teaching content is important, but I also had a strong desire to wake up my students. Even on the first day of school, I wanted to question them, but I was also aware that I could get fired for talking about vulnerable topics that had nothing to do with chemistry such as being involved in gangs. The first day came and I thought, "Oh, well. I'm going to take a leap of faith." I was committed to starting the first day of school in a way that would address and awaken the minds of my students beyond the chemistry curriculum and that is what I did.

I followed Ariana's approach by sharing a piece of my counter-story without telling them who the author was. Through journaling, I then challenged my students to question why they were at school, who they were here for, and what they wanted to accomplish. I told them that my class would challenge them, and that when they wanted to give up, they should look back at their journals. Their responses were varied, some were open and honest while others were more reserved and were holding back. This led me to reflect on their responses. An excerpt from my own journal:

> I recall being astonished by their journal entries and I knew I had made the right choice when I read the stories about my students. Some talked about the sacrifices their family made to migrate from Mexico to the United States while others talked about their father's ambivalence toward education and future goals. While my students come to school because they want an education, they are also aware of how society is treating them differently, and specifically as lesser. They are challenging the low expectations that have been imposed on them and are determined to prove teachers, administrators, and even family wrong. One story I will never forget was about a boy who had tattoos of gang signs on his hands and arms. He wrote about how he was looked down on by teachers and administrators. He was determined to prove that he was more than the gang sign tattoos, that he would go to college or the military to make his family proud. He was fully aware of how he was being treated, how he wished that people would stop judging him and would instead ask him about his life.

To this day, as a teacher, I continue to ask my students who they are and why they are here at school and in my class. When I see my female students excelling in chemistry, I tell them about the statistics pertaining to Hispanic females graduating in chemistry or a science technology, engineering, and mathematics (STEM) career and they are shocked. As a teacher, I understand that my job is more than just teaching chemistry content, it is also about caring as much about the decisions they make and who are they going to be when they walk out of my class as I do about their performance in class.

My purpose is reflected in my commitment to the whole student, rather than just teaching the chemistry content. My sense of social justice stems from my commitment to really knowing my students and creating a safe classroom culture that allows students to express who they really are. My competence developed from my autoethnography in which I observed that male students were called upon more frequently than females in high school chemistry. I recognize that gender bias begins early and contributes to the underrepresentation of females in many STEM disciplines.

My autonomy is shown in my awareness of school culture and power relationships between the principal and students who have been marginalized. I also work on developing resilience in my students by asking them to look back at their journals when they are challenged or frustrated and understand the importance of my relationship with them (more than the content). I am a strong reflexive practitioner as I continually examine and reexamine my behaviors and assumptions about my students, and the effect of my behavior, beliefs, and assumptions have on my students in different contexts.

Implications for Teacher Education in a HSCOE

The federal definition of Hispanic-Serving Institution (HSI) is "an institution of higher education that has an enrollment of undergraduate full-time equivalent students that is at least 25 percent Hispanic students" (DOE, 2016). While HSIs make up 15% of institutions of higher education, they enroll more than 66% of Hispanic students (HACU, 2019). Thus, HSIs play a significant role in the education of Latinx students.

The College of Education & P-6 Integration at UTRGV considers itself to be a HSCOE. Our HSCOE's responsibility is to produce teachers who will eventually teach in Hispanic-Serving school districts comprised of predominately Hispanic students. While many of the PK-12 students face discrimination and oppression because of their language, race, gender, and immigration status, it is perilous to assume that HSCOE program graduates will automatically know to acknowledge these inequities and the effect they have on their students. As such, it is the responsibility of our college to engage in culturally sustaining pedagogies that address issues of students, in this case preservice teachers, who have been marginalized. In addition, it is our responsibility to ensure that graduates leave our teacher preparation program with an understanding of the responsibility they have in working with their own Latinx students so that they will transition into higher education with a sense of purpose and agency that Felicia and Ariana didn't have. As a college that prepares science teachers or teachers who will be teaching in STEM fields for predominantly Latinx populations there are additional factors, such as the intersection of gender and ethnicity, that also demand attention. The inequities that exist in science and math classrooms have historically marginalized females and students of color and are evidenced by the underrepresentation of Latinx people earning doctorates in a STEM field (HACU, 2019; Lee & Buxton, 2010).

It is critical for our science preservice teachers to have an awareness of the social, cultural, political, and historical factors that have led to systemic inequitable practices, and to be provided with the knowledge and tools to challenge and change these practices as teacher agents. One way to do this is by helping STEM preservice teachers develop critical and reflective practices. Ariana discusses this in her thesis (Garza Garcia, 2018, p. 49):

> My personal experience as trying to use my light complexion to pass for white and (students) trying to hide his or her Spanish accent are examples of assimilation (Berry, et al, 2006)...also impact future decisions, like choosing a college to attend. This is important because the college we choose to attend and where we choose to live will most definitely have an impact on our identity. I know that my identity would not be the same had I chosen to attend a different college. Just as I know that my identity was influenced by my parent's decision for us to move to the U.S. I can't help but wonder if I would have pursued a master's degree had I had we stayed in Mexico. And I also believe I am the person I am today because of how I have reacted to the oppression and marginalization I experienced as a Mexican immigrant female in a STEM field. This emphasizes the need for our schools to provide guidance, support, and safe outlets for immigrant students to discuss their concerns and issues.

Ariana and Felicia's autoethnographies show how their personal experiences growing up an immigrant or migrant in the public school system led to a lack of a sense of belonging and to feeling the need to mask who they were. As teachers we will continue to have students in our classrooms who have been disenfranchised because they are immigrants, migrants, or native Spanish speakers. For this reason, teacher educators in our college need to create a climate for preservice teachers that promotes sense of belonging and support in a way that models it for their future practice. One way to do that is through the autoethnographic counter-storytelling in a research CoP as described in this chapter.

Questioning and challenging social injustices is a hallmark of critical race theory and LatCrit (Ladson-Billings & Tate, 1995; Solórzano & Bernal, 2001; Solórzano & Yasso, 2002), and is necessary for developing critical consciousness and agency (Torre 1999; Urrieta, 2007). Through a process of counter-storytelling, we have done just that. Bartolome (2004) argues that exemplary teachers are those that connect their own personal inequitable experiences to their classroom teaching. It is critical to prepare teachers who provide a classroom culture that offers all students the opportunity for success in the classroom and beyond. We do this through an ethic of care, community, inquiry, and agency that resonates with our community and empowers preservice teachers as change agents.

References

Bartolome, L. I. (2004). Critical pedagogy and teacher education: Radicalizing prospective teachers. *Teacher Education Quarterly, 31*(1), 97–122.

Berry, J. W., Phinney, J. S., Sam, D. L., & Vedder, P. (2006). Immigrant youth: Acculturation, identity, and adaptation. *Applied Psychology, 55*(3), 303–332.

Biesta, G., & Tedder, M. (2007). Agency and learning in the lifecourse: Towards an ecological perspective. *Studies in the Education of Adults, 39*(2), 132–149.

Department of Education. (2016). Retrieved from https://www2.ed.gov/print/programs/idueshi/definition.html

Ellis, C., Adams, T. E., & Bochner, A. P. (2011). Autoethnography: An overview. *Historical Social Research/Historische Sozialforschung, 36*, 273–290.

Freire, P. (1970). *Pedagogy of the oppressed.* New York, NY: Bloomsbury Publishing.

Garza Garcia, A. (2018) *Ojos vendados: An ethnographic approach to understanding how immigration status and language influence the identity of high school students in the Rio Grande Valley* (Unpublished master's thesis). University of Texas Rio Grande Valley, Edinburg, TX.

Hispanic Association of Colleges and Universities. (2019). Retrieved from https://www.hacu.net/hacu/default.asp

Hernandez, C. M., Morales, A. R., & Shroyer, M. G. (2013). The development of a model of culturally responsive science and mathematics teaching. *Cultural Studies of Science Education, 8*(4), 803–820.

Hughes, S., & Pennington, J. (2017). *Autoethnography: process, product, and possibility for critical social research.* Los Angeles, CA: SAGE Publishing.

Ladson-Billings, G., & Tate, W. F. (1995). Toward a critical race theory of education. *Teachers College Record, 97*(1), 47.

Lee, O., & Buxton, C. A. (2010). *Diversity and equity in science education: Research, policy, and practice.* Multicultural Education Series. New York, NY: Teachers College Press.

Matthews, B., & Jessel, J. (1998). Reflective and reflexive practice in initial teacher education: A critical case study. *Teaching in Higher Education, 3*(2), 231–243.

Pantić, N. (2015). A model for study of teacher agency for social justice. *Teachers and Teaching, 21*(6), 759–778.

Solórzano, D. G., & Bernal, D. D. (2001). Examining transformational resistance through a critical race and LatCrit theory framework. *Urban Education, 36*(3), 308–342.

Solórzano, D. G., & Yasso, T. J. (2002). Critical race methodology: Counter-storytelling as an analytical framework for education research. *Qualitative Inquiry, 8*(1), 23–44.

Torre, A. A. N. L. (1999). Developing voice: Teacher research in bilingual classrooms. *Bilingual Research Journal, 23*(4), 451–470.

Toyosaki, S., Pensoneau-Conway, S. L., Wendt, N. A., & Leathers, K. (2009). Community autoethnography: Compiling the personal and resituating whiteness. *Cultural Studies Critical Methodologies, 9*(1), 56–83.

Urrieta, L. (2007). Identity production in figured worlds: How some Mexican Americans become Chicana/o activist educators. *The Urban Review, 39*(2), 117–144.

Wenger, E. (2006). Communities of practice: A brief introduction. Retrieved January 25, 2008, from http://www.ewenger.com/theory/communities_of_practice_intro.htm

9 How Autobiographies of Latinx Preservice Teachers Build Culturally Relevant Instruction for the Nature of Science

Noushin Nouri, Jair J. Aguilar
and Patricia Ramirez-Biondolillo

One aim of science education is to develop more equitable undergraduate science learning, including making science more accessible for diverse learners. Since Latinx students are underrepresented in science (Riegle-Crumb, Moore,& Ramos-Wada, 2011), there is an immediate need to consider differentiated instructional approaches in order to increase their engagement in it, especially in Hispanic-Serving Institutions (HSIs). To do this, we argue that preparing teachers to teach science in a culturally relevant context by developing their understanding of how sociocultural factors shape both their own and their students' learning is a powerful place to begin. Latinx preservice teachers (LPSTs) come into education programs as learners with existing cultural understandings and experiences. These can be drawn from and made explicit to produce more culturally responsive teachers. One way to build a strong foundation of culturally responsive instruction is to collect and examine LPSTs' autobiographies about their own science education. In this chapter, we, therefore, present and analyze the results of LPSTs' autobiographical descriptions of their experience with science from early childhood into adulthood, paying specific attention to how their cultures shaped those experiences. This study took place at a four-year HSI with the highest Hispanic undergraduate student enrollment in the state of Texas (Excelencia in Education, 2018). The fact that the majority of our students (almost 92%) are Latinx makes it crucial for us, as STEM educators, to hear their voices and integrate them into our educational programs as a Hispanic-Serving College of Education (HSCOE).

Literature Review

The need to develop more equitable undergraduate science education by making science relevant to all students led to the National Science Foundation (NSF) (1996, 2017) to call on communities of scientists and science educators for assistance. According to Santiago, Calderón, and Taylor (2015), the Latinx population is the largest growing ethnic group in the U.S., and is projected to become approximately 30% of the entire population by 2050. If a group this large is not effectively exposed to a high-quality education, fostering skill and interest in science and technology, the U.S. will have a shortage of individuals working in STEM careers. Currently, 66% of all Latinx undergraduate students are served at HSIs (Excelencia in Education, 2018); thus, HSIs have the potential to be leaders in developing curricula that can increase Latinx participation in and contributions to science on a national level. To increase the number of Latinx students in STEM, we argue teachers must be better prepared to engage these students in science and related fields beginning in or before elementary school, by implementing teaching and learning techniques and approaches that are more relevant to the students' backgrounds, experiences, and cultural orientations (Kelly-Jackson & Jackson, 2011). Research suggests teachers, particularly those in early education, are reluctant to implement high-quality science lessons due to poor preparation in teaching science, lack of knowledge of or experience regarding science, or simply because of mistaken beliefs and attitudes toward the nature of science or NOS (Greenfield et al., 2009). Consequently, there is an urgent need to identify and understand culturally shaped beliefs, as well as the strengths and barriers that foster or hinder interest in and engagement with science within Latinx communities.

Culturally Relevant Pedagogy

Culturally relevant pedagogy (CRP) is a method of teaching in a cross- or multicultural setting that encourages students to relate course content to their cultural background. Often, course material is presented in a mainstream idiom, or with underlying mainstream assumptions that hamper learning. CRP proposes a theory in which students develop both their critical skills and cultural competencies at the same time, thus attaining better academic success (Ladson-Billings, 1995). Ladson-Billings states that to achieve this, teachers who advocate for CRP must have a clear conception of self and others, as well as how understanding social relationships impact their relationship with others. In this regard, Lee and Luykx (2007) conclude that teachers who promote, use, and advocate for CRPs must see themselves as part of a larger learning community in which (a) they have a necessity to give back, (b) they believe all their students can achieve their goals, and (c) their instruction is always evolving.

These ideas are synthesized into the three main characteristics of CRPs (Morrison, Robbins, & Rose, 2008) as follows: academic success, cultural competence, and critical consciousness. Morrison et al. define the first as teachers maintaining high expectations for their students' success, without compromising or losing cultural identity. The second requires teachers to provide encouragement and support to their students so that they maintain their cultural identity while achieving academic success. They do this by reshaping the prescribed curriculum, building on students' prior experiences and knowledge, and encouraging relationships between schools and communities. Finally, Johnson (2011) defines critical consciousness as students' ability to "identify, understand, and critique societal issues and inequities" (p. 173). Unfortunately, according to Buxton (2009), this last is often the least addressed aspect of CRPs, especially in high-poverty low-performing schools, where students lack access to high-quality teachers, teaching, and resources.

The Nature of Science

The NOS is "a rich description of what science is, how it works, how scientists operate as a social group, and how society itself both directs and reacts to scientific endeavors" (McComas, Clough, & Almazroa, 1998, p. 4). When teaching about NOS, several important aspects should be included: scientific knowledge is tentative (subject to change), empirically based, and subjectively shaped (i.e., involves personal background, biases, and/or is theory-laden). The subjective aspect involves human inference, imagination, and creativity, which includes the invention of explanations that are socially and culturally embedded. Additionally, the distinction between observations and inferences, and the functions of and the relationship between scientific theories and laws should also be considered (Lederman, 2007).

There are many reasons for including NOS in school curriculums and, therefore, in teacher preparation programs. Bravo, Merce, and Anna (2001) believe that understanding what science is, how it has progressed through history, and its relationship with society and culture are essential to be an educated citizen of the 21st century. The lack of deep understanding of NOS leads teachers to present science as a collection of facts instead of as a discipline (Abd-El-Khalick & Lederman, 2000). Meyer and Crawford (2011) highlight that "viewing science as culture creates the space for examining science learning, and inquiry, as a borderland of cultural interaction" (p. 531). Specifically, communicating the culture of science helps populations whose cultural understanding or interpretation of science is not aligned with the cultural attitudes and practices of the scientific community (Lee, 2003). In this regard, Meyer and Crawford (2011) state that when NOS is included in the instruction, students come to see how their cultural views about science differ from the "values of schools-based science" (p. 544). Meyer and Crawford argue further that this strategy explicitly helps diverse learners reach a better understanding and ownership of scientific concepts that don't align with their cultural backgrounds.

Unfortunately, despite the importance of NOS and its effective role in implementing a CRP, only 3% of research about NOS is related to ethnic groups other than whites (Walls, 2012). In one study of bilingual fifth graders of mostly Puerto Rican backgrounds, Meyer and Crawford (2011) combined inquiry instruction and NOS to show that, while students acknowledged science as a way of knowing, they distinguished it from their families' views about it. Similarly, the limited research specifically investigating Spanish preservice teachers' knowledge of NOS has concluded that these populations have misconceptions about science (Vázquez-Alonso, García-Carmona, Manassero-Mas, & Bennassar-Roig, 2013), but does not offer correctives of this problem. To help Latinx populations create stronger connections to and develop an interest in science, it is critical to link their cultures with the culture of science and NOS.

Theoretical Framework

The research we present here considers and adopts a framework developed by Lee and Fradd (1998) that argues for modifying instruction to fit students' existing conceptions of science. Lee and Fradd introduced the concept of "instructional congruence to indicate the process of mediating the nature of academic content with students' language and cultural experiences [so as] to make such content (e.g., science) accessible, meaningful, and relevant for diverse students" (p. 13). Further, they emphasize that instructional congruency is impossible to achieve in science unless teachers understand NOS as an integral part of knowing how to guide students in developing an understanding of science. In other words, teachers need to know "what the nature of science is and what kinds of language and cultural experiences the students bring to the learning process" (p. 14). Lee (2003) further explains that cultural congruency, i.e. compatibility between students' culture and the culture of science, is also needed for integrating science with students' cultural experiences in order to encourage and enable better levels of achievement and interest in science. Following these ideas of cultural and instructional congruency, we begin our present research examining LPSTs' cultural experiences and combining them with teaching NOS.

Methods

As a method of inquiry, an autobiography is a narrative form that provides stories as data, wherein each person shares his or her experience as a kind of a story that can be analyzed (Merriam, 2002). Autobiography shows a person's perspective in a precise and specific context, with precise and specific connections to the situations they describe (Manning & Cullum-Swan, 1994).

Gathering learners' autobiographies can help educators take learners' culture and experience into account when designing curriculum or methods of instruction. When students are not part of mainstream culture, their stories are significant because they highlight the differences between how mainstream and non-mainstream students learn. Meyer and Crawford (2011) emphasize the role of these experiences in science learning, connecting their neglect to underrepresentation:

> Without directing greater attention to students' actual experiences in school, science and how science may or may not align with students' diverse racial, cultural, and linguistic backgrounds and understandings, these student groups will likely remain underrepresented in the sciences.
>
> (p. 530)

Therefore, autobiographies were chosen as a methodological strategy and used to collect student's experiences in science.

Participants

Ten LPSTs were recruited from our current preservice population. All ten preservice teachers were Latinx female preservice teachers who were between the ages of 19 and 22.

Data Collection and Analysis

The participants were asked to write their "science-life story" reflecting on experiences that impacted their attitudes toward science as well as their understanding of the NOS. To help guide their autobiographies, participants were provided a set of guiding questions (Table 9.1) that were adopted and modified from Krause and Maldonado (2019). Participants were free to expand beyond the topics within the guiding questions.

Because many preservice teachers are not familiar with the term Nature of Science, we purposefully did not refer to this phrase directly in the guiding questions (e.g., question 10).

Researchers coded the date using two coding methods: In vivo and domain and taxonomic coding (Saldaña, 2015). The rationale for using in vivo coding was because it considers the use of words or short phrases "from the participant's own language in the data record as code" (Saldaña, 2015, p. 294) and it reflected our desire to emphasize the actual words used by the participants. As we were also interested in extracting cultural aspects, we used domain and taxonomic coding based on its usefulness for "discovering the cultural knowledge people use to organize their behavior and interpret their experiences" (Saldaña, 2015, p. 292). At the beginning researchers independently coded the data. In analyzing these narratives, we sought to uncover both strengths and barriers that facilitated or hindered science learning.

Table 9.1 List of guiding questions for the autobiographies

Number	List of Questions
1	What do you remember most about learning science in elementary or middle school?
2	How do you feel about science? How have your feelings changed over time?
3	How do you think your school science experiences impacted your understanding of science? What experiences made it easier/harder for you to learn science?
4	What did your teachers do or not do to connect science to your home/cultural/community experiences? How do you think this impacted your experience?
5	How was your science learning supported at home and in your community? Did your parents or other family members engage in activities involving science? Did you do any activities that involved or applied science outside of school (e.g., sports, hobbies, and games)?
6	If you received science instruction in a language other than your home language, what was your experience like? What did teachers do or not do to support your learning?
7	Do you remember any memory from your science teacher that made you interested/hated on science?
8	Are there any elements in your culture that can be considered as a barrier to learn science or pursue a career in science?
9	Are there any elements in your culture that can be considered as a benefit to learn science or pursue a career in science?
10	To what extent did your science teachers go beyond the content and to help you to know how science generally works?

After coding all the data independently, researchers convened to determine percent of agreement (85%) and engaged in discussion to reach consensus on final coding.

Results

The topics that emerged from the students' autobiographies were categorized around eight major themes: family involvement, linguistic barriers, cultural relevance, conflicts between science and religion, gender stereotypes, early experiences with science education, the impact of teachers' attitudes and methods, and standardized tests. Following, we provide more details, with direct student quotations and examples of each theme.

Family Involvement

One of the positive aspects of Latinx culture is a deep loyalty to family (Quintos, 2008), and this was revealed to be a powerful motivation for science learning for many LPST students. For example, Alondra[1] explained that being good in science and math while her sibling and cousins struggled continually encouraged her to learn more in order to help them. Similarly, Emma, who enjoys science a great deal, discussed how her family always encouraged her to pursue science, how her parents were actively involved in her science fair projects, and how her brother studying science were important motivating factors for her. Opportunities to help siblings, positive parental encouragement, and important role models within the family setting were highlighted in many of the LPST autobiographies.

Yet, while many LPSTs acknowledged that their families strongly encouraged their continued engagement in science education, some also revealed that it was difficult for their families to provide support in learning science due to language barriers (e.g., parents who were monolingual Spanish-speakers), lack of resources, and parents' educational background. These LPSTs identified a lack of role models and a lack of familiarity with science-related careers as primary reasons why they were not interested in pursuing a career in science. Some narratives described a generational impact, wherein the parents' level of formal education acted as a barrier for an LPST's own aspirations, curtailed access to educational resources, and prevented access to benefits conferred by higher socioeconomic standing, as explained by Erica:

> In my culture, I do feel there are barriers to pursuing a degree or career in science. A lot of times, students in our culture are not able to go to college because of family. Some are expected to start working straight out of high school to help out with family bills and the household. I know there are a lot of careers that we can pursue that involve science. I think, in order to help our students, we need to be able to tell our life story at the beginning of the year, so they know it is possible [for them] to become anything they want.

Linguistic Barriers

Participants in this study all came from Latinx families who speak Spanish at home. Since Spanish was their first language, participants revealed that the English language was often a linguistic barrier for learning the scientific language, as well as other subjects. Some participants stated that although they were placed in bilingual programs, these often did not provide enough support to help them build cognitive academic language proficiency in English. Bilingual programs often offer the instruction both in English and students' native language (in this case Spanish) while English as a second language (ESL) classes help students with improving their English skills. In both cases, students may need specific support for making necessary connections between scientific academic language and conversational English. Due to the lack of resources and support specific to science, many students struggled with science terminology and this affected their attitude toward science. Julia called science terminology "a nightmare." Mira expressed concern about lack of supportive bilingual programs in the upper levels, saying "Even though the district had a high Spanish speaking population, they only offered bilingual education at the elementary level and the upper levels had ESL programs. It was evident that some of my peers struggled with language barriers."

From these perspectives, ESL classes are not successful in scaffolding students' linguistic needs in science. Mira complained, "when I was struggling with difficult science terminology, my bilingual class was teaching me colors in English." In some cases, although the students were willing to learn and build their scientific literacy, their respective schools did not offer enough support or resources for them to refine their academic scientific language and conceptual understanding of science.

Cultural Relevance

The integration of culturally relevant instruction in the classroom allows students to use experiences and concepts to build on their schema. Some LPSTs stated that culturally relevant lessons helped them understand the content being taught. Similarly, some LPSTs claimed that the lack of cultural relevance is the reason they did not understand science and thus began to dislike it. For example, Julia explained, "The only teacher I had [that I] really learned from was a physics teacher because of her incorporating a lot of culturally relevant examples."

Some LPSTs wrote about lack of experiences connecting science to their actual life and their community, and this makes the importance of including this experience in teacher preparation programs more critical. Consider this quote from Karen:

> I can't really think of ways my teachers connected science to my everyday life. Maybe, when we got to bring something from home and do a show-and-tell, some people would bring animals. Again, I don't recall science being supported, promoted or further touched upon outside the classroom. I used to be a part of the Boys and Girls club and we would do some activities in there, but for the most part, I do not remember any science.

In addition, while some LPSTs appreciated teachers who connected their lessons to the community, Sarah criticized her teachers for not including any activity related to the community in their lesson plans:

> I don't remember any of my teachers throughout my school years who even tried to connect science to my community, school, or culture. If I had had some connections between science and my personal life, I think I would have definitely been more interested in the subject.

It is important for HSIs to recognize the need to incorporate culturally relevant instructional approaches to foster an environment that inspires students to take ownership of their learning and growth. These narratives imply that the shift for incorporating more culturally responsive pedagogy into the classroom must occur if we want to bridge the gaps in science education.

Conflicts between Science and Religion

Some LPSTs mentioned that scientific principles often conflicted with the religious traditions of their culture, claiming this was a challenge for them and a reason for being apprehensive toward science. The families of these LPSTs' feared that the knowledge of science would interfere with their child's religious faith. For example, Jessi mentioned:

> Hispanic culture traditionally stems from cornerstone ideas of religious dedication, machismo attitudes, and dedication to the family above anything. I was told by many of my own family to abandon ideas in conflict with my religion if I wanted to support my family.

In addition, many LPSTs shared several examples of conflicts between theological perspectives and scientific principles in their autobiographies, though it should be highlighted that occasionally LPSTs had misconceptions about scientific principles. For example, Nicole wrote:

> I was challenging what I was taught at home with what I was learning at school. In school, I was learning that science is part of everything, from our creation to evolution, to health and wellness. This created a conflict with my Hispanic heritage because, according to my parents, I was created by a greater being. Yet, according to my textbook I was created by organisms.

After sharing her own experience that "my mom used to say science is against my faith," Nicole offered her idea about teacher preparation programs' responsibilities:

> I think it is important that an educator establishes an understanding with parents who feel that science instruction goes against religious beliefs to reassure that what is being taught is to help develop their child's understanding when it comes to science.

Gender Stereotypes

Science is often depicted as a male-dominated field. These stereotypes have a negative effect on young girls who are subsequently dissuaded from taking an interest in science. For example, Sarah stated that

"I think science is not for girls." Stereotypes informed by sociocultural factors associated with ethnicity, socioeconomic status, and age directly influence how people feel about their own identities and gender roles. Some participants stated that they felt gender played a latent role in their desire to pursue science or not. Monica wrote in her narrative: "As a Hispanic female, I feel that careers in scientific fields are not always encouraged." In addition to this perspective, in some of LPSTs' minds, the social environment discriminated against them in accordance with this mindset, as in this quote from Jessi, "along the way, throughout high school, I met other people who would bring me down because I was a girl, and girls weren't as involved in scientific fields."

Early Experiences with Science Education

While some of our LPSTs mentioned the positive impact of early exposure to science on their later science success, in some narratives LPSTs indicated not being exposed to science prior to fifth grade, which is the first grade level that science is assessed by a state-mandated standardized test in Texas. We found multiple narratives that contained statements along the lines of: "I cannot recall any science in elementary."

Conversely, some of the narratives described some of the science experiences in elementary or middle school as enjoyable. Emma who was, in fact, exposed to science during those years recalls it fondly.

> My elementary and middle school experiences had a positive impact on my attitude towards science because I used to enjoy science classes. But once I started high school, the pressure of getting a good grade and the language barrier made it hard for me to understand the science classes and I stopped enjoying them.

Lack of exposure to science in early education also led to a lack of foundation for learning more advanced science in the higher grades, turning science into a "difficult" subject. In some autobiographies, we noticed LPSTs starting to dislike science beginning in middle school, which, among other factors, was rooted in the lack of foundation from early childhood as exemplified by the comment, "in middle school, the science began getting tougher for me, the words grew more complex and it took me longer to process the information that was being given to me, so I began to dislike the subject."

The Impact of Teachers' Attitudes and Methods

Many of the LPST narratives reveal that both teachers' attitudes and methods can significantly affect a student's interest in science. As an example of the first, Alondra wrote: "My teacher seemed like she was someone who loved teaching the subject. Things changed after that.

I started to like science." By contrast, Erica criticized her teacher's attitude saying, "It was clear my teacher did not enjoy what she did." As a result, Erica showed a more negative attitude toward science, which she sought to correct, or at least mask, in her own teaching. "I would try a different way. I would not want my negative attitude toward the subject to come across to the students."

Participants' narratives also reflected both positive and negative experiences about instructional approaches. These narratives describe how "authentic" approaches like hands on activities and similar methods made science engaging, and how a lack of the same made the classes difficult and boring. For example, Nicole wrote, "I loved hands-on activities but hated lectures and worksheets." Or, "I loved her classes. Her lesson plans used engaging ways to incorporate science [in]to our daily life. We even had a part called 'science in the kitchen'". By contrast, Karen explained:

> What made it harder for me was ... going through a long chapter in the science textbook every class period...[it] made me dread going to that class.

Other narratives depicted how rote memorization and the lack of authentic, engaging experiences affected how the LPSTs felt about learning science. They described feeling discouraged due to didactic learning and a lack of active participation in their classes. As Sarah stated, "most of the time it was lectures and non-sense [sic] worksheets." Further many described an emphasis on formulas rather than the concept of science in their classroom.

While lack of "authentic" approaches suggests a disconnect between science and its pragmatic uses in everyday life, the LPSTs' teacher's failure to contextualize the whys and wherefores of science—i.e., the NOS—hindered students' comprehension of the concept of scientific facts, theories, and laws. Rebeca wrote, "I enjoyed experimenting and things like dissecting, but I dreaded going to science class to learn about laws and equations simply because I couldn't understand them or make sense of them." When students do not understand the reason why something is a law and why something else is a theory, everything can seem like nonsense.

In the excerpts above, we can ascertain that teachers play an important role in helping shape the science identity of students. Teachers who incorporated hands-on activities made a strong positive impact on their students' attitude toward science.

Standardized Tests

The narratives also described how high-stakes testing affected the quality of instruction students received. The LPSTs reported that teachers were focused on teaching to the test and did not engage in inquiry-based learning. Thus, LPSTs revealed how they started to become more disengaged from science by associating it with high-stakes testing. According to Rebeca:

> I feel as though many students during my time in elementary through high school can agree on the fact that during this time is when state exams became the focal point of all instruction. Therefore, we were not being taught how to think but more of what to think.

The last sentence of this narrative alone is telling as to the extent to which emphasizing the test can go against the NOS, which encourages critical thinking and provokes asking questions.

Discussion

Often, working in an HSCOE/HSI means focusing on enrollment (Garcia, 2017). In order to think beyond this narrow scope, we examined LPSTs' experiences in their own science education to provide a better picture of LPSTs needs to create a culturally relevant teacher preparation program. The CRP has proven to be an effective teaching approach, particularly to many of the science and mathematics (Jackson & Boutte, 2009; Kelly-Jackson & Jackson, 2011) subjects students tend to avoid in their STEM pipeline.

The results presented in this project highlight some of the factors that can interfere in the learning and teaching of science from the perspective, background, and experience of LPSTs through a process of self-narratives captured as autobiography (Manning & Cullum-Swan, 1994; Merriam, 2002). The experiences of LPSTs who participated in this project show that exposure to science instruction in early elementary years can promote interest in science later in life. In the state of Texas, elementary students do not take standardized tests in science until fifth grade (Texas Education Agency, 2012). This, according to our students, led to many teachers in early education to be reluctant to teach science. However, students must learn from childhood the basics and fundamentals of science in order to reach the level of scientific knowledge needed for a good quality science education that lasts a lifetime (Lederman & Abd-El-Khalick, 1998).

Moreover, the LPSTs revealed in their autobiographies how their science teachers were unable to connect science instruction with the LPSTs' own cultural contexts, backgrounds, and experiences. When teachers use CRPs (Kelly-Jackson& Jackson, 2011), they are not only considering the students' backgrounds and experiences in their instruction, but also connecting, engaging, and motivating students by referencing a culture they know and understand (Williams & Rudge, 2016). As a result, students are less reluctant to engage in classroom activities, responding with a more positive attitude and an interest in the learning process. In addition, when teachers connect their instruction culturally, they can address and include social and religious aspects that help students from different cultures and conditions feel they belong to a science community (Hernandez, 2001).

For example, the LPSTs explained that religion played a major role in their academic scientific growth––negatively—by preferring faith-based explanations that rendered real-life events, easily clarified by science, "unexplainable" (Taber, 2017). Therefore, teachers must find cultural opportunities (e.g., in Latinx culture) to make connections that could be highlighted in a science class, which in the end would help students overcome some of the misunderstandings and barriers they may have toward the learning of science (Billingsley, Brock, Taber, & Riga, 2016).

Another aspect that the LPSTs externalized in their narratives was how gender stereotypes are prominent in their families and community. This played a significant role that either weakened or completely hampered any desire to pursue a career in a science-related field. Students should be exposed to the experience and expertise of science professionals, particularly women, with the aim of breaking the false stigma that science is a single-gender profession and showing that anyone can pursue a career in any STEM-related field (Stout, Dasgupta, Hunsinger, & McManus, 2011).

Teacher preparation programs, in particular those rooted in HSIs, should include examples of CRP, community involvement projects, authentic science, and the NOS (McComas et al., 1998) in their programs of study.

Implications for HSCOEs

In answering the call for HSIs to examine the ways in which they serve their Latinx students (Garcia, 2017), we provide a list of suggestions based on the outcomes of our project.

1   It is important to expose LPSTs to culturally relevant science instruction, so they may utilize these concepts in their own teaching. This helps increase best practices in early childhood education that can promote interest and skills in science that can be used later in life. Elementary students in Texas not being assessed in science until upper grades (Texas Education Agency, 2012) has impacted the extent to which science education is addressed in the early grades; however, students must learn from early childhood the fundamentals of science required to foster scientific knowledge (Lederman & Abd-El-Khalick,1998).

2   Students in our study reported that most of their science instruction, especially in high school, was boring lectures, resulting in students

not enjoying their teachers' attitude. Despite the strong emphasis on the importance of inquiry-based science teaching and NOS, according to our participants, most teachers still prefer to lecture in their classrooms. Conceptual learning, science and engineering practice, science process skills, and the NOS should be emphasized in teacher preparation science courses.

3   Culturally relevant science education and community connections are necessary to help students from each culture and background feel they belong to a science community. Latinx students' cultures have many aspects that can be highlighted in science classes.

4   In an HSCOE, students often come from religious families (Gonzalez, 2008). The discussion should be held in science methods courses about the differences between science and religion, which is a component of NOS.

5   All classrooms in the community should address gender disparities by inviting Latinx women who work in different scientific fields to discuss career opportunities.

6   NOS should be an important part of science classes along with science content. Understanding NOS would allow students to recognize why they are doing science and why learning about it is meaningful. In addition, learning about science process skills provides lifelong lessons for students, and recalling and associating science as a context that helped them to learn these skills increases positive feelings about science in society.

As final words, in the discipline of science, the answer to what it means to be an HSCOE is the importance of teaching science in a way that emphasizes culturally sustaining practices with implementing CRP, community involvement projects, authentic science, and the NOS in degree programs. Furthermore, education programs should utilize specific strategies to communicate science terminology with bilingual students. Finally, science and education departments should work together to make sure teachers have a proper pedagogical content knowledge to teach science. This collaboration should be expanded to involve some of our preservice teachers in scientific research, providing them with authentic experiences in doing science, specifically when research is related to their cultural community and environment. "Having a Latinx-serving identity is based on both outcomes and culture" (Garcia, 2017, p. 128). Let us aim for the best outcome for our students by preparing them with respect to their culture.

Note

1 All names are pseudonyms.

References

Abd-El-Khalick, F., & Lederman, N. (2000). The influence of history of science courses on students' views of nature of science. *Journal of Research in Science Teaching, 37*(10), 1057–1095.

Billingsley, B., Brock, R., Taber, K. S., & Riga, F. (2016). How students view the boundaries between their science and religious education concerning the origins of life and the universe. *Science Education, 100*(3), 459–482.

Bravo, A. A., Merce, I., & Anna, E. (2001). *A characterisation of practical proposals to teach the philosophy of science to prospective science teachers.* Paper Presented at the IOSTE Symposium, Paralimni, Cyprus.

Buxton, C. (2009). Science inquiry, academic language, and civic engagement. *Democracy in Education, 18*(3), 17–22.

Excelencia in Education. (2018). *Hispanic-serving institutions (HSIs): 2017–2018.* Washington, DC: Excelencia in Education.

Garcia, G. A. (2017). Defined by outcomes or culture? Constructing an organizational identity for Hispanic-serving institutions. *American Educational Research Journal, 54*(1_suppl), 111S–134S.

Greenfield, D. B., Jirout, J., Dominguez, X., Greenberg, A., Maier, M., & Fuccillo, J. (2009). Science in the preschool classroom: A programmatic research agenda to improve science readiness. *Early Education and Development, 20*(2), 238–264.

Gonzalez, R. G. (2008). College student spirituality at a Hispanic serving institution. *Journal of College and Character, 9*(4), 1–26.

Hernandez, H. (2001). *Multicultural education: A teacher's guide to linking context, process, and content.* New York, NY: Merrill/Prentice Hall.

Jackson, T. O., & Boutte, G. S. (2009). Liberation literature: Positive cultural messages in children's and young adult literature at freedom schools. *Language Arts, 87*(2), 108.

Johnson, C. C. (2011). The road to culturally relevant science: Exploring how teachers navigate change in pedagogy. *Journal of Research in Science Teaching, 48*(2), 170–198.

Kelly-Jackson, C., & Jackson, T. (2011). Meeting their fullest potential: The beliefs and teaching of a culturally relevant science teacher. *Creative Education, 2*(4), 408–413. doi:10.4236/ce.2011.24059

Krause, G., & Maldonado, L. (2019). Our linguistic and cultural resources: The experiences of bilingual pre-service teachers in mathematics autobiographies. In T. G. Bartell, C. Drake, A. Roth McDuffie, J. M. Aguirre, E. E. Turner, & M. Q. Foote (Eds.), *Transforming mathematics teacher education: An equity-based approach.* Cham, Switzerland: Springer.

Ladson-Billings, G. (1995). Toward a theory of culturally relevant pedagogy. *American Educational Research Journal, 32*(3), 465–491.

Lederman, N.G. (2007). Nature of science: Past, present, and future. In S.K. Abell & N.G. Lederman (Eds.), *Handbook of research on science education* (pp. 831–880). Mahwah, NJ: Erlbaum.

Lederman, N. G., & Abd-El-Khalick, F. (1998). Avoiding de-natured science: Activities thatpromote understandings of the nature of science. In W. F. McComas (Ed.), *The nature of science in science education* (pp. 83–126). Dordrecht, The Netherlands: Springer.

Lee, O. (2003). Equity for linguistically and culturally diverse students in science education: A research agenda. *Teachers College Record,* 105, 465–489.

Lee, O., & Fradd, S. H. (1998). Science for all, including students from non-English-language backgrounds. *Educational Researcher,* 27(4), 12–21.

Lee, O., & Luykx, A. (2007). Science education and student diversity: Race/ethnicity, language, culture, and socioeconomic status. *Handbook of Research on Science Education,1,* 171–197.

Manning, P. K., & Cullum-Swan, B. (1994). Narrative, context and semiotic analysis. In N. K. Denzin & Y.S. Lincoln (Eds.), *Handbook of qualitative research* (pp. 463–477). Thousand Oaks, CA: Sage Publications.

McComas, W. F., Clough, M. P., & Almazroa, H. (1998). The role and character of the nature of science in science education. In W. F. McComas (Ed.), *The nature of science in science education* (pp. 3–39). Dordrecht, The Netherlands: Springer.

Meyer, X., & Crawford, B. A. (2011). Teaching science as a cultural way of knowing: Merging authentic inquiry, nature of science, and multicultural strategies. *Cultural Studies of Science Education,* 6(3), 525–547.

Merriam, S. B. (2002). Introduction to qualitative research. *Qualitative Research in Practice: Examples for Discussion and Analysis,1,* 1–17.

Morrison, K. A., Robbins, H. H., & Rose, D. G. (2008). Operationalizing culturally relevant pedagogy: A synthesis of classroom-based research. *Equity and Excellence in Education,* 41(4), 433–452.

National Science Foundation. (1996). *Shaping the future: New expectations for undergraduate education in science, mathematics, engineering, and technology.* Arlington, VA. Retrieved from https://www.nsf.gov/pubs/1998/nsf98128/nsf98128.pdf

National Science Foundation, National Center for Science and Engineering Statistics. (2017). *Women, minorities, and persons with disabilities in science and engineering: 2017.* Special Report NSF 17–310. Arlington, VA. Retrieved from www.nsf.gov/statistics/wmpd/

Quintos, B. (2008).*Culture+pedagogy+mathematics: Multiple perspectives in a Latino community* (Doctor) of philosophy dissertation), The University of Arizona, Arizona Open Repository. Retrieved from http://arizona.openrepository.com/arizona/bitstream/10150/194393/1/azu_etd_2714_sip1_m.pdf

Riegle-Crumb, C., Moore, C., & Ramos-Wada, A. (2011). Who wants to have a career in science or math? Exploring adolescents' future aspirations by gender and race/ethnicity. *Science Education,* 95(3), 458–476.

Saldaña, J. (2015). *The coding manual for qualitative researchers.* London, UK: Sage.

Santiago, D. A., Calderón, G. E., & Taylor, M. (2015). *Factbook 2015: The condition of Latinos in education.* Washington, DC: Excelencia in Education.

Taber, K. S. (2017). The relationship between science and religion: A contentious and complex issue facing science education. In B. Akpan (Ed.), *Science education: A global perspective* (pp. 45–69). Cham, Switzerland: Springer

Stout, J. G., Dasgupta, N., Hunsinger, M., & McManus, M. A. (2011). STEMing the tide: Using ingroup experts to inoculate women's self-concept in science, technology, engineering, and mathematics (STEM). *Journal of Personality and Social Psychology,* 100(2), 255–270.

Texas Education Agency (TEA). (2012). STAAR general resources. Retrieved from https://tea.texas.gov/student.assessment/staar/

Vázquez-Alonso, Á., García-Carmona, A., Manassero-Mas, M. A., & Bennassar-Roig, A. (2013). Spanish secondary-school science teachers' beliefs about Science-Technology-Society (STS) Issues. *Science & Education, 22*(5), 1191–1218.

Walls, L. (2012). Third grade African American students' views of the nature of science. *Journal of Research in Science Teaching,49*(1), 1–37.

Williams, C.T., & Rudge, D.W. (2016). Emphasizing the history of genetics in an explicit and reflective approach to teaching the nature of science: A pilot study. *Science & Education, 25*, 407–427.

10 Bilingual Teacher Educators at an HSI

A Border Pedagogy for Latinx Teacher Development

Alcione N. Ostorga, Christian E. Zúñiga and Kip Austin Hinton

The U.S. borderlands are a unique geopolitical space that requires context-specific pedagogies (Reza-López, Huerta Charles, & Reyes, 2014), such as specific practices for strengthening academic and linguistic readiness (Flores, Clark, Claeys, & Villarreal, 2007; Guerrero & Guerrero, 2017) and for developing a critical consciousness in order to ensure educational quality (Ostorga & Farruggio, 2018). As we develop these special pedagogies, it is important for us to consider the specific diversities of our communities within our border context. The Rio Grande Valley (RGV) is a fast-growing area spanning four counties along the northern margin of the Rio Grande. Most unique to our region is the fluidity of its border with Mexico, where bilingualism and biculturalism are common and where living often spans across two countries, as people commute to work and visit families or shop. Our Latinx[1] student population consists mostly of U.S.-born Mexican Americans, Mexican immigrants, and transnational students with daily commutes between the U.S. and Mexico. These aspects of our students' lives interact with their identity development in unique ways. Therefore, we aim to develop pedagogies for promoting professional growth in our preservice teachers based on the specific contextual factors of our region and other regions along the U.S. southern border.

As a borderlands institution, we are developing a mission and vision for our Hispanic-Serving Institution (HSI) identity in the College of Education and P-16 Integration, as well as in our university. We envision pedagogical practices embedded in our teacher preparation that are context-specific to our bilingual, biliterate, and bicultural communities; one that not only prepares preservice teachers to effectively teach all students, but also promotes strong values for equity and social justice. For our Latinx preservice teachers, this aim has two purposes: (1) to tailor our educational practices capitalizing on their unique strengths and addressing possible challenges in their professional development, and (2) to prepare them to successfully promote their students' academic achievement through rigorous, culturally appropriate, and sustainable practices (Paris, 2012).

We draw on a growing body of seminal work in Latinx teacher preparation to theorize a set of border pedagogies for our context. These represent specific pedagogies that foster the development of Latinx teachers who are knowledgeable of the appropriate teaching practices for all types of students. Furthermore, we pursue practices that can help our students develop into advocates for social justice, aware of the many social and political forces impacting the schools where they will serve. These specific practices should take into consideration the specific cultural and professional identities of our preservice teachers. As a special interest research group within our college, aiming to develop an HSI identity that is context-based, we engaged in a meta-synthesis of professional literature that includes empirical research and theoretical work about the preparation of Latinx preservice teachers in our border region. We foresee the application of these pedagogies for other regions where Latinx preservice teachers can benefit, and envision furthering our research in the future to explore metaphorical borders, including Latinx preservice teachers' hybrid transcultural identities outside our geographical border.

The Need for Border Pedagogies in Latinx Teacher Preparation

There is a significant shortage of teachers from minoritized populations nationwide. In the state of Texas, white children already make up less than half of the school-age population; non-white children constitute a growing majority in cities across Texas, and in much of the U.S. (Mordechay & Orfield, 2017). Though these statistical trends are more drastic in Texas, due perhaps to its size and proximity to the border, only 27% of the teaching workforce in the state is Latinx (Parker, 2018). Nationwide, the number is even more alarming as Latinx teachers make up only 9.2% of the teaching workforce. The implication, then, is that we have a growing need for a body of knowledge that focuses on Latinx teacher preparation to address the growing population of Latinx K-12 students.

In the RGV, the demographics are quite different from the rest of state and the nation, with Latinx representing 97% of students and 89% of the teachers (RGV Focus, 2019). Because our preservice teachers come from the local communities and will return as to their communities as teachers upon certification, this has huge implications for our role in the transformation of education for all children in the area. As an HSI in the RGV, we believe we are in a position to make significant contributions in the area of Latinx teacher preparation by developing border pedagogies that specifically fit the social, historical, and cultural context of the RGV.

Within our context, particular concerns are related to the effects of subtractive schooling (Valenzuela, 2004) and hegemonic practices that impacted the identity and academic development of our preservice teachers during their P-12 education. For example, Flores and Riojas (1997) documented issues related to the high incidence of failure in certification exams among minority preservice teachers in the state of Texas. This continues to be an area of concern today. Significant concerns documented pertain the Spanish proficiency test required for the certification of bilingual teachers (Guerrero & Guerrero, 2017). Other areas of concern include promoting critical awareness, deconstructing the effects of hegemonic practices preservice teachers experienced through schooling (Ostorga & Farruggio, 2018), and developing advocacy and agency (Palmer, 2018).

Across time, research in teacher preparation demonstrates that the ultimate goal has been to promote student success by teaching research-based practices. Thus, teacher preparation has focused on educating preservice teachers about pedagogy, or the most effective methods for their instructional practices. In addition, preservice teacher preparation includes knowledge of the various content areas that students must learn. Thus, the body of research has led to specific approaches in teacher preparation, such as the implementation of high leverage practices (Ball, Sleep, Boerst, & Bass, 2009), development of a critical reflective stance (Brookfield, 2017), and teacher inquiry (Cochran-Smith & Lytle, 2009), to name a few. Yet, the body of knowledge on teacher preparation tends to assume a "one-size-fits-all" approach anchored in monolingual English, white, middle-class contexts (Ladson-Billings, 2005).

Though the term *Border Pedagogies for Teacher Development* has not been used directly by other scholars in the field, there is nevertheless an emerging focus in investigating practices for Latinx teachers. For example, we see this trend in the works of scholars at other HSIs, such as the University of Texas (UT) at San Antonio (Flores et al., 2007) and UT El Paso (Reza-López et al., 2014), as well as at UTRGV (Guerrero & Guerrero, 2017; Ostorga & Farruggio, 2014; Rodríguez & Musanti, 2014). Research in this area has also been conducted beyond the state of Texas, such as the work of Garrity, Aquino-Sterling, Van Liew, and Day (2016) and Wong, Athanases, and Banes (2017) in California. The emergence of this focus across different geographical areas points to the need for a coherent investigation in order to develop these appropriate pedagogies for Latinx preservice teachers.

Our Research Journey

Our journey begins with who we are within this context. We combine our three different perspectives as:

- a native Portuguese speaker from Brazil, who immigrated to the U.S. during adolescence, experiencing English immersion and culture shock,

- a Latina, RGV native with simultaneous bilingual development, and
- a white native English speaker, not born in a border state, who learned Spanish as a teenager.

Our process can be best understood as an organic grounded theory approach (Charmaz, 2006) where the field of educator preparation for Latinx preservice teachers was a setting to be explored so that we could develop an understanding of the ways and means developed by these future practitioners. If we envision the entire field of teacher preparation for Latinx as the research setting, and the published work as our data, we can then understand the need to examine all types of evidence to decipher the pedagogies developed and the reasoning behind their development. For our purposes, this includes empirical and theoretical works. Given our individual experiences and our awareness of how life experiences impacted our own identity development, along with the ample research to support this awareness (Achugar, 2006; Haddix, 2010; Varghese, Morgan, Johnston, & Johnson, 2005), we can conclude that professional identity development is not just based on broad principles for all preservice teachers. Instead, we must also consider the contextual mitigating factors (CMFs) (Gallard Martinez, Pitts, Brkich, & de Robles, 2018) that contribute to our preservice teachers' formation. CMFs refer to the "...set of socio-historical-political contextual constructs..., simultaneously interweaving community, education, family, gender/identity, and other socially constructed domains" (p. 3). Important CMFs to consider in preservice teachers' development may include their experiences in schooling and their cultural and linguistic development, as they often come from a cultural and linguistic background that is different from the dominant culture and language experienced in schools.

Based on these ideas, and with the intent of building on the research of others who have worked with similar populations, we decided to investigate peer-reviewed empirical studies that examined the challenges and opportunities encountered in the preparation of Latinx preservice teachers. We were aware that being of an exploratory nature, most of these studies would make use of qualitative methodologies. Therefore, with the intentions of being systematic, before actually engaging in the literature review, we first explored specific methods available to us and found that meta-analysis of qualitative research would be our best choice at this initial stage. This exploration represented our act of studying the map for our journey, so we identified mentor texts (Ke, 2009; Reljić, Ferring, & Martin, 2015) that might help guide our literature analysis. This step was particularly helpful in guiding us toward a systematic process of identification and selection of studies in our meta-analysis. We made conscious decisions about the search engines and the specific terms used in our searches. We used a total of 70 search terms in six categories, which included identity/demographics, geographic location, teacher education, labels of bilingual students, P-12 programs, and other concepts (see Table 10.1). Then, we narrowed our search to empirical work focused on teacher preparation at the preservice level within the four U.S.-Mexico border states based on the unique contextual factors present in the borderlands. As we progressed in the investigation, we also searched for the appropriate studies referenced in the original articles we examined. Our initial compilation consisted of 84 publications.

Table 10.1 List of search terms: total of 70 terms

Identity/demographics 15	Geographic location 17	Teacher ed 11
Latino	Borderlands	Teacher education
Latina	Border	Teacher preparation
Latinos	Southwest	Teacher training
Latinx	Texas	Teacher certification
Hispanic	New Mexico	Teacher licensure
Chicano	Arizona	Educator preparation
Chicana	California	Preservice teacher
Mexican American	Tamaulipas	Teacher educator
Mexican	Coahuila	Paraprofessional
Indigenous	Nuevo León	
Native American	Chihuahua	
	Sonora	
	Baja California Norte	
In Spanish:	*In Spanish:*	*In Spanish:*
Mexicano	Frontera	Normalista
Mexicana	Fronteras	Escuela normal
Indígena	Neplanta	
Indio	Neplantera	

Labels of bilingual students 6	P-12 programs 12	Other concepts 9
Emergent bilinguals	Bilingual education	Identity
English Language Learners	Dual language	Border pedagogy
Limited English Proficient	Double immersion	Hybridity
Spanish speakers	English as a Second Language	Grow your own
Nahuatl	English Language Development	Culturally relevant pedagogy
	Mexican American Studies	Culturally responsive
	Chicano Studies	
	Raza Studies	Funds of knowledge
	Tribal education	Bilingualism
		Spanish
In Spanish:	*In Spanish:*	
Bilingüe	Educación bilingüe	
	Intercultural bilingüe	
	Doble inmersión	

Our studied body of work expanded to include three edited volumes (Guerrero, Guerrero, Soltero-Gonzalez, & Escamilla, 2017; Flores, Sheets, & Clark, 2010; Ramirez, Faltis, & De Jong, 2018), some of which was published during our investigation.

Among the relevant publications, we also found work that was theoretical in nature. Although these publications were not reporting the results of specific empirical work, they synthesized an extensive body of research on converging areas that impact the identity formation, ideologies, and professional formation of Latinx preservice teachers. These often provided a foundation for much of the research that was being conducted (Flores et al., 2010; Palmer & Martinez, 2013; Reza-López et al., 2014). Furthermore, we realized that our work was moving beyond a mere meta-analysis to summarize findings. Instead, we discovered the need to synthesize a whole body of knowledge and felt compelled to include theoretical work, as well as the analysis of empirical work, to develop a theory of border pedagogies for teacher preparation. Our emerging theory was founded on the last 30+ years of teacher education work with Latinx preservice teachers. For example, the work of Flores et al. (2010), an edited volume, presented a synthesis of much of the research conducted at the University of Texas San Antonio, of which eight studies are included in our meta-analysis. Also, included was an article by Reza-López et al. (2014), which synthesizes works of Anzaldua and Freire, among others, to explain what they call a Nepantlera pedagogy. Their synthesis illuminates theoretical concepts used by other researchers in our analysis, such as Caldas Chumbes (2016), Rodríguez and Musanti (2014), Sarmiento-Arribalzaga and Murillo (2010). We therefore needed more than a simple meta-analysis of qualitative research in our theorizing process and discovered Sandelowski and Barroso's (2006) model for meta-synthesis of qualitative research. Though systematic and worthy as a method for a meta-synthesis of qualitative work, we found it was too limiting for our purposes because if strictly followed, it would lead us to exclude the significant work, as explained above, that should be included in our research to get a more comprehensive picture of the border pedagogies developed. Therefore, as we shifted our research approach and explored the possibility of using a meta-synthesis methodology, we further expanded our method toward a different kind of meta-synthesis. Our meta-synthesis includes theoretical, qualitative, and quantitative studies to synthesize and build a more complete understanding of the pedagogies developed by others, and to create a formal theory based on the current body of knowledge on this topic, a theory of *Border Pedagogies for Teacher Development*. For the purposes of this chapter, we focus here only on our analysis of the empirical work.

Our analytical process led to the discovery of emergent themes among the studies and relationships among them, as well as an examination of our positionalities as participant researchers within the context of teacher preparation along this border community. As we analyzed the different publications through our bi-weekly conversations, we discovered that teacher education faculty and preservice teachers are players within different micro contexts: (1) the P-12 school system where preservice teachers attended and will return upon graduation, (2) the local communities, and (3) the university-based teacher preparation program (see Figure 10.1). In turn, these micro contexts interact with the macro sociopolitical/educational context of which they are a part. As teacher educators, many of us have been the products of educational contexts similar to the educational context in which our preservice teachers will exercise their professional practices. Yet, many teacher educators are not familiar with the CMFs that have impacted our preservice teachers, and they should engage in experiential work at the local communities and local schools to become informed of these important factors in the identity formation. Thus, in essence, university teacher preparation sits at the center of this cyclical journey in Latinx teacher preparation. Furthermore, the three stakeholders in this journey such as students in P-12 schools, preservice teachers who are future teachers, and teacher educators in an HSI within the border live and engage with each other as

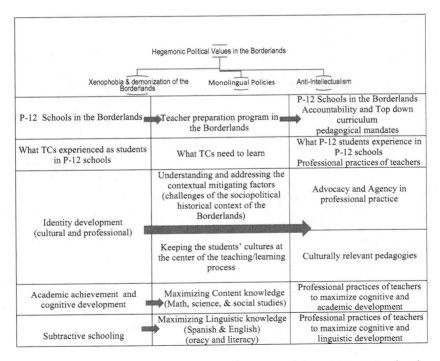

Figure 10.1 Emerging conceptualization of contextual factors impacting border pedagogies for Latinx teacher preparation.

they interact within the contextual sociopolitical setting of our society and our nation.

The picture we present here attempts to illustrate the relationships among these multiple stakeholders and the multiplicity of factors in their journey, yet we realize that this picture is not linear but three-dimensional, with the relationships going in different directions. For example, our practices will impact the school setting in the future, as our preservice teachers become teachers, but their practices are also impacted by their past experiences, when they were students in schools. Likewise, the sociopolitical context of schools influences our pedagogies as educators since we attempt to promote what we view as positive changes. We also tailor our practices based on our past experiences as students and our current knowledge of the forces acting upon the education of all children. Certainly, the diagram presented, which is a work in progress, signifies our evolving view of the complexities of these intermingled forces and evolving pedagogies: knowledge of the forces acting upon the education of all children. At this point in our study, we theorized the following elements and the relationships among them.

The emergent pedagogies for our context can be divided into four categories:

- Understanding and addressing CMFs present in the context of the borderlands,
- Keeping students' cultures at the center of the teaching/learning process,
- Maximizing content knowledge (discipline-specific instructional approaches related to math, science, and social studies knowledge),
- Maximizing linguistic knowledge (development of the four language domains – oracy and literacy – in Spanish and English).

It is important to note that these categories are not isolated units but interact with each other in the development and application of the specific pedagogies. For example, in the study by Rodríguez and Musanti (2014), their developed pedagogies addressed both the maximization of content knowledge and linguistic knowledge since it used an instructional approach where language is taught through content. This fosters the development of English as a second language (ESL) while promoting conceptualization of specific disciplines such as mathematics or science.

Addressing the CMFs to Foster Professional Readiness

This first category is at the heart of teacher educators' work with Latinx preservice teachers as they facilitate the development of the teacher's professional identities. Some important elements identified by teacher educators in the professional formation of teachers are a critical reflective stance (Brookfield, 2017), a value for social justice, a strong inquiry stance (Cochran-Smith & Lytle, 2009), and a teacher agency (Palmer & Martinez, 2013). Though content knowledge and pedagogical knowledge are crucial in effective teaching practices, professional values and ideology ultimately are the forces that drive the teaching practice. This is why it is not enough to transmit the knowledge of the best teaching practices for future teachers, for we must also work toward the development of a professional identity. For Latinx preservice teachers, this work includes awareness about their cultural identities, and the values and dispositions that lay at the foundation of their cultural selves, especially those values that may be in misalignment with the values from a majority culture. For example, the development of professional values that include an inquiry stance or a willingness to engage in critical reflection, advocacy, and agency are dependent on the self-identity of the teacher and in some ways, may be in opposition to the Latinx preservice teachers' cultural values, which is made clear when we closely examine the process of identity formation.

Our understanding of professional identity refers to how teachers define themselves as professionals. We develop an identity by associating with particular groups, beliefs, and ways of being and by rejecting other values. Our individual identity is the nexus where we negotiate our different ways of being in the world. Thus, our professional practices emerge from our pedagogical knowledge as it interacts with our value systems (personal and professional) and our professional identities. Professional identities are continuously evolving (Flores & Day, 2006) concepts or images of self that strongly influence the way individuals develop as teachers. Therefore, we can understand that identity formation is the result of a person's experiences across time and their responses to these experiences.

Professional identity is also woven with the cultural identity forged from personal values. This is a complex process when personal values come from a minoritized culture. In situating our work within the research about bilingual teacher preparation along border states, we find that our Latinx preservice teachers have commonalities in the CMFs from experiences that have impacted the formation of their personal and cultural identities. Among the commonalities in their identity formation, which differs from preservice teachers from dominant cultures, are bilingualism, biculturalism, and the sociopolitical context they experience as members of a minoritized ethnicity, among others.

Bilingualism and Biculturalism in Identity Formation

During their early school experiences in the U.S., many preservice teachers in bilingual education programs across the southern border states experienced transitional bilingual education. In this subtractive approach (Valenzuela, 2004), students are rushed out of bilingual education as early as possible and into English immersion programs where they are subject to losing their native language, and likely to fail to succeed academically compared with their monolingual, native English-speaking peers (National Center for Education Statistics, 2013). In addition, they often learn to devalue their language and culture (Sarmiento-Arribalzaga & Murillo, 2010), a stance that is in opposition to teacher preparation for additive bilingualism and social justice. Furthermore, due to the social context of schooling and society in general, when Latinx preservice teachers come into our programs, we find that they are not always aware of the forces that contributed to the social inequities they experienced.

In addition, unlike white American children raised on individualistic values and nurtured into becoming independent, as children, Latinx preservice teachers were taught based on collectivist/familist values (Rinderle & Montoya, 2008) and were often taught to respect authority. This may be why Latinx preservice teachers are not always ready to challenge traditional practices (Weisman & Hansen, 2008) or engage in critical reflection, which requires them to question the status quo for the benefit of their students because these behaviors are in opposition to their values, especially since as P-12 students they were typically not engaged in critical thinking and were often expected to be generally submissive in the classroom settings.

Also, agency is an important stance for teachers who work with minoritized populations, especially emergent bilinguals. They must be in a position to challenge the practices imposed and base their decisions on their own data and a professional knowledge that combines research with personal insight into the contextual factors that impact learning. The achievement gap between white and Hispanic students has persisted across the last three decades (U.S. Department of Education, 2015) despite educational policies which were supposedly created to dismantle the statistical gap. Latinx preservice teachers must be able to bring their unique perspectives, critically examining school practices and outcomes, and seek to innovate these practices to address their students' needs and talents. Specific pedagogies for Latinx preservice teachers, therefore, must aim to promote their professional development by facilitating in them the complex process of identity reconstruction (Torres & Baxter-Magolda, 2004); one that helps them to make sense of their interweaving cultural and professional identities, preparing them to engage in teacher agency and advocacy for their students.

This category of studies identifies pedagogies to address CMFs particular to the border region and is unique to the preparation of Latinx teachers who have experienced schooling in bilingual and bicultural settings. This is the area most investigated in the studies we examined, though many of them only identified CMFs without actually developing the appropriate practices to address them.

Among the challenges resulting from CMFs identified in the reviewed studies were the need for cultural relevancy (Wong, Athanases, & Banes, 2017). Other studies identified the presence of contradictory discourses between family and school, which eventually led to the adoption of hegemonic school values (Aguilar, MacGillivray, & Walker, 2003; Garrity et al., 2016). These responses to CMFs often impacted language ideologies that promote monolingualism and deficit views of self. Another response to CMFs was the silencing of contradictory discourses, which eventually led to feelings of inadequacy and fear of seeking help in school, which sometimes may lead to dropping out due to academic failure. A complete analysis of this category is beyond the purposes of this chapter. Instead, we focus here on specific border pedagogies to address these and other CMFs experienced by Latinx preservice teachers through their life experiences in a border context.

Among the border pedagogies developed in the empirical research, we investigated is the exposure to contradictions in the field and specific activities that allows preservice teachers to examine tacit ideologies and to engage in critical analysis and self-reflexive assignments allowing them to reconstruct their identities to one that includes agency and advocacy. Exposure to contradictions were present in the work of Caldas Chumbes (2016) and Ostorga and Farruggio (2014). For example, Caldas Chumbes taught a course where she made use of a drama-based activity called counter-storytelling. In this activity, preservice teachers were presented with narratives of seasoned bilingual teachers that exposed the challenges they faced in schools as they grappled with social inequities. The counter-storytelling took place in the form of performances where preservice teachers practiced their responses to the challenges they would face in the future, particularly in the discrepancies between professional knowledge imparted in their teacher preparation courses and the realities of the bilingual education school context. The preparation for the counter-storytelling included the use of semi-structured conversations where the preservice teachers explored their perceptions of themselves as advocates and their ideologies related to language. The learning activities also included opportunity for reflections where preservice teachers experienced shifts in their ideology as demonstrated through the shifts in discourse. As explained by Caldas Chumbes, this pedagogy has the "… potential to imprint in the body—as well as in the intellect—a developing political clarity" (p. 256). It merged counter-storytelling and performance through Theater of the Oppressed as a pedagogy that "blurred the lines between the lessons learned" from past experiences and the rehearsal of future stories that could represent a way to resist the subtractive practices in bilingual education.

These are among the border pedagogies developed to counteract the effects of CMFs in an overarching way. Other pedagogies to address CMFs will be specifically described in the next three sections of this chapter since they address CMFs by specifically maximizing content and linguistic knowledge, and by identifying practices that are culturally relevant and sustainable (Paris, 2012).

Keeping Culture at the Center for Preservice Teachers and Their Future Students

Integrating culture into the teaching and learning process is significant for both preservice teachers and their future students. Given the diversity of student populations across our nation, this has been recognized as an important kind of knowledge for all teachers. Due to their cultural experiences and ethnic identity, Latinx can be resourceful in integrating culture into their teaching practices. One study by Téllez (1999) demonstrates that during student teaching, preservice teachers of Mexican American descent found creative ways of infusing culture into their teaching despite the limitations imposed by prescribed curricula in the schools, demonstrating their special resourcefulness in keeping culture at the center to make teaching appropriate for their students.

An example of pedagogies for culturally relevant pedagogy for preservice teachers and students was described in the work of Ostorga and Farruggio (2014). The program combined the use of structures that capitalized on the preservice teachers' cultural strengths. In their third semester in the preparation program, preservice teachers engaged in a summer library program for language minority students where they experienced the freedom to apply what they learned in their courses without the supervision of a mentor teacher, or the limitations of a school setting. They created thematic units based on the children's interests and cultures. The experience was followed by a regular student teaching semester. This combination of activities provided a stark contrast and exposure to contradictions leading them toward paradigm shifts and critical reflection similar to what occurred in the study by Caldas Chumbes (2016). As part of the coursework, reflective assignments took place within a dialogical space where faculty and preservice teachers had evolved together, learning from each other. The work included a pedagogy of cariño described by Bartolomé (2008), a culturally relevant pedagogy for preservice teachers who have been marginalized by their school experiences and who thrive in collaborative environments. This counter hegemonic pedagogy combines academic rigor and liberatory practices. The preservice teachers in this program became aware of the inequitable subtractive practices they had experienced and learned ways to develop their own practices for the benefit of their students.

Some of the pedagogies developed in programs described in the other categories also address the need for cultural relevancy such as translanguaging practices to leverage linguistic repertoire in two languages to further develop their linguistic abilities in Spanish (Musanti & Rodríguez, 2017). This study demonstrates that while linguistic connections are important for students' conceptualization in schools, they are also culturally relevant and especially significant for preservice teachers who experienced the negative effects of CMFs as described in the previous section.

Practices for Maximizing Content Knowledge

In preparing teachers to lead their students to academic success, we should find effective ways of developing preservice teachers' own knowledge of these disciplines, as well as the skills to teach them. There is a scarcity of studies in this area for Latinx preservice teachers' development. Notable research includes an examination of preservice teachers' ability to ask high-order thinking questions in language arts and mathematics (Diaz, Whitacre, Esquierdo, & Ruiz-Escalante, 2013), and Rodríguez and Musanti's (2014) work on language use during instruction. Their work combines instructional practices that teach language through content and the use of translanguaging, where the first language becomes a resource to maximize the learning of content in a new language. The study by Diaz et al. described areas that need to be addressed but did not specifically develop pedagogies to address these challenges. However, Rodríguez' and Musanti's work on translanguaging practices may be developed as a border pedagogy to promote linguistic development of both students and preservice teachers. Obviously, there is a need for research to examine pedagogies for Latinx preservice teachers that maximize content knowledge for all learners within our local borderlands schools.

A fourth study (Flores et al., 2007) specifically addressed the need to maximize preservice teachers' success through support for academic and professional development, including their knowledge of the disciplines. This border pedagogy developed at the University of Texas San Antonio created a multilevel system of support for students with one of the goals being specifically to maximize the quality of programing and the retention of preservice teachers during their preparation and through induction for one year. The most significant component of this complex border pedagogy was the creation of the Academy for Teacher Excellence (ATE), which had five components, including faculty and peer support through the ATE Teacher Academy Learning Community. The collaborative approach provided academic, emotional, and professional support. The program demonstrated success in increasing recruitment and retention of preservice teachers, as well as successful completion of their professional preparation. Evidently, this approach deserves a more in-depth look so it can be duplicated at other HSIs to address similar challenges.

Pedagogies for Maximizing Linguistic Knowledge

This category, which includes oracy (listening and speaking) and literacy (reading and writing), though a goal for the preparation of all teachers, is differentiated for Latinx preservice teachers, especially for those who will work with Latinx emergent bilingual students. For them, linguistic knowledge is bilingual, including the (cross) linguistic knowledge of Spanish and English, along with the knowledge of bilingual development. Nine studies addressed this theme. We detail the most notable work in this category.

Specific pedagogies in this category included the work presented by López and Assaf (2014). It consisted of a combination of field-based and service-learning components in conjunction with coursework focused on literacy practices that included reading and writing for emergent bilinguals. The field-based component allowed preservice teachers to integrate theory to practice within a formal school setting in collaboration with a mentor teacher. Conversely, the service-learning component, which took place after school and allowed preservice teachers to experience the freedom to apply principles learned in the coursework, led to the development of generative knowledge (Ball et al., 2009), which is the teacher's ability to apply their professional knowledge and understandings to new situations.

Another pedagogy in this category was explained in the work of Milk (1990). The focus of this study was to analyze a specific course that integrated instructional methods for content and language taught in Spanish to both ESL and bilingual preservice teachers. The language used in the course aimed to meet the differing Spanish language proficiency needs of both types of preservice teachers, while also preparing them to implement content-based strategies for learning language. ESL specialists received an immersion experience in Spanish that provided them with meaningful experiences for their future practices. Bilingual education specialists were provided opportunities to enhance their proficiency in academic Spanish. The course included simulated classroom experiences with small group, content-based instruction using a heterogeneous collaborative learning approach. The findings in this study are inconclusive due to the short-term duration of the course during the summer term. Nevertheless, the results are promising, and further research may lead us to a meaningful pedagogy for our HSI context.

Another noteworthy border pedagogy was developed at the University of California, Davis, (Banes et al., 2016) and focuses on the use of self-reflexive inquiry into language and culture. The study describes this border pedagogy as a key assignment in a course on cultural diversity and education for preservice teachers. Findings include the development of metalinguistic awareness, and the promotion of appropriate ideological clarity to shape their practices, which lead to agentic decision-making aimed at meeting the needs of their students. Through the assignment, preservice teachers learned to leverage their resources as multilingual individuals who make use of their experiences to connect with students and develop responsive teaching.

Implications for Hispanic-Serving Colleges of Education

Through our analysis, we found support for some of our own experiences in working with Latinx preservice teachers within the RGV. These include the importance of understanding the sociopolitical context of the borderlands and developing the knowledge of students' languages and development—which need to be an integral part of the preparation of Latinx preservice teachers—in addition to the rigorous knowledge of the disciplines they will teach to their future students. Consequently, these teacher educators' practices must evolve through personal explorations of the educational context within RGV communities, especially for those who did not grow up within the region. Then, we can consciously play our role as practitioners within the middle space between the school contexts that impacted our preservice teachers and the school context that can be transformed by their practices when they graduate and become certified. Furthermore, this is how we teacher educators can engage in the practices that deconstruct the effects of the hegemonic practices preservice teachers have experienced through schooling so they can develop as strong advocates and critical pedagogues in the local schools and communities, as well as outside our region. Our analysis and theorizing process pointed to the following specific principles to be present in teacher preparation programs within HSIs:

- Include elements aimed at raising awareness of tacit ideologies and sociopolitical contextual factors that impacted on the formation of their own identities,
- Build upon ethnic identity and a strong self-concept promoting the readiness to engage in agency and advocacy,
- Provide support through university structures and learning communities with spaces for dialogue among faculty and students about the important issues in their developmental journey,
- Include opportunities for maximizing linguistic development in Spanish and English,
- Ensure that the resources and knowledge acquired can be sustained after graduation, perhaps through support structures during their first year as professionals.

Though we derived important knowledge from the synthesis of the work already conducted, we realize that our work is just beginning. There are many gaps to be addressed. For example, we still need to examine teacher preparation pedagogies for Latinx preservice teachers outside our geographical border. Additionally, practices for the inclusion of culturally relevant instruction and for maximizing linguistic and academic success in all content areas still need to be explored further. We invite teacher educators everywhere to join us as we seek the appropriate practices that transform education for Latinx students and teachers across our nation.

Note

1 The inclusive term Latinx, comprising multiple cultures, races, and ethnicities who either originated or descended from Latin America, is the term used in this chapter, instead of Hispanic.

References

Achugar, M. (2006). Writers on the borderlands: Constructing a bilingual identity in Southwest Texas. *Journal of Language, Identity, and Education, 5*(2), 97–122.

Aguilar, J. A., MacGillivray, L., & Walker, N. T. (2003). Latina educators and school discourse: Dealing with tension on the path to success. *Journal of Latinos and Education, 2*(2), 89–100.

Ball, D. L., Sleep, L., Boerst, T. A., & Bass, H. (2009). Combining the development of practice and the practice of development in teacher education. *The Elementary School Journal, 109*(5), 458–474.

Banes, L. C., Martinez, D. C., Athanases, S. Z., & Wong, J. W. (2016). Self-reflexive inquiry into language use and beliefs: Toward more expansive language ideologies. *International Multilingual Research Journal, 10*(3), 168–187.

Bartolomé, L. (2008). Authentic cariño and respect in minority education: The political and ideological dimensions of love. *International Journal of Critical Pedagogy, 1*(1), 1–17.

Brookfield, S. D. (2017). *Becoming a critically reflective teacher.* San Francisco, CA: John Wiley & Sons.

Caldas Chumbes, B. G. (2016). *Performing the advocate bilingual teacher: Drama-based interventions for future story-making* (Doctoral Dissertation). University of Texas, Austin.

Charmaz, K. (2006). *Constructing grounded theory: A practical guide through qualitative analysis.* London, UK: SAGE.

Cochran-Smith, M., & Lytle, S. L. (2009). *Inquiry as stance: Practitioner research for the next generation.* New York, NY: Teachers College Press.

Diaz, Z., Whitacre, M., Esquierdo, J., & Ruiz-Escalante, J. (2013). Why did I ask that question? Bilingual/ESL preservice teachers' insights. *International Journal of Instruction, 6*(2), 164–176.

Flores, B. B., Clark, E. R., Claeys, L., & Villarreal, A. (2007). Academy for teacher excellence: Recruiting, preparing, and retaining Latino teachers through learning communities. *Teacher Education Quarterly, 34*(4), 53–69.

Flores, B. B., & Riojas, E. (1997). High-stakes testing: Barriers for prospective bilingual education teachers. *Bilingual Research Journal, 21*(4), 345–357.

Flores, B. B., Sheets, R. H., & Clark, E. R. (Eds.). (2010). *Teacher preparation for bilingual student populations: Educar para Transformar* (1 ed.). New York, NY: Routledge.

Flores, M. A., & Day, C. (2006). Contexts which shape and reshape new teachers' identities: A multi-perspective study. *Teaching and Teacher Education, 22*(2), 219–232.

Gallard Martínez, A. J., Pitts, W. B., Brkich, K. M., & de Robles, S. L. R. (2018). How does one recognize contextual mitigating factors (CMFs) as a basis to understand and arrive at better approaches to research designs? *Cultural Studies of Science Education.* DOI: 10.1007/s11422-018-9872-2

Garrity, S., Aquino-Sterling, C. R., Van Liew, C., & Day, A. (2016). Beliefs about bilingualism, bilingual education, and dual language development of early childhood preservice teachers raised in a Prop 227 environment. *International Journal of Bilingual Education and Bilingualism, 21*(2), 176–196.

Guerrero, M. D., Guerrero, M. C., Soltero-Gonzalez, L., & Escamilla, K. (Eds.). (2017). *Abriendo brecha: Antología crítica sobre la educación bilingüe de doble inmersión.* Albuquerque, NM: Fuente Press.

Guerrero, M. D., & Guerrero, M. C. (2017). Competing discourses of academic Spanish in the Texas-Mexico borderlands. *Bilingual Research Journal, 40*(1), 5–19.

Haddix, M. (2010). No longer on the margins: Researching the hybrid literate identities of Black and Latina preservice teachers. *Research in the Teaching of English, 45*(2), 97–123.

Ke, F. (2009). A qualitative meta-analysis of computer games as learning tools. *Handbook of Research on Effective Electronic Gaming in Education, 1,* 1–32.

Ladson-Billings, G. J. (2005). Is the team all right? Diversity and teacher education. *Journal of Teacher Education, 56*(3), 229–234.

López, M. M., & Assaf, L. C. (2014). Developing deeper understandings of diversity: Service learning and field experiences combine for generative learning of bilingual/ESL preservice teachers. In *Research on Preparing Preservice Teachers to Work Effectively with Emergent Bilinguals* (Vol. 21, pp. 31–57). Emerald Group Publishing Limited. https://doi.org/10.1108/S1479-368720140000021000

Milk, R. (1990). Preparing ESL and bilingual teachers for changing roles: Immersion for teachers of LEP children. *TESOL Quarterly, 24*(3), 407–426.

Mordechay, K., & Orfield, G. (2017). Demographic transformation in a policy vacuum: The changing face of US metropolitan society and challenges for public schools. *The Educational Forum, 81,* 193–203.

Musanti, S. I., & Rodríguez, A. D. (2017). Translanguaging in bilingual teacher preparation: Exploring pre-service bilingual teachers' academic writing. *Bilingual Research Journal, 40*(1), 38–54.

National Center for Education Statistics. (2013). *Trends in academic progress 2012.* Institute of Education Sciences U.S. Department of Education, Washington, DC.

Ostorga, A. N., & Farruggio, P. (2014). Discovering best practices for bilingual teacher preparation: A pedagogy for the border. In Y. Freeman & D. Freeman (Eds.), *Advances in Research on Teaching* (vol. 21, pp. 113–136). Bingley, UK: Emerald Group Publishing Limited.

Ostorga, A. N., & Farruggio, P. (2018). Preparing bilingual teachers on the U.S./Mexico border: Including the voices of emergent bilinguals. *International Journal of Bilingual Education and Bilingualism.* DOI: 10.1080/13670050.2018.1438348

Palmer, D. K. (2018). Supporting bilingual teachers to be leaders for social change: "*I must create advocates for biliteracy.*" *International Multilingual Research Journal, 12*(3), 203–216. DOI: 10.1080/19313152.2018.1474063

Palmer, D. K., & Martinez, R. (2013). Teacher agency in bilingual spaces: A fresh look at preparing teachers to education Latino/a children. *Review of Research in Education, 37,* 269–297.

Paris, D. (2012). Culturally sustaining pedagogy: A needed change in stance, terminology, and practice. *Educational Researcher, 41*(3), 93–97. https://doi.org/10.3102/0013189X12441244

Parker, C. (2018, June 26). Educator reports and data. Retrieved January 2, 2019, from https://tea.texas.gov/Reports_and_Data/Educator_Data/Educator_Reports_and_Data/

Ramirez, P. C., Faltis, C. J., & De Jong, E. J. (Eds.). (2018). *Learning from emergent bilingual Latinx learners in K-12: Critical teacher education.* New York, NY: Routledge.

Reljić, G., Ferring, D., & Martin, R. (2015). A meta-analysis on the effectiveness of bilingual programs in Europe. *Review of Educational Research, 85*(1), 92–128.

Reza-López, E., Huerta Charles, L., & Reyes, L. V. (2014). Nepantlera pedagogy: An axiological posture for preparing critically conscious teachers in the borderlands. *Journal of Latinos and Education, 13*(2), 107–119.

RGV Focus. (2019). *Teacher landscape data* – unpublished.

Rinderle, S., & Montoya, D. (2008). Hispanic/Latino identity labels: An examination of cultural values and personal experiences. *Howard Journal of Communications, 19*(2), 144–164. https://doi.org/10.1080/10646170801990953

Rodríguez, A. D., & Musanti, S. I. (2014). Preparing Latina/o bilingual teachers to teach content in Spanish to emergent bilingual students on the U.S.-Mexico border. In Y. S. Freeman & D. E. Freeman (Eds.), *Research on preparing preservice teachers to work effectively with emergent bilinguals* (Vol. 21, pp. 201–232). Bingley, UK: Emerald Group Publishing Limited.

Sandelowski, M., & Barroso, J. (2006). *Handbook for synthesizing qualitative research.* New York, NY: Springer Publishing Company.

Sarmiento-Arribalzaga, M. A., & Murillo, L. A. (2010). Pre-service bilingual teachers and their invisible scars: Implications for preparation programs. *SRATE Journal, 19*(1), 61–69.

Téllez, K. (1999). Mexican-American preservice teachers and the intransigency of the elementary school curriculum. *Teaching and Teacher Education, 15,* 555–570.

Torres, V., & Baxter-Magolda, (2004). Reconstructing Latino identity: The influence of cognitive development on the ethnic identity process of Latino students. *Journal of College Student Development, 45*(3), 333–347.

U.S. Department of Education, Institute of Education Sciences, National Center for Education Statistics, National Assessment of Educational Progress (NAEP), various years, 2002–2015 Reading Assessments.

Valenzuela, A. (2004). *Leaving children behind: How Texas style accountability fails Latino youth.* Albany, NY: SUNY Press.

Varghese, M., Morgan, B., Johnston, B., & Johnson, K. A. (2005). Theorizing language teacher identity: Three perspectives and beyond. *Journal of Language, Identity, and Education, 4*(1), 21–44.

Weisman, E. M., & Hansen, L. E. (2008.) Student teaching in urban and suburban schools: Perspectives of Latino preservice teachers. *Urban Education, 43*(3), 653–670.

Wong, J. W., Athanases, S. Z., & Banes, L. C. (2017). Developing as an agentive bilingual teacher: self-reflexive and student-learning inquiry as teacher education resources. *International Journal of Bilingual Education and Bilingualism.* DOI: 10.1080/13670050.2017.1345850

11 Building Meaning for an HSCOE Designation

Learnings and Proximations

Patricia Alvarez McHatton, Eugenio Longoria Sáenz and Janine M. Schall

After completing three cycles of the Hispanic-Serving Institution Special Interest Research Group (HSI SIRG) initiative, we have come to some understandings but know that there is more work to do. We embarked on our journey because of a deep commitment to our students and our community. We are well aware that our community, by virtue of its history and the ways in which it is often characterized (e.g., through educational attainment, socioeconomic status), is often perceived from a deficit lens. We fully recognize the strengths and assets our community and therefore our students possess and the ways in which we can utilize our students' cultural and linguistic capital to ensure positive academic and affective outcomes. These beliefs led us to an exploration of what it means to be a Hispanic-Serving College of Education (HSCOE) in which we engaged in collaborative self-reflection leading to positive change in the ways in which we serve our students.

Initially, our search for an answer to what it means to be an HSCOE was informed by our desire to replicate and enhance in our own institution the pride and strength of culture found at HBCUs and Tribal Colleges and the belief that a strong collective understanding of what it means to be an HSI would strengthen our student success efforts. During our first year of exploration, we soon realized that there is no *one* identity to be had or found. Rather, we came to a deep understanding of the heterogeneity of HSCOEs by virtue not only of the diversity within and across the groups that comprise a Hispanic designation but also of the differences that abound based on the percentage of Latinx students that reside within and beyond an institution of higher education.

We came to understand that our journey was an opportunity to build our own identity as an HSCOE and to operationalize what that demanded of us. Subsequently, we began to intentionally and explicitly weave a culturally and linguistically sustaining and affirming narrative through our practice at the College of Education and P-16 Integration (CEP). This narrative was born from our own becoming and focused on an asset-based paradigm, which challenged ideas of success of Latinx students defined in the context of predominately white institutions. Finally, this narrative was about more than achieving equity for Latinx students in relationship to their higher education achievement; it was about disrupting a culture of complicity at HSIs when it came to serving Latinx students in the absence of an HSI identity.

The Facilitators and the Voices that Brought Us to this Critical Conversation

As described in the first chapter, we—the three co-editors of this book—came to this work as a result of our own lived experiences. While varied, those experiences highlighted a commitment to the success of the students and communities we serve. We each had our own personal narrative we re-visited in relationship to some abstract value proposition regarding the identity and responsibility of an HSCOE in preparing educators that would further this commitment. For Patty, as the inaugural Dean of the CEP at an HSI, it has always been about exploring the question of what it means to be an HSCOE. Being in a location that is predominately Latinx does not mean that the practices and approaches we employ to meet students' needs will be automatically fully aligned to our population. Deep introspection, critical reflection, and substantive collective dialogue are essential if we are to embody what it means to be an HSCOE. For Janine, as chair in a new department that housed courses about multicultural and bilingual education, there was a strong need to help build research capacity within her faculty and support the desire to become a premiere bilingual, bicultural, and biliterate HSI. For Eugenio, exploring our identity as an HSCOE was an opportunity to develop a new counter-narrative about the people and place in which he was raised.

Lessons Learned

Our goals for the project were multi-faceted: (1) advancing a learning and learned community focused on what it truly means to be an HSI in general and an HSCOE specifically; (2) facilitating a culture and community of inquiry maximizing student success; and (3) developing a counter-narrative regarding the strengths and assets of our students and communities. We began the work somewhat naïvely, believing that we would find an answer to the question and that everyone entered the work from the same or similar stance.

As evidenced by the variety of topics encompassed in the chapters within this text, participants approached the questions from different vantage points and with different methodologies. As we progressed through each cycle, we came to realize that there were four interrelated cross-cutting themes which were threaded throughout each of the projects. We addressed these as ethics, or principles of conduct (Merriam-Webster, 2019), that guide our work as an HSCOE. These consisted of an ethic of care, an ethic of community, an ethic of inquiry, and an ethic of agency.

The Ethic of Care

Noddings (2001) proposes that care is a basic need grounded in relationships in which individual needs and perspectives are acknowledged and nurtured. Care is crafted over time and through mutual respect. While some well-meaning people may succumb to the pobrecito syndrome, a belief that educators need to go easy on learners who are poor and/or culturally and linguistically diverse resulting in low expectations of students (Noguera, 2010), care is about warm demanders (Bondy & Ross, 2008), individuals who take a "…stance that communicates both warmth and a nonnegotiable demand for student effort and mutual respect" (p. 54).

We have begun to think critically about how care is enacted at our HSCOE. As an HSCOE we need to understand who our students are, the assets they bring with them, and the challenges they face. With this knowledge we can consciously and deliberately build authentic relationships with our students, leverage their strengths, and attend to their needs. As we have moved into new SIRG cycles and expanded the work, we remind and encourage ourselves to keep our ears open to the language we use within and beyond our institution when we talk about our population and our students. And importantly, we have come to realize that an ethic of care does not only apply to our students and their families, it also applies to our interactions with each other and our colleagues.

The Ethic of Community

The HSI SIRG initiative intentionally fostered a learning and learned community among our participants on the belief that a mutually supportive group is stronger than the individual. Furman (2004) furthered Starratt's (2004) work on ethical leadership, which called for an ethic of care, an ethic of justice, and an ethic of critique as necessary for authentic leadership in PK-12 settings. While essential, she found them insufficient in that they focused on the individual. She posits the importance of a relational praxis and proposed an ethic of community rooted in an "ongoing process of communication, dialogue and collaboration" (p. 221). Our internal HSI SIRG was comprised of a diverse group of colleagues who were engaging in a process of communication, dialogue, and collaboration as we explored our guiding question. An ethic of care was essential as we built our community, negotiated differences of opinion, and gently guided each other to different ways of knowing.

Our HSCOE incorporates or belongs to various communities beyond the research initiative. For example, the HSCOE community as a whole includes all our students, faculty, and staff, but people also belong to communities in the Rio Grande Valley beyond the university. Living out this ethic means that our HSCOE must consciously and thoughtfully build collaborative, mutually beneficial relationships with the people, school districts, colonias, towns, and cities across the Rio Grande Valley.

The Ethic of Inquiry

Inquiry is a process of seeking knowledge, asking questions, and engaging in systematic investigation as we move away from anecdotal stories to data-informed spaces. It is about being curious and exploring the world in which we live and learning more about the lived experiences of our students, communities, and colleagues. As an HSCOE, inquiry requires introspection and critical self-reflection about our own practices as we investigate issues of equity and access and our role in ensuring both for our students. This comes with the understanding that faculty and staff must identify and confront our own personal biases and instances of complicity in maintaining the status quo. Of course, the ethic of inquiry extends to our students. Our HSCOE must develop and sustain curricular and pedagogical practices that support student inquiry. As we create structures that support deliberate, critical, and reflective inquiry, we also must accept the inherent risk and messiness of doing this work; an ethic of care and an ethic of community are essential if we are to submerge ourselves fully in an ethic of inquiry.

The Ethic of Agency

Schlosser (2015) defines an agent as "a being with the capacity to act" and agency as "the exercise or manifestation of this capacity" (¶ 1). He goes on to state, "The former construes action in terms of intentionality, the latter explains the intentionality of action in terms of causation by the agent's mental states and events" (¶ 1). As each of the SIRGs and ourselves engaged in dialogue and debate on the overarching question of what it means to be an HSCOE, the notion of agency moved to the forefront of our discussions. We came to understand our responsibilities as faculty in an HSCOE as agentic beings who must take action to transform the experience of our Latinx students in educator preparation programs. While we have been exploring what it means to be an HSI, it is vitally important to move toward what we need to *do* in order to serve our students.

Through our HSI SIRG initiative we endeavored to support each other as we encountered instances of dissonance or situations in which our beliefs were challenged or at times brought to light by virtue of the collective. As we move beyond the research initiative, our HSCOE must also consider how we support students as they develop a sense of agency during their teacher preparation program. As we explored the overarching question of what it means to be an HSCOE and how we can make that term meaningful, an ethic of care supported our evolution. An ethic of community made us aware that we were not alone in our efforts. An ethic of inquiry identified topics pertinent to the group and the students and communities we serve. Finally, an ethic of agency made clear the role we must assume as an HSCOE.

Why This Work Matters

During a professional development session with school-based leadership teams from school districts throughout our region, the following question was asked, "How many of you have graduated from UTRGV or one of its' legacy institutions' educator preparation programs?" Every single person in the room raised his or her hand. We had often talked about being the primary institution responsible for the talent development of the region's education workforce, but we were honestly astounded to see 100% of the people in a room full of school leaders raise their hands. This moment signified the importance of our role as an HSCOE. We are not only preparing our high school graduates to serve as future teachers in the RGV, we are also preparing our teachers to serve as future leaders, either as principals and/or educators, as well as future faculty. Being consciously aware of this recursive cycle made clear our impact in the region and beyond and the responsibility that comes as a result.

However, transforming the education of Latinx students has importance beyond the RGV. Along with the moral imperative of providing all students with a high-quality, equitable, culturally sustaining and affirming education is the fact that shifting demographics of the U.S. mean that Latinx people will play an important and growing role in the cultural, social, economic, and political outcomes of our country. An HSI that truly *serves* its students will be able to produce positive outcomes such as graduation and employment rates while recognizing and valuing the cultural and linguistic capital that students possess. Where Predominately White Institutions may implicitly or explicitly promote the need to assimilate in order to find success, HSIs should develop an identity that encourages and affirms Latinx student identities while confronting and deconstructing institutional legacies of oppression, disenfranchisement, and marginalization. These legacies, then, can be replaced with programs, policies, pedagogy, and curriculum built upon culturally affirming and sustaining practices which recognize and value the cultural, social, and linguistic capitals of the students.

Discovering Versus Building Identity

Our original intention was to find this elusive identity because our original question prefaced what it meant to be an HSI rather than what it meant to become one. In everything we verbalized, there was an underlying assumption that being an HSCOE was something tangible that we needed to find, catch, and release at our own institution. It took us a year to realize that this intention was misguided by what we thought we knew about what it meant to be an HBCU or Tribal College.

HBCUs and Tribal Colleges have always *been*. HSIs have only ever been in the process of *becoming*. Coming to this realization dramatically changed that of which we were in pursuit. After the first year of the SIRG initiative we reframed our questions to explore the opportunity to build identity rather than seek it. The question of what it meant to be an HSI is now informed by a new and different set of assumptions, rooted in the premise that the meaning of being an HSI is to be identity builders rather than identity seekers.

The most recent iteration of our question in this work has evolved from what it means to be an HSI to what we do as a HSI and as faculty in an HSI to ensure the success of our student population in our university and the communities they come from. We now clearly know that our identity as an HSI is manifested in what we do as well as the number of Latinx learners we serve.

It Depends and Just Imagine

When we are asked what it means to be an HSCOE, we respond with, "It depends." It depends on whether the Latinx population is 26% of your total student population or 92%. It depends if you are in a suburban, urban, or rural area, or along the U.S./Mexico border. It depends on who your faculty are. It depends. And it changes. It is an ever-evolving process. Where we were yesterday as an HSCOE is not where we will be tomorrow as an HSCOE.

UTRGV's HSCOE believes it has the propensity and responsibility to be a national and international leader in what it means to be an HSI where Latinx learners are succeeding and making an impact on their community, region, and beyond. That is our mandate. In closing, we urge the faculty, staff, and students at HSIs and HSCOEs to ask, "How am I enacting an ethic of care? How am I building community? How can inquiry help with the situation at hand? And how am I demonstrating my role as an agentic being?" If you ask yourself these four questions every time you engage with someone—students, faculty, colleagues, or strangers, you will embody what it means to be an HSCOE.

References

Bondy, E., & Ross, D. D. (2008). The teacher as warm demander. *The Positive Classroom, 66*(1), 54–58.

Furman, G. (2004). The ethic of community. *Journal of Educational Adminis-tration, 42*(2), 215–235. DOI: 10.1108/09578230410525612

Merriam-Webster Dictionary. (2019). Ethics definition. Retrieved from https://www.merriam-webster.com/dictionary/ethic

Noddings, N. (2001). Care and coercion in school reform. *Journal of Educational Change, 2,* 35–43.

Noguera, P. (2010). *What it takes to leave no child behind.* RAPSA: Reaching At-Promise Student Association Conference, San Diego, CA.

Schlosser, M. (2015). Agency. In E. N. Zalta (Ed.), *The Stanford encyclopedia of philosophy.* Retrieved from https://plato.stanford.edu/archives/fall2015/entries/agency/

Starratt, R. J. (2004). *Ethical leadership.* San Francisco, CA: Jossey-Bass.

Appendix 1

Example of Hispanic-Serving Institution Request for Proposals

The University of Texas
Rio Grande Valley

College of Education
& P-16 Integration

**Request for Proposals
2018–2019 Academic Year**

Hispanic-Serving Institution SIRG Research Initiative

The U.S. Department of Education defines Hispanic-Serving Institutions (HSIs) as "an institution of higher education that....has an enrollment of undergraduate full-time equivalent students that is at least 25 percent Hispanic students..." (www2.ed.gov/programs/idueshsi/definition.html). The University of Texas Rio Grande Valley (UTRGV) is currently the second largest HSI in the U.S., with 89% of students overall and 92% of College of Education and P-16 students identifying as Hispanic. UTRGV's mission is:

> To be one of the nation's leaders in higher education, its premier Hispanic-serving institution, and a highly engaged bilingual university, with exceptional educational, research, and creative opportunities that serve as catalysts for transformation in the Rio Grande Valley and beyond.

While the designation of HSI is clearly central to UTRGV's developing identity and the identity of the College of Education and P-16 Integration (CEP), as an academic institution we are working to articulate what this designation means for our college and how we can support this identity through our curriculum, pedagogy, scholarship, and community engagement. What does it mean to serve a population of primarily Hispanic undergraduate and graduate students?

Because becoming a premier HSI is a current high priority, the CEP established a research initiative to support faculty teams in Special Interest Research Groups (SIRGs) as they explore various aspects of the overarching question: What does it mean to be a Hispanic-Serving College of Education, and how do we make this term meaningful for postsecondary education?

Using this overarching question as a guide, research teams should develop a focus for in-depth exploration. For example, one SIRG may focus on leadership preparation within an HSI while another SIRG examines the needs of transnational preservice teachers. Although each SIRG will have a different focus, we expect all SIRGs to struggle with broad questions such as the following:

- How do we support the identity that is being an HSI for UTRGV?
- How is an HSI different from other institutions?
- How is a College of Education at an HSI different from other Colleges of Education?
- How do we effectively address the unique student population at an HSI?
- How does an HSI designation affect recruitment, college readiness, and the teacher pipeline?
- What are the initiatives within an HSI that can inform our work with educator preparation?

The goal of the SIRG Research Initiative is to struggle with questions such as these; to create meaning from that struggle; and then to shape that meaning into new learnings that will lead our region in innovation, thought, and educator preparation.

SIRGs provide a forum within the CEP for the involvement of individuals drawn together by a common interest in a field of study, teaching, or research. For the 2018–2019 academic year, we will fund five new SIRGs. Each new SIRG will receive $1,250 to further the work of the SIRG (e.g., purchase books, cover travel costs, pay for professional development). In addition, SIRGs that were funded in 2017–2018 are eligible to continue as part of this learning community. Continuing SIRGs will receive $500 to further the work of the SIRG.

New SIRGs

Expectations

It is expected that all SIRGs will provide deliverables including presenting at the end of year SIRG exhibition, conference presentations, and manuscript submissions by the end of the academic year.

- All proposals must address the following question: What does it mean to be a Hispanic-Serving College of Education, and how do we make this term meaningful for postsecondary education?
- All SIRG members **must:**
  - Attend all SIRG events, including the two-day retreat, pulse check, and SIRG exhibition.
  - Present the SIRG outcomes at the SIRG exhibition.

- Each SIRG **must:**
  - Maintain documentation on meeting agendas and minutes to chronicle their efforts.
  - Meet proposed outcomes.
  - Submit a final report detailing outcomes.

Composition

The SIRG **must** consist of a minimum of three and a maximum of five members. Members could be comprised from multiple disciplines or a single discipline. A SIRG is participatory; we encourage you to include faculty from other colleges although the expectation is that the majority of the members are from CEP. SIRGs are also encouraged to include student members at either the undergraduate or graduate level. They may also consist of Holmes Cadets (i.e., high school students).

Application Process

Applications are limited to five double-spaced pages (not including references or appendix) and must include:

- **SIRG Name.**
- **SIRG Members and Affiliations:** Include which member will be the point of contact.
- **Executive Summary:** A concise description of your research that includes major activities and outcomes as well as an explanation of how the SIRG addresses the following question: What does it mean to be a Hispanic-Serving College of Education, and how do we make this term meaningful for postsecondary education? Your summary should be linear and descriptive. The purpose of this section is to provide the review committee with a broad factual overview of your research project, its activities, and summative goals.
- **Research Questions:** A listing of your questions of study.
- **Methodology:** A brief description of the methodology used in this research project. Discuss the techniques that will be used to address the research questions.
- **Impact Statement:** A description of the significance and impact of this scholarly activity on the profession or research area. Statement of need and/or gap that the research addresses connected to the guiding question (What does it mean to be a Hispanic-Serving College of Education, and how do we make this term meaningful for postsecondary education?).
- **Alignment to CEP and UTRGV mission and vision, as well as UTRGV strategic plan:** Explain the connection between the missions and visions of the CEP and UTRGV, as well as UTRGV's strategic plan.

- **Dissemination**: Identify potential journal(s) and conference(s) as anticipated venues for the dissemination of your research.
- **Appendix**: Include in the appendix a brief (one paragraph) bio of each SIRG member including expected contribution to the SIRG goals and objectives.

Email your application to the Dean's Office by September 3, 2018, 5:00 PM.

Awards

A total of five SIRGs will be awarded. Each SIRG will receive $1,250.00 to assist with their research initiative. A committee will review the applications and make recommendations to the Dean. See attached rubric.

Timeline

Objective	Location	Date	Time
SIRG Q&A	Zoom	8-15-18	9:00–10:00 AM
Proposal Submission Due	N/A	9-3-18	5:00 PM
Proposal Review and Award Announcement	N/A	9-14-18	5:00 PM
SIRG Kickoff Retreat	TBD	9-22-18	9:00–5:00 PM
		9-27-18*	1:00–4:00 PM
SIRG Pulse Check (Brunch)	TBD	1-19-19	9:00–12:00 PM
SIRG Exhibition (Reception)	TBD	4-27-19	4:00–6:00 PM

*All SIRG members are expected to attend unless they are scheduled to teach during this time.

Continuing SIRGs

HSI SIRGs that were funded in 2017–2018 can continue to be part of this learning community by submitting a proposal for continuation or expansion of the work completed this past year.

Awards

Continuing SIRGs will receive $500.00 to assist with their research initiative. A committee will review the applications and make recommendations to the Dean.

Expectations for Continuing SIRGs

It is expected that all SIRGs will provide deliverables including presenting at the end of year SIRG exhibition, conference presentations, and manuscript submissions by the end of the academic year.

- All proposals must address the following question: What does it mean to be a Hispanic-Serving College of Education, and how do we make this term meaningful for postsecondary education?
- All SIRG members must:
  - Attend all SIRG events (i.e., one day of two-day retreat, pulse check, and exhibition).
  - Present the SIRG outcomes at the SIRG exhibition.
- Each SIRG must:
  - Maintain documentation on meeting agendas and minutes to chronicle their efforts.
  - Meet proposed outcomes.
  - Submit a final report detailing outcomes.

Composition

Continuing SIRGs should consist of original members. Addition of new members is acceptable if it would further the research goals of the SIRG. The lead for the SIRGs must be faculty within CEP.

Application Process

Applications are limited to five double-spaced pages (not including references and appendix) and must include:

- **Executive Summary:** A concise description of your research that includes major activities and outcomes. Specifically addresses your previous SIRG accomplishments and how you will build upon them. Your summary should be linear and descriptive. The purpose of this section is to provide the review committee with a broad factual overview of your research project, its activities, and summative goals. **Note: Proposals must address the focus of the call.**
- **Research Questions:** A listing of your questions of study.
- **Methodology:** A brief description of the methodology used in this research project. Discuss the techniques that will be used to address the research questions.
- **Impact Statement:** A description of the significance and impact of this scholarly activity on the profession or research area. Statement of need and/or gap that the research addresses connected to the guiding question (What does it mean to be a Hispanic-Serving College of Education, and how do we make this term meaningful for postsecondary education?).
- **Alignment to CEP and UTRGV missions:** Explain the connection between the missions of the CEP and UTRGV and the research project. An explanation of how the SIRG addresses the following question: What does it mean to be a Hispanic-Serving College of

Education, and how do we make this term meaningful for postsecondary education?

- **Dissemination:** Identify potential journal(s) and conference(s) as anticipated venues for the dissemination of your research.
- **Appendix:** Include in the appendix a brief (one paragraph) bio of each SIRG member including expected contribution to the SIRG goals and objectives.

Timeline

Objective	Location	Date	Time
SIRG Q&A	Zoom	8-15-18	9:00–10:00 AM
Proposal Submission Due	N/A	9-3-18	5:00 PM
Proposal Review and Award Announcement	N/A	9-14-18	5:00 PM
SIRG Kickoff Retreat	TBD	9-22-18	9:00–5:00 PM
		9-27-18*	1:00–4:00 PM
SIRG Pulse Check (Brunch)	TBD	1-19-19	9:00–12:00 PM
SIRG Exhibition (Reception)	TBD	4-27-19	4:00–6:00 PM

*All SIRG members are expected to attend unless they are scheduled to teach during this time.

Appendix 2

Evaluation Rubric for Hispanic-Serving Institution Special Interest Research Group Proposals

The University of Texas
Rio Grande Valley
College of Education
& P-16 Integration

Evaluation Rubric for SIRG Proposals

	Minimal	*Adequate*	*Strong*	*Points*
Research Questions and Methodology	The rationale is not stated nor supported by the literature, and lacks clear intent of research questions/issues being addressed. Research questions and/or design for conducting research are unclear, underdeveloped, or inappropriate for the study. (0–2 pts)	The rationale is somewhat clear and/or lacks full support from the literature and clear intent of the research questions/issues being addressed. Research questions and/or design for conducting research that are basically sound, though, may need minor revisions. (3–4 pts)	The rationale is clearly stated, is fully supported by the literature, and provides clear intent of the research questions/issues being addressed. Research questions and/or design for conducting research are clearly articulated, thorough, and coherent. (5–6 pts)	
Focus of SIRG*	The focus is unclear and does not align with the purpose of the initiative. (0–1 pt)	The focus is somewhat clear and/or alignment with the purpose of the initiative needs additional support. (2 pts)	The focus is clearly articulated and fully aligns with the purpose of the initiative. (3 pts)	

(Continued)

	Minimal	Adequate	Strong	Points
Impact & Alignment to CEP/UTRGV Mission & Strategic Plan	Alignments and/or potential contributions to the field are unstated or unclear. (0–1 pt)	Alignments and/or potential contributions to the field are only somewhat stated and clear. (2 pts)	Alignments and/or potential contributions to the field are clearly articulated. (3 pts)	
Expected Outcomes and Metrics for Success	Outcomes are not clear and/or appropriate or realistic to the tasks and funding cycle. (0–1 pt)	Outcomes are somewhat clear and/or not fully aligned, appropriate, or realistic to the tasks and funding cycle. (2 pts)	Outcomes are clear, fully aligned, appropriate, and realistic to the tasks and funding cycle. (3 pts)	
Total Score				

*Proposals must be aligned to the purpose of the HSI SIRG Initiative in order to be funded.

Appendix 3
Funded Projects

Collaborative research groups are awarded funding through a competitive proposal process each cycle. Awarded projects include the following:

Cycle Four Projects (2019–2020)

Proposing a Culturally Relevant Framework and Assessments for Teaching Nature of Science and Authentic Science to Latinx Preservice Teachers
Research Team: Dr. Noushin Nouri, Dr. Angela Chapman, Dr. Mingstan Lu, Leslie Garrido

Despite major efforts that have been undertaken to enhance science teachers' NOS/AS views, contextualizing NOS/AS instruction for a Latinx population and the crucial component of assessing learners' NOS/AS views in a culturally relevant context remains an issue. This proposal seeks to answer this need for a new NOS/AS questionnaire which will be designed and validated with the aim of investigating Latinx preservice teachers understanding of NOS and AS.

Deep Dive into HSI Students' Testimonios to Build and Learn Our Faculty Paths
Research Team: Dr. Karin A. Lewis, Dr. Miryam Espinosa-Dulanto, Dr. Vejoya Viren, Juana Dolores Montiel

Embracing and including indigenous knowledges, challenging the contrived separation between academic work and community involvement, and deconstructing racism in the academy must be part of the work of HSIs. In this project we gather *testimonios* of resilience, challenges, and successes from students before and within their UTRGV/HSI experience.

Latinx Pre-Service Bilingual Elementary Teachers: Exploring the Intersections of Mathematical Proficiency, Language Use, Self-efficacy, and Problem-Solving
Research Team: Dr. Jair J. Aguilar, Dr. Maria Diaz, Victor M. Vizcaino

The purpose of this study is to examine Latinx preservice bilingual elementary teachers' development of mathematical proficiency and self-efficacy for problem-solving as they are exposed to a series of non-routine mathematical tasks. In addition, the study seeks to explore the effects of language when communicating mathematics.

(Continued)

Researching Our Identity as an HSI: A Significant Case Study of How and What Faculty, Administrators, and Staff Do to Improve Student Success
Research Team: Dr. Israel Aguilar, Dr. Jesus Abrego, Dr. Federico Guerra

A significant case study of one exemplar HSI will help to identify ways leaders among faculty, administrators, and staff are helping to ameliorate the pattern of low performance among Hispanic students.

Graduate Counseling Students' Perception of Their Preparedness to Practice Play Therapy
Research Team: Dr. Clarissa Salinas, Dr. Eunice Lerma, Dr. Yih-Jiun Shen, Dr. Diana Delinda Ruiz

Cultural and linguistic competence is integral in providing multiculturally appropriate services to the Spanish-speaking population. However, there is a disparity of Spanish-speaking mental health professionals and service delivery. This proposal is to address the need for trained Play Therapists in the Rio Grande Valley. The researchers plan to use the results to develop a training model for teaching counseling student's basic knowledge and skills in Play Therapy methods.

The Experiences of Women Faculty of Color Within and Beyond the College of Education at Hispanic-Serving Institutions
Research Team: Dr. Elena Venegas, Dr. Jacqueline Koonce, Lorenza Lancaster, Julissa Bazan

The purpose of this qualitative study is to identify the experiences of women faculty of color, who are not Latina, both within and beyond Colleges of Education at Hispanic-Serving Institutions.

Developing a Border Pedagogy for Teacher Preparation
Research Team: Dr. Alcione Ostorga, Dr. Kip Hinton, Dr. Christian Zúñiga

In this meta-analysis of the professional literature we examine border pedagogy, particularly focusing on the following questions: What is border pedagogy and how is it defined or understood? What are border pedagogical practices for Latinx teacher preparation?

Assessing the Effects of a Basic Communication Course on Students' Communication Competence and Intercultural Effectiveness in a Hispanic Serving Institution
Research Team: Dr. Wan-Lin Chang, Jennifer Lemanski, Po-Yi Chen

The purpose of this study is to explore how a basic communication course helps students at a Hispanic-Serving Institution to increase their communication competence, and which kind of communication competence abilities (interpersonal communication, small group communication, public speaking) students gain most after taking a basic communication course. Furthermore, the study will allow investigation into how culture and a bilingual environment may impact students' communication competence.

Cycle Four Projects (2019–2020)

Connecting with Students Through Social Justice and Diversity @ UTRGV
Research Team: Carlos E. Cuellar, Natasha Altema McNeely, Ruby Charak

UTRGV ranked third in the nation in awarding Bachelor's degrees to Latino/a students which suggests that it is providing this population with unprecedented opportunities for upward mobility. However, *what does UTRGV do that is unique in contributing to their educational experiences?* This research proposes to analyze the common approaches in pedagogy and curricular design focused on incorporating issues of social justice and racial/ethnic diversity at UTRGV. Additionally, this research will evaluate the extent to which programs, courses, and faculty that incorporate issues of social justice and diversity impact student outcomes related to agency, academic achievement, and civic engagement.

Cycle Three Projects (2018–2019)

Agency and Identity among Math and Science Teachers in the Borderlands
Research Team: Dr. Angela Chapman, Ariana Garza, Felicia Rodriguez, Johanna Esparza, Alicia Cronkhite

Math/science educator identity influences classroom culture. However, power structures in RGV schools encourage dominant American cultures even though the majority of teachers and students are Hispanic. This SIRG seeks to investigate ways to help secondary teachers develop a strong identity and agency as a means of transforming their classroom culture.

Science Is Socially and Culturally Embedded: How It Is Useful for Hispanic Elementary Teachers in the RGV
Research Team: Dr. Noushin Nouri, Vero G. Frady, Patricia Ramirez

This project has been designed to increase Hispanic preservice teachers' understanding of nature of science and to improve their attitude toward science and the teaching of science.

Developing a Border Pedagogy for Teacher Preparation
Research Team: Dr. Alcione Ostorga, Dr. Kip Hinton, Dr. Christian Zúñiga

In this meta-analysis of the professional literature we examine border pedagogy, particularly focusing on the following questions: What is border pedagogy and how is it defined or understood? What are border pedagogical practices for Latinx teacher preparation?

(Continued)

Listening to HSI students' Testimonios to build and learn our OWN paths.

Research Team: Dr. Miryam Espinosa-Dulanto, Dr. Karin Lewis, Dr. Vejoya Viren

Deconstructing racism in higher education must be part of the institutional identity of HSIs as well as embracing and including indigenous knowledges and rejecting the separation between academic work and community involvement. This project will share students' voices through their testimonios of resilience, challenges, and success before, within, and after their UTRGV/HSI experiences, locating these experiences within the Latinx tradition of political struggle and pride to help to develop strategies for social change and an opportunity for decolonizing and transcontinental (South-North) understandings based on indigenous-mestizo wisdom and ethics of communality.

Investigating Hispanic Serving College of Education Students' Perspectives and Experiences Regarding High Impact Practices: Latinx Success Stories

Research Team: Dr. Ming-Tsan Lu, Dr. María Díaz, Dr. Johanna Esquivel

The purpose of this mixed methods study is to investigate CEP students' perspectives and experiences with high-impact practices.

The Experiences of Women Faculty of Color Within and Beyond the College of Education at Hispanic-Serving Institutions

Research Team: Dr. Elena Venegas, Dr. Jacqueline Koonce, Lorenza Lancaster, Julissa Bazan

The purpose of this qualitative study is to identify the experiences of women faculty of color, who are not Latina, both within and beyond Colleges of Education at Hispanic Serving Institutions

---

Transforming Teacher Preparation in HSIs: Exploring Translanguaging

Research Team: Dr. Sandra Musanti, Dr. Alma Rodríguez, Dr. Alyssa Cavazos

Translanguaging is a natural occurring phenomenon in bi/multilingual communities and an identity marker of the community in the RGV. This SIRG seeks to investigate how translanguaging pedagogies at an HSI impact bilingual and writing teacher candidates' perceptions of linguistically inclusive literacy instruction to improve teacher preparation.

Hispanic Family Engagement Practice Through Mixed Reality Simulation
Research Team: Dr. Hsuying Ward, Dr. Ignacio Rodriguez, Leticia Frias-Perez

This study describes how we provide mixed-reality IEP learning opportunities to prepare students to advocate social justice and become culturally responsive scholars toward the education of their PK-12 pupils with disabilities. This research investigates the effect of intervention using MRS—TeachLive™ as the tool to help practitioners see how their words and actions effect their collaboration with Hispanic parents of children with disabilities.

Reflections on Teacher Education Practices of First-Year Tenure Track Professors at an HSI
Research Team: Dr. Gilberto Lara, Dr. Hitomi Kambara, Dr. Maria Leija, Dr. Gerardo Aponte Martinez

The objective of the SIRG is to reflect on our teacher education practices as first-year tenure track professors at an HSI. In this research project, we wrestle with the following questions: What does it mean to be a professor at an HSI? How am I inclusive of my students' knowledge, experiences, language, and culture? What activities do I engage in as I work toward becoming a professor that encourages the sustainment of my students' culture and language?

Transformative Practice through Technology Integration: How to Leverage the CEP HSI Frames of Reference
Research Team: Dr. Leticia De Leon, Dr. Zulmaris Diaz, Dr. Michael Whitacre, Dr. Janet Martinez

Perception of technology competence and university instructor use of instructional technology play a vital role in preservice teachers' willingness to use it in their own practice. In this SIRG, we explore the question, *Will technology integration in learning transform student frames of reference in a HSCOE?*

Science Is Socially and Culturally Embedded: How It Is Useful for Hispanic Elementary teachers in the RGV
Research Team: Dr. Noushin Nouri, Dr. Jair Aguilar, Patricia Ramirez

This project has been designed to increase Hispanic preservice teachers' understanding of nature of science and to improve their attitude toward science and the teaching of science.

Developing a Border Pedagogy for Teacher Preparation
Research Team: Dr. Alcione Ostorga, Dr. Kip Hinton, Dr. Christian Zúñiga

In this meta-analysis of the professional literature we examine border pedagogy, particularly focusing on the following questions: What is border pedagogy and how is it defined or understood? What are border pedagogical practices for Latinx teacher preparation?

Agency and Identity among Math and Science Teachers in the Borderlands
Research Team: Dr. Angela Chapman, Ariana Garza, Felicia Rodriguez

Math/science educator identity influences classroom culture. However, power structures in RGV schools encourage dominant American cultures even though the majority of teachers and students are Hispanic. This SIRG seeks to investigate ways to help secondary teachers develop a strong identity and agency as a means of transforming their classroom culture.

(Continued)

Cycle Two Projects (2017–2018)

Language and Literacy Practices of CEP Students at an HSI
Research Team: Dr. Janine M. Schall, Dr. Veronica Estrada, Dr. Elena Venegas

Language and literacy practices play an essential role in academic success, yet we know little about how undergraduate CEP students use language and literacy practices to navigate their personal, work, and academic lives. This exploratory study will use student surveys and focus groups to explore this question.

Cycle One Projects (Spring 2017)

Agency and Identity among Math and Science Teachers in the Borderlands
Research Team: Dr. Angela Chapman, Ariana Garza, Felicia Rodriguez

Math/science educator identity influences classroom culture. However, power structures in RGV schools encourage dominant American cultures even though the majority of teachers and students are Hispanic. This SIRG seeks to investigate ways to help secondary teachers develop a strong identity and agency as a means of transforming their classroom culture.

Language and Literacy Practices of CEP Students at an HSI
Research Team: Dr. Janine M. Schall, Dr. Leticia De Leon, Dr. Veronica Estrada

Language and literacy practices play an essential role in academic success, yet we know little about how undergraduate CEP students use language and literacy practices to navigate their personal, work, and academic lives. This exploratory study will use student surveys and focus groups to explore this question.

Exploring and Sharing an Ethic of Care in Critical Pedagogy: Outsiders/Non-Hispanic Faculty at an HSI
Research Team: Dr. Karin Lewis, Dr. Jacqueline Koonce, Dr. Vejoya Viren, Dr. Miryam Espinosa-Dulanto

This qualitative study explores the intersectionality of diverse professor and student cross-cultural, racial, social, and linguistic differences and offers ways to cultivate an ethic of care in critical pedagogy at a Hispanic-Serving Institution in order to transcend boundaries; bridge insider-outsider epistemologies; engender trust; and develop mutual understanding, respect, reciprocity, and empathic teaching-learning relationships.

Literacy 2.0: Family and Community Literacy
Research Team: Dr. Cinthya Saavedra, Dr. Joy Esquierdo, Dr. Isela Almaguer, Dr. Dagoberto Ramirez

The purpose of Literacy 2.0 SIRG is to examine the organic literacies of Hispanic families living in the Edinburg Housing Authority public housing as a way to address the development of literacy skills for Hispanic families through the creation of a culturally relevant literacy center that will produce digital and print bilingual stories.

Index